Excuse me, are you Jewish?

Excuse me, are you Jewish?

PUBLISHED AND COPYRIGHTED © BY:
Emet Publications
Jerusalem 2006/5766

DISTRIBUTED EXCLUSIVELY BY:
Jonathan David Publishers, Inc.
68-22 Eliot Avenue, Middle Village, New York 11379, USA
TELEPHONE: 718-456-8611 • www.jdbooks.com

ACKNOWLEDGEMENTS:
EDITORS: Gershom Gale, Ora Elper
PROOFREADING: Menucha Kaplan, Esther Herskovics
TYPESETTING: S. Kim Glassman

COVER DESIGN BY: S. Kim Glassman
PICTURES: Sukkah, Chabad House of Venice
Menorah, Chabad House of Bangkok
Tefillin, Chabad House of Ancorage
Purim, Chabad House of Eilat

For orders, comments and stories for future editions,
see us on the web at: www.areyoujewish.net

ISBN 0-8246-0467-9

Excuse me, are you Jewish?

STORIES OF CHABAD-LUBAVITCH OUTREACH AROUND THE WORLD

Malka Touger

Published by Emet Publications

Distributed Exclusively by Jonathan David Publishers, Inc.

Foreword

*T*wo *yeshivah* students found themselves in the outback area of Queensland, Australia. They had been part of a team of young men who drove the Chabad *mitzvah* mobiles[1] for weeks in the summer to outlying areas. Evidently they had taken a wrong turn and ended up far away from their intended destination.

A man, surprised to see *yeshivah* students in this remote area, asked: "What are two nice Jewish boys doing here?"

"Actually," one of them replied, "we were asking ourselves the same question. But now that we have met you, we know exactly why we're here. Excuse me, are you Jewish? Would you like to put on *tefillin*?"

*   *   *

These questions have been asked countless times over the last four decades. As various branches of the Chabad-Lubavitch movement have spread their outreach activities throughout the world, their representatives have encountered Jewish men and women everywhere, even in the most unexpected places, and time and again, they have asked: "Excuse me, are you Jewish?"

---

1. The mobile units manned by Chabad students which have enabled Jewish outreach activities to be taken to the streets of many major cities.

In keeping with the Jewish tradition that a question can be answered with a question, the response has often been: "Why do you ask?"

The answers are many.

We ask because we care.

We ask because we have something to share.

We ask because the Torah teaches us that the Jewish people are an indivisible whole and each of us has a responsibility towards our fellow man.

We ask because it's the most straightforward way to begin a conversation about what it means to be Jewish.

We ask because we are on a mission.

The Hebrew term for mission, *shlichus,* and the terms *shaliach* and *shluchah,* the masculine and feminine for an agent charged with carrying out a mission, recur frequently throughout this book, for the concept of living one's life as a mission lies at the core of the chassidic movement. As Rabbi Yosef Yitzchak Schneerson[2] taught: "It is incumbent on every person to know that, wherever he is located, he is an agent of the Master of all things, [charged with the mission of] revealing G-d's will and His intent in creating the world – to illuminate the world through the light of the Torah and Divine service."[3]

This mission is often directed outwards, as the Baal Shem Tov, the founder of Chassidism, taught his followers: "A soul may descend to this world and live seventy or eighty years" just to do a favor for another Jew, be it something material, or how much more so, something spiritual."[4]

---

2. The Rebbe Rayatz, the sixth Lubavitch Rebbe.

3. The *Igros Kodesh* of the Rebbe Rayatz, Vol. III, p. 70.

4. Quoted *ibid.,* Letters, No. 750-751 {translated as *The Making of Chassidim* (SIE, 5756)}; *Sefer HaSichos* 5701, p. 65-66; explained in *Likutei Sichos,* Vol. I, p. 32-33, *et al.*

The Lubavitcher Rebbe, Rabbi Menachem M. Schneerson, institutionalized the above concepts, sending out shluchim, young men and women, to distant communities to help others.[5] In part, their mission involves helping people materially, but their mission is primarily a spiritual one.

When the Rebbe assumed leadership of the Lubavitch movement, assimilation was spreading rapidly within the Jewish community and demographers spoke of "the vanishing American Jew." The Rebbe sent emissaries to cities and countries where a proud show of Jewish identity would have been considered unthinkable and there they lit sparks within Jewish hearts, showing men and women how to connect to their spiritual roots.

Rather than wait for Jews to come to the synagogues, *yeshivos,* and Jewish schools, the Rebbe instructed his shluchim to go out to homes, places of business, and college campuses, and acquaint them with their heritage. He emphasized that each one of us possesses a soul that is "an actual part of G-d."[6] As a result, "No Jew desires – and no Jew can – remain separate from G-dliness,"[7] and, if given the chance to identify with his or her spiritual birthright, would respond. Due to his requests, teachings, and example, thousands of people have undertaken this mission.

Everywhere.

From Anchorage, Alaska, to Surfers Paradise, Australia;

---

5. In truth, the Rebbe's predecessor, Rabbi Yosef Yitzchak Schneerson, pioneered the concept of *shlichus* during the ten years (1941–1950) that he spent in the u.s., but both conceptually and in practice, it was the Rebbe who transformed *shlichus* into the primary thrust of Lubavitch and a major force in contemporary Jewish life.

6. *Tanya,* ch. 2.

7. The *Igros Kodesh* of the Rebbe *Rayatz,* Vol. IV, p. 384.

from Novosibirsk, Siberia, to Rio de Janeiro, Brazil; from Kinshasa, Congo, to Beijing, China – and everywhere in between.

Although they have been successful in sparking spiritual revolutions within individuals and communities, these men and women don't see their achievements as a result of their individual gifts or efforts. On the contrary, whenever they speak of their work, they emphasize in homely Yiddish that all they accomplish is due to *der Rebbe's kochos* ("to the Rebbe's power").

We are all familiar with motifs of empowerment. When we look up to a person with well-earned respect and feel that he truly knows us and believes in us, it is natural that one should try to live up to his expectations. Because we have identified with an ideal such a person has taught, we dedicate ourselves to the tasks necessary to achieve it, without thinking of ourselves and our limitations. And as a consequence, we are not bound by them.

But on *shlichus*, something deeper is involved. When Rabbi Gershon Mendel Garelik first went out on shlichus almost 50 years ago, a local Jew was surprised to see a Chassid on the streets of Milan. "This is not such a clean city," he exclaimed. "What is a person like you doing here?"

"The Rebbe wants to tidy it up," Rabbi Garelik replied. "I am the Rebbe's broom."

That calls to mind an old Yiddish adage, "When G-d wishes, even a broom can shoot." When a person sees himself as no more than a broom and, without shirking responsibility, does not rely on his own unaided power, he opens himself up to a much greater force. He becomes aware that something much larger than himself is working through him. This is

what the shluchim mean when they attribute their success to
the Rebbe.

*F*or many years, I have been listening to stories of
shlichus and I have never ceased to be amazed – at the
unseen hand of Divine Providence which makes things
happen, how the hearts of Jews are alive and seek to identify
with their heritage, and how each one of us, if we just set
ourselves to the task, can bring about miracles in microcosm.

I felt strongly that these stories should be shared, not
only in chassidic gatherings, but in printed form. I decided to
compile an anthology that would enable a reader to glimpse
into the work of these shluchim. I did not see this as a literary
endeavor, but more like a candid-camera snapshot of how these
men, women, and children live their lives on this mission.

And so I set about contacting shluchim and shluchos all
over the world. Knowing that people do not always respond
to an impersonal email, I opted to call people individually and
request stories. Preparing to make these calls, I opened the
Shluchim Directory. There they were – pages upon pages of
names, addresses and telephone numbers. Many names were
familiar, many were not. I began to make contact and present
the idea of the book. Instantly, the names evolved into live hu-
man beings. They varied in age, background, number of years on
shlichus, nature of activities, size of community and just about
everything else. But the unwavering commitment was global
and I knew that the task ahead of me would be fascinating,
even if not necessarily easy.

First, there was the need to plan the phone calls according
to the differences in international time zones. And then, the

repeated attempts to reach the busy shaliach or his wife, and the quick course I received in learning how to ask the local housekeeper: "Is the rabbi or his wife there? When will they be home?" in Russian, Spanish, French, Portuguese, Georgian, etc. (I thanked G-d for my knowledge of Hebrew and Yiddish).

Perhaps the most difficult part of the process was getting the shaliach or shluchah to tell the story. In stark contrast to the natural tendency to maximize and publicize one's accomplishments, they would often say: "I don't really have any outstanding story of Divine Providence. I know that many people do, but for me the most outstanding Divine Providence is that I, my spouse and our children are living on shlichus and doing our best to fulfill our mission successfully."

So often, their humility made the greatest sacrifices seem matter-of-fact. As many shluchim replied: "I am honored that you have called me, but honestly, you would do much better contacting the well-known, successful shluchim who have built multi-purpose complexes. They probably have inspiring tales to tell. I am just a 'little guy shaliach' in a small community who is just trying to get my job done."

Or as Rabbi Yosef Yitzchak Eidelman said: "You are asking for an outstanding story from Casablanca, Morocco, where my parents have been on shlichus for over forty years? When I was growing up in Morocco, I didn't think there was anything extraordinary about a Russian couple settling in a third-world Muslim country, raising a Chassidic family and going about their daily task of promoting Judaism in a hostile and often dangerous environment."

And there were the numerous shluchim who answered: "Here, speak to my wife. She's the one that makes things happen here."

At times, the reason for a shaliach's humble response could be his lack of awareness of the impact he had. For example, a college student once participated in a "weekend with Chabad." She was inspired, but not motivated enough to seek more information about Judaism. The following year, in graduate school in another city, she spotted a rabbi on campus. His appearance reminded her of the rabbi she had met on the weekend the year before. So, from afar, she followed the black hat and coat and thus found her way to Chabad House. Today, she is living a full Torah lifestyle and raising her own jolly bunch of 'black hatters.'

In the same vein, a few high school girls were standing on the street corner in Brighton Beach, Brooklyn, handing out candles and brochures about candle-lighting. A girl approached a woman passerby and began conversing with her. Before she could hand her a brochure, the woman became intimidated and turned quickly away. Undaunted, the girl and her friends continued their efforts for a while, then they boarded a bus to go home.

Without their knowing, the woman who had initially rejected their gesture had actually not gone far. She had watched the girls and waited until they left the scene. Then, she returned and picked up a pamphlet that someone else had taken, but later put down. She read its contents as she walked away. Sometime later, she called the telephone number on the brochure and she was directed to contact the local shaliach in her neighborhood. This led to an invitation for the upcoming holiday of Pesach which was followed by an open invitation for Shabbos. The woman and her mother now observe Shabbos on their own.

Nevertheless, while every individual example of how they have inspired a person may not have been noticed, by and large, the contribution of the shluchim is recognized and appreciated in their local communities. Ask one of the mailmen in Afula, Israel, who delivered a letter to the local Chabad House.

"I wasn't sure what to do with this letter," he told the shluchim Rabbi Shlomo and Chedva Segal, a bit awkwardly. "But I know that you have this sign outside your center, that states: 'The address for all your Jewish needs.' I guess this is the only place I could deliver this letter."

The address on the envelope stated: To G-d, somewhere up there in the Garden of Eden.

Hearing the shluchim's stories was obviously inspiring. But I enjoyed speaking with the shluchim and shluchos even if they did not share a story. They were always encouraging; they were understanding, even if their story was not included. They were forgiving, even as I persisted, calling again and again.

As the stories were being told, I had a sense that the teller was reliving the episode. When the story was about a person in need, vibes of genuine empathy were conveyed along with vivid details. While depicting an episode that brought success to the shlichus or to a fellow Jew, the teller's gratitude and joy were almost tangible. As the shaliach related the punch lines of his story, I could hear him marveling at G-d's hidden ways. And as I listened to events that were overwhelming with challenge, it seemed that the shluchah had enough trust and belief to go around for many, including myself.

I also discovered that many of these dedicated people are extremely talented story-tellers! In writing the stories, I have tried a 'just-the-facts-ma'am' approach and refrained from extensive flowery descriptions or trying to point to lessons and morals. On the other hand, I felt it my duty to include the nuances that the teller conveyed.

One of the delightful experiences in the process of putting

together this volume was the pleasure of discovering that, unintentionally, often in the course of one evening's random calling, I had called several members of one family consecutively. In one chain of calls, I had spoken to three generations of shluchim from one family who live in different places in the world. True, with communications being what they are today, that's not such a big deal. But still, there were many heartwarming moments as I related regards back and forth world-wide. Some were thankful because they had been too busy lately to call family.

In a larger sense, all of the shluchim see themselves as part of one large family and look to each other for strength and inspiration. In that vein, Rabbi Yehudah Teichtel of Berlin, Germany, related that when he was just starting out, he knew he had to cover all bases of possible exposure. He faithfully attended city fairs, bazaars and public events, set up his *tefillin* booth, manning it alone throughout the day in his attempt to contact local Jews.

Once, as he prepared for this tedious and often unsuccessful all-day activity, he felt it difficult to muster inner conviction and energy. In his mind, he sought encouragement. His thoughts took him back to the summers of his younger days in California. He recalled the image of the indefatigable chassid, Rabbi Shmuel David Raichik, standing for hours in the hot sun on the street corners of Los Angeles, eagerly searching for Jews with whom he could put on tefillin.

That was just the inspiration he needed. With renewed motivation, he went on his mission. It was precisely that day that he met, on the street corner, a local Jew who proved to be one of Chabad's ardent supporters in Berlin.

Many of the stories recorded in this volume tug at the soul. But shluchim also shared the lighter side of their ongoing encounters.

Since many shluchim live in countries whose language is not their mother tongue, there can be moments of public oops! It was a humored crowd that smiled and forgave their rabbi when he addressed the dignitaries present at the public Menorah lighting ceremony as "the extinguished guests."

And there was a reluctant gentleman whom the shaliach was trying to attract to his Chabad House who insisted, "Rabbi, I have a strong sense of my Jewishness, but I am really not drawn to organized religion."

"In that case," shot back the rabbi earnestly and straight from the hip, "this is just the place for you! Ask anyone, I am the most disorganized person you'll ever meet."

And a shluchah in the New York area related that, for one of her programs, she hired an instructor to teach the women Jewish dances. Unfortunately, the woman got lost and could not find the Chabad House. After circling the area unsuccessfully for quite a while, she finally parked in front of a store.

"Would you happen to know where this address is?" she asked, showing the owner the card.

"Sure, it's right nearby. I'll show you," he answered. "You must be Jewish. Many people come in here to ask about that place. It's where all the lost Jews go."

Shlichus is not merely the job of a rabbi or even a post he and his wife share. It is a family endeavor – and often that of a large family.

Once Rabbi Eliezer and Rochi Shemtov of Montevideo, Uruguay, took their children for a trip to the local science museum.

Seeing the sizeable group, the guard shook his head. "Sorry, there are no school tours on Sunday," he informed them.

Humor aside, perhaps the greatest concern of the shluchim is their children. The extremely busy and often hectic schedule of any Chabad House is not the easiest environment in which to raise children. And raising chassidic children in distant places rather than in the protected environment of a chassidic community is no small feat. Nevertheless, the children identify with the shlichus and actively participate in the activities. As one young Yosef Yitzchak responded when asked how he could spend an entire day on the street, shaking *lulav* and *esrog* with passersby on Sukkos: "It's easy; I was born a shaliach."

Rabbi Yehuda and Devorah Weg of Tulsa, Oklahoma, relate that their eight-year-old son, Mendy, was their right-hand man as they built the local *mikveh*. As part of his home schooling program (and for lack of fulltime occupation), Mendy accompanied his father throughout the process.

At some later point, it was decided to send Mendy to study at the Chabad yeshivah in Crown Heights, Brooklyn. Mendy was a bit intimidated by the knowledge his classmates had. He realized he had much to catch up on and he shared his frustrations with his parents.

"You should see what these kids know!" he exclaimed with an obvious tinge of envy. "They read the Torah and commentary perfectly and they have already learned many chassidic texts. What do I know compared to my classmates? All I know is how to build a *mikveh*."

Soon, however, one of his teachers discovered Mendy's knowledge and hence he was nicknamed the *'mikveh maiven.'*

Perhaps the most moving statement I have heard in the course of this project came from Mrs. Rochel Pinson, who is on shlichus in Tunisia with her husband, Rabbi Nissan. I had the good fortune of meeting her in my hometown, Jerusalem. This afforded me the pleasure of a face-to-face conversation, a pleasant respite from the overseas phone calls. She shared an incident which is included in the book. But I regret that the written story does not do ample justice to this remarkable woman. With the regal aura she projects and with genuine humility packaged in true joy, she said, "If someone would ask me if I would do it all over again, in the incredible, but difficult place of Tunisia, I would say wholeheartedly, Yes! Yes to all forty-four years of our shlichus."

* * *

I would like to thank all the shluchim and shluchos for providing me with the material for this book. Whether or not your story is included, I thank each one of you and appreciate the time and patience you granted me in relating the stories and checking and rechecking the details. And I apologize to all those who have stories to share, but with whom I was not able to connect; perhaps in a second volume.

I would also like to express my gratitude to all the people whose stories have appeared in this book. Though most of the names are authentic, in a few instances pseudonyms have been used.

My thanks to Sichos in English, and its director, Rabbi Yonah Avtzon for permission to use the explanatory material that appeared in their works.

I would like to express appreciation to my husband, Rabbi Eli Touger, who has assisted me greatly in working on this project. And of course, my children, who have been valuable partners in this endeavor, serving as sounding boards for the stories and providing insight and encouragement. Their cooperation has enabled this book to be written. May they all merit to join the ranks of shluchim worldwide and continue to ask, "Excuse me, are you Jewish?"

Malka Touger
Yerushalayim
Rosh Chodesh Kislev, 5766

*B*efore Rabbi Chezki Lifshitz and his wife Chanah embarked on shlichus in Katmandu, Nepal, they were assisting the shluchim in Bangkok. One day, while riding in a taxi stuck in heavy Bangkok traffic, Rabbi Lifshitz correctly calculated that it would take less time to walk to his destination. He paid the fare and got out. As he walked down the street, a well-dressed foreigner approached him.

"Excuse me for stopping you on the street like this," the man began. Introducing himself as David, he continued, "it's just that you look like you could advise me. My wife and I are from America, and we have a business here. We're expecting the birth of a baby boy any day now. Where would we be able to find a *mohel*[8] to perform the circumcision?"

"I am a *mohel*," Rabbi Lifshitz replied with a smile, "and I'll be happy to be of service."

Later, David told him that, the day before they had met, his wife had asked him if he had done anything more to find a *mohel*. Anxiously, she had questioned him: "What do you expect? Do you think you'll bump into a *mohel* on the streets of Bangkok?"

*C*ongregants attending Yom Kippur services are usually tired, hungry, and not particularly attentive as the fast nears its end. But in this instance, the rabbi was saying

---

8. One who performs a *bris,* a ritual circumcision.

something that succeeded in arousing their interest. Rabbi Yehoshuah Binyamin Gordon, who is on shlichus with his wife Devorah in Encino, California, was voicing an appeal just before the evening *Neilah* Service. Rabbis often make appeals at that time, but this one was unlike the usual request for donations.

"I use precious moments such as those to make a 'mitzvah appeal,'" explains Rabbi Gordon. "I describe and explain the Rebbe's mitzvah campaign, and encourage people to take on an added commitment in their service of G-d. It is a very auspicious time when our focus should be on a soul commitment rather than on a monetary pledge."

That Yom Kippur, Rabbi Gordon didn't know how far-reaching his appeal would be. He certainly had no idea that it would go as far as Italy!

* * *

The guard posted at the main entrance to the annual Cosmetics Fair in Bologna, Italy, checked the foreign passport and overseas address, and then handed a pass to the bearded man who was tugging a large suitcase on wheels. Everything seemed in order, as many of the exhibitors were lugging cases of merchandise into the fairgrounds. The guard couldn't know that this case held 'goods' of a different sort.

But Rabbi Dovid Borenstein who is on shlichus with his wife, Mindy, in Bologna, was not really concerned about what the guard knew or didn't know. All he cared about was being able to distribute his merchandise – kosher sandwiches!

It isn't always this hard to provide kosher food for the Jews who attend the various business fairs in Italy. For example, in Vicenza, a two-hour drive from Bologna, three major jewelry fairs take place every year. The promoters are well aware of the numerous Jews in the jewelry business who attend and require kosher food. There, a place has been set aside for

Rabbi Borenstein and his helpers, enabling them to provide food, prayer accommodations and a meeting venue for the Jewish participants.

Cosmetics, though, are not jewelry, and there is no conspicuous Jewish presence at the annual Cosmetics Fair in Bologna. But Rabbi Borenstein knows that, whether visible or not, Jews do attend, and kosher food should be available for them. He packs the varied sandwiches prepared by his wife into the special case purchased just for this "businessman" role and gains entrance to the fairgrounds. The fact that his hometown is Montreal, Canada, entitles him to a foreign passport, and his parents' address serves as the overseas location of origin.

"The fair is located in a complex containing a number of buildings," explains Rabbi Borenstein. "I *shlep* my case in and out of those buildings, trying to 'sniff out' Jewish people. I listen for Hebrew, which is obvious, but of course English speakers who attend may also be Jewish. Over the years, I've become acquainted with numerous Jewish exhibitors and leave them some sandwiches to distribute to their Jewish patrons. In addition, the exhibition booths often state the exhibitor's country of origin, so whenever I see the "IL" notation, I stop, knowing it stands for Israel."

Making his way through the fairgrounds one day, Rabbi Borenstein was exiting Building 21 on his way to Building 22 when he saw a man and woman who had just walked out of that building. The rabbi and the couple exchanged glances. It was a moment of mutual recognition, one Jew identifying with another. The man sized up the rabbi, assuming that he was a foreigner who could use some assistance. He recalled a recent encounter on a train, when his knowledge of Hebrew and Italian had enabled him to help a rabbi from Israel who was lost.

"Can I help you?" the man asked in Hebrew.

"No, thanks," replied the rabbi. "Actually, I'm here to help you."

"How can you help us?" the man asked, puzzled.

"Well," said the rabbi with a big smile, "I have a hunch you might be a bit hungry. Am I correct?"

The man and woman looked at each other in astonishment. "This is unbelievable," he heard the couple muttering to one another. Rabbi Borenstein was used to people's surprise at his unexpected offer, but it wasn't quite clear why this couple was so taken aback.

"Hungry?!" the man replied. "We're famished!"

"Well then, let's not waste time. We'll move out of the flow of traffic and get you and your wife something to eat."

Soon, Rabbi Borenstein had his suitcase wide open.

"What would you like? Salami? Corned beef? Tuna? Egg salad? Lettuce and tomato? Take your pick."

But instead of taking a sandwich, the man took Rabbi Borenstein's hand and shook it vigorously. Then he took hold of his shoulders and literally hugged him. "Thank you, thank you! You are an angel! No, you are Elijah the prophet, that's who you are!" The couple took a sandwich each while Rabbi Borenstein urged them to take more for later in the day.

"A rabbi with a suitcase full of sandwiches! Kosher salami at the fair in Bologna! Who are you?" they asked in amazement. "What brought you here just when we needed you most?"

After Rabbi Bornstein explained who he was and what his objectives were, he inquired, "And who are you?"

"My name is Shlomo Mansano, and this is my wife, Shoshanah. We are make-up artists from Encino, California. We travel extensively and work with Hollywood stars and other people all over the world."

"Encino? Do you know Rabbi Josh Gordon?"

"Of course we know him! He's our rabbi! But how do you know him?"

"We went to the Chabad rabbinical school together in Montreal in our youth. We're still good friends."

Shlomo and his wife then left the rabbi, after thanking him profusely once again. Rabbi Borenstein wondered why the couple had been so inordinately grateful, but contented himself with noting how satisfying it was to meet people who so obviously appreciated his efforts.

He continued his work, with a lighter step and a suitcase that seemed a little easier to lug around.

* * *

When the Mansanos returned to California, Shlomo went straight to see his rabbi. Rabbi Gordon could see that he was eager to talk, and wondered what it was all about.

"Rabbi," Shlomo began, "when you spoke this past Yom Kippur at *Neilah* about accepting a new mitzvah, something stirred in me, and I decided to increase our observance of eating kosher. My wife Shoshanah and I had begun to keep kosher at home some years earlier, but not always outside the home. With our extensive traveling, we found keeping kosher in other countries very difficult, if not impossible. But following your *Neilah* mitzvah appeal, we both decided that the time had come for us to make the move. Our new mitzvah for the New Year became to keep kosher even outside our home.

"We were loyal to our commitment until the day we arrived at the annual Cosmetics Fair in Bologna. We took our usual room at the bed-and-breakfast, figuring that the bread and jam they serve in the morning would be basically kosher, and hoped that we would find something acceptable to eat during the rest of the day. As lunch hour approached, we started to feel hungry. There were food booths all around us, their aromas quite intoxicating.

"But a commitment is a commitment! A Diet Coke might be good enough for lunch, but what would we do for dinner? We really didn't know. I must confess, rabbi, that my favorite food is hot dogs and hamburgers. Actually there's one food I like even more, salami. My wife and I grew hungrier and hungrier. The smell of the hot dogs and burgers was really getting to us.

"Would G-d really care if we just had some lunch?" we wondered. "What choice do we have, after all? Even the Rebbe, whose mitzvah campaign we had become part of, would surely understand. We were not in Jerusalem or Tel Aviv. We were not in New York, or even in Los Angeles. We were in a convention center in Bologna, Italy… Shoshanah and I were rapidly growing dizzy and weak; the tempting aromas were almost overwhelming. Then, as if from heaven, this rabbi appeared with kosher food, and what's more, he's your friend!"

"Rabbi, we were the beneficiaries of an open miracle. We had taken upon ourselves to keep kosher even there, in the middle of nowhere. Why? Because you encouraged us in your *Neilah* appeal to take part in the Rebbe's mitzvah campaign. And the Rebbe sent us his shaliach, who found us in the middle of a large convention center, and brought us kosher food just at our weakest moment!"

Settling comfortably into her couch late one Thursday night, Mrs. Dini Freundlich sighed in relief. "Thank G-d, this will be a regular weekend," she thought. "Living here on shlichus is a challenge and an inspiration, but I could really use a break."

By "here" she meant Beijing, China, where she and her husband, Shimon, run the Chabad House, and "a regular weekend" means only fifty or sixty guests at their Shabbos meals.

It was two weeks after Pesach, and the past days had been especially taxing. Bi-annually, a large, two-week fair is held in Guanzhou (Canton), and Jewish businessmen from around the world attend it. Chabad of China provides kosher food, services and a spiritual respite for the participants. Mrs. Freundlich had been cooking, packaging and sending food for over two hundred people.

As she was resting, the telephone rang. Her husband took the call.

"Hello, this is Rabbi Mendel Gurewitz from Brunoy, France," said the voice at the other end. "A Chabad supporter from France, Mr. Greene, and a small group of associates are now in China on business. They are planning to spend Shabbos at the Great Wall and are wondering if you could send a few Jews to spend the day with them."

"I would like to help," responded Rabbi Freundlich, "but there really isn't anyone to send. You know, Beijing doesn't yet have a thriving Jewish community. To be honest, I'm not clear as to what 'Shabbos at the Great Wall' means; there are no hotels there. Why don't you give me Mr. Greene's number and I will contact him directly to see if I can be of assistance."

Rabbi Gurewitz readily gave him the number. After inquiries, Rabbi Freundlich discovered that Mr. Greene was planning to spend Friday celebrating a recent corporate merger together with his Chinese business partners. "They should have at least some semblance of Shabbos," thought Rabbi Freundlich. Nodding encouragingly at his wife, as she would have to do all this last minute baking, he offered to bring Mr. Greene and his associates *challah* and wine. Mr. Greene was very touched by the gesture, and they arranged to meet early Friday morning, before the group set out for the Great Wall.

"I groaned inwardly," recalled Mrs. Freundlich, "because it meant I would have to make the batch of dough right away. At that moment, I thought I would not have had the strength to budge even if the Great Wall was to come tumbling down on top of me!"

But of course the dough was made, and the next morning twelve freshly baked, golden *challos* were ready. As she handed the neatly packed bags to her husband, a weary Mrs. Freundlich muttered under her breath: "No one could appreciate the true cost of these *challos*."

"At least one person can," her understanding husband smiled warmly as he thanked her for her efforts.

An hour later, Rabbi Freundlich called his wife from the hotel.

"Mr. Greene would like to know how much you think your *challos* are worth?" he said. "He thinks they're worth a Torah scroll!"

Mrs. Freundlich could hardly believe her ears. Their Chabad House had been using a small scroll, which her parents, the Lipskars of Johannesburg, South Africa, had lent them. Chabad House of Beijing desperately needed its own scroll.

Later, Rabbi Freundlich related what had happened.

"Mr. Greene was very moved by our efforts to provide him with *challos* and wine. They were still warm from the oven and the aroma permeated the hotel lobby. He asked about our activities in Beijing, and how we managed to sustain and spread Judaism here. He inquired about our Chabad House – do we have a *minyan*, a Torah scroll and so on. I told him about our need, and he informed me that he had had two Torah scrolls written recently, and was planning to donate one to a worth-while institution."

Mrs. Freundlich adds: "The mantle for the Torah scroll has two *challos* embroidered on it. This is a reminder to myself and others that, when we meet a challenge, others often appreciate it, and our efforts are blessed by G-d."

The Alter Rebbe, Rabbi Schneur Zalman of Liadi, founder of the Chabad-Lubavitch chassidic movement, lived on the lower floor of a two-story home. His son, later to succeed him and to become known as the Mitteler Rebbe, lived on the upper floor.

Once the Mitteler Rebbe's baby son fell out of the cradle and began to cry. The Mitteler Rebbe was so absorbed in his studies, he did not even hear the baby's cries.

The Alter Rebbe was also studying. Nevertheless, he heard the baby and went upstairs to tend to the infant. Later he reprimanded his own son: "How could you have left the baby crying?"

The Mitteler Rebbe explained that he simply hadn't heard. He had been so engrossed in his studies that he was oblivious to everything else.

But the Alter Rebbe was not satisfied: "You should never be so involved in your own spiritual endeavors that you fail to hear the cry of a Jewish child."

When our Rebbe repeated this story, he explained that there are children who cry out because of physical discomfort or need and others whose need is spiritual. Sometimes, a person may not consciously know that he is in need, but his inner heart is crying. Our responsibility, he explained, is to listen carefully and be sensitive to this inner call.

*L*azer Sholokov was twelve-and-a-half when he attended the Chabad camp at Nizhny Novgorod, Russia. The shlichim and camp directors, Rabbi Shimon and Yael Bergman, had already noticed his innate sensitivity to Judaism during the past year of his participation in Chabad programs. And so Rabbi Bergman decided to broach the subject of his upcoming thirteenth birthday. He explained the meaning of the bar mitzvah ceremony and offered to prepare him for the event. Lazer was grateful to the rabbi, for his family knew little of Jewish practice.

"Lazer was a willing student," recalls Rabbi Bergman. "Still, I wanted him to know how fully I recognized his dedication in committing himself to learn how to read from the Torah and deliver a chassidic discourse by heart; this is not what typical twelve-year-old Russian boys of limited Jewish background usually choose to do. For that reason, I told him that gifts were also part of the celebration. I promised him a gift of his choice for his diligence and performance.

"Lazer did us all proud and fulfilled his role beautifully. His bar mitzvah was a moving experience for all those who attended." A few days later, Lazer paid the rabbi a visit. Rabbi Bergman was expecting him.

"Lazer," he exclaimed warmly, "you did wonderfully! You certainly earned the gift I promised. Just tell me what you want." Rabbi Bergman was sure Lazer would ask for some computer game or electronic gadget, as would any young boy from an underprivileged family. He would be only too happy to oblige. But he was unprepared for what followed.

"Rabbi," Lazer began with a slight quiver in his voice, "you have been very kind and generous to me, and since you promised me a gift, I feel it's all right to make this request. I hope it will not be asking too much. You see, I have a sixteen-year-old brother who became interested in putting on *tefillin* when I began to. We both have to leave the house early in the morning to get to school, and often there isn't enough time for both of us to put on *tefillin*. So for my gift, I would like to ask for a pair of *tefillin* for my brother."

Camp Gan Israel of Long Beach, California, directed by the shluchim Rabbi Moshe and Nechamah Engel, went to a baseball game. The campers were scurrying to find their seats, when Rabbi Engel heard his name being shouted across the stadium filled with forty thousand fans.

"Hey, Rabbi Engel, look here!" came the shrill call of a nine-year-old. The boy, who had attended camp the previous year, was waving his fringes. "See? I'm still wearing my *tzizis!*"

When Perla Cohen arrived at the home of Rabbi Shmuel and Sara Gurewitz in Lyon, France, she had all the tools for learning in hand. Born in Morocco, Perla was a full-time science student at La Doua University, and studying was simply what she did. And so, when the rabbi who would be officiating at her upcoming marriage informed her of the French Orthodox Rabbinical Union requirement that prospective couples become acquainted with the laws concerning Jewish family life, she scheduled a class with enthusiasm.

Mrs. Gurewitz, appreciated Perla's intelligence and curiosity and broadened the scope of their classes, teaching her about other aspects of setting up a Jewish home as well. She broached the topic of the *mezuzah*, explaining that this mitzvah is among the foremost signs of a Jewish household.

"Perla, you don't have to wait until you're married," Mrs. Gurewitz told her. "You can put a *mezuzah* on the door post of the apartment you live in right now."

"Mrs. Gurewitz," Perla responded, "I enjoy learning with you and understand the concept of this mitzvah, but I just don't think it's a good idea at the moment. You see, I live alone in the Les Brotteaux neighborhood of the sixth *arrondissement*. You must know that that's a very posh, non-Jewish area. I don't have to tell you about the anti-Semitism in France. I'm not sure it's safe to display my religion so openly."

Mrs. Gurewitz reiterated that the very essence of this mitzvah is safety and security, and from time to time she brought up the topic again. Eventually, Perla decided to put up a *mezuzah*, but on the inside of her door; she was still worried about attracting attention. It took a few more weeks before she gathered the courage to put up a *mezuzah* on the outside.

At winter break, Perla left Lyon to visit her family in Morocco. When she mentioned the *mezuzah* she had put up, however, she was confronted with opposition. Her family echoed her own original apprehensiveness and convinced her that she was compromising her safety. And so the *mezuzah* came down.

Shortly afterwards, though, Perla called to tell Mrs. Gurewitz that she had put the *mezuzah* back up on the outside of her door. Mrs. Gurewitz was surprised. Ever since she had learned of the parents' adamant protest, Mrs. Gurewitz had not brought up the topic again, hoping to find an appropriate time in the future, perhaps. What had made Perla change her mind?

Perla recounted that, a few days earlier, an elderly man had come to her door and introduced himself as her downstairs neighbor. She barely knew him, aside from the one time he had come up to give her a piece of mail that had mistakenly been put in his box.

The man had a pained look in his eyes. "Why did you take off the *mezuzah*?" he had asked in a troubled voice. "Please don't think badly of me for intruding on your privacy but, you see, I'm a Holocaust survivor. I came from a large, proud and observant Jewish family. In the war I lost everyone and everything. I married a non-Jewish woman and have drifted far away from my heritage.

"When I came up to deliver your mail that day and saw a *mezuzah* on the door, it reminded me of my childhood, my family and my religion. Instinctively, I reached up to kiss it, and that brought a flow of tears as I recalled my long-lost mother, father, brother and sisters. Ever since then, I had been taking the elevator up to your floor every day just to kiss the *mezuzah*. It has comforted me and enabled me to reconnect with my past. Why did you take it away?"

*I*t was the final Shabbos of the Jewish year, and a group of rabbinical students had flown in from New York to assist Rabbi Moshe and Matty Bryski of Agoura Hills, California, with the junior congregation program for the upcoming High Holy Days.

On the way back from the morning services, two of the students noticed a moving van parked in front of a house in the neighborhood. Guiding the truck into the driveway were a man and a young girl.

Spontaneously, the boys approached them.

"Hello! Welcome to the neighborhood," they called out cheerfully. "We're from New York and are guests of the local rabbi. Are you Jewish?"

"Yes, I am, in fact," replied the man. "My name's Jeff and this is my daughter, Rebeccah."

"Come and join us for the Shabbos meal," suggested the boys. "We're on our way to pick up another member of the community right now, and our hosts love to have guests!"

The man was clearly taken aback by their gesture. He looked around hesitantly, first at the movers, then at his daughter, at his new home, and back at the friendly young men. As he stood there, a bit overwhelmed, one of the boys approached the movers and made a similar inquiry. Soon, the man, his daughter and the movers – who turned out to be Israelis – were sitting around the same Shabbos table eating *cholent*, saying *l'chayim*, and singing songs.

As Shabbos came to an end, and it was time for the Saturday night services, Rabbi Bryski realized that they could have a *minyan* right on the premises. It was quite a mixed bunch that gathered for the evening *maariv* service and the *havdalah* ceremony that followed. As if on cue, singing and dancing erupted, joining together the muscle-bound Israeli movers, the newcomer, the young chassidic men and the rabbi.

A few days later, an envelope arrived at the Chabad House. It was a thank-you note from Jeff, expressing his appreciation for the warm welcome.

"I want you to know," he wrote, "that before I moved, I had prayed that I would be able to connect to Jewish people and find a community. I never imagined that my prayers would be answered quite so quickly, and so extensively!"

Jeff began attending some of the Chabad programs. One

evening, Rabbi Bryski was giving a class on the subject of "Faith and Suffering." Jeff was there, listening attentively and wiping tears from his eyes. After the class he came up to the rabbi and embraced him, unable to hold back his sobbing. Gently, Rabbi Bryski invited him to his office, and Jeff began to tell his story.

"A year before I moved to Agoura, my family fell apart due to unfortunate circumstances. I couldn't bear the pain of loss, nor cope with my depression. I was angry at G-d and hated myself. My emotions were so out of hand that I decided to end my life.

"But I wanted to leave my one daughter with a positive memory of me, so I took her out to the movies, planning to bid this miserable world farewell that night after she fell asleep. We made our way to the Mountaingate Plaza Cinema in the Simi Valley Mall.

"As we entered the mall, we heard some Jewish-sounding music and were surprised to see a Jewish group singing and dancing right in front of the theater. There was a large menorah burning brightly in the background, and I suddenly remembered that it was Chanukah. Before I knew it, one of the dancers drew us into the circle. And there I was – on the night I had planned to end my life, I found myself dancing and celebrating!

"The irony of the situation throttled me and I knew then and there I couldn't go through with my plan. I resolved to give life another try. I would move and find a new home, a new community and a new life. I found a house here in Agoura Hills and prayed that it would work out. And there you were, the very day I moved in."

Rabbi Bryski listened attentively to Jeff's story, and could hardly contain his inner tumult. He grasped Jeff's hand and held it tightly for a moment. Then he said: "Please wait here. I'll be right back."

"I ran to my bedroom," recalls Rabbi Bryski, "and pulled out some photo albums, looking for the volume with Chanukah pictures. I searched through the photos, flipping the pages back and forth in a frenzy. Then I found it! Chanukah at the Simi Valley Mall... We were the people dancing there. That year we had decided to add another city to our list of Chanukah lighting celebrations. Why Simi Valley? Why Mountaingate Mall? I don't know. Why did we grab a total stranger and get him to dance? Why not? It was Chanukah, after all, and we shouldn't be the only ones celebrating.

"And yes! There was the picture of the man and his daughter dancing with us that night! A snapshot of life...."

When Rabbi Menachem Brod entered the Yad Labonim hall in Rechovot, Israel, he was met by a crestfallen group of organizers. The local schluchim had worked hard to organize what they had hoped would be a successful event. They had invited Rabbi Brod, a gifted speaker and the spokesman for Chabad in Israel. He in turn had prepared a powerful address on Chabad philosophy, incorporating an audiovisual program. The program also featured musical entertainment and, all in all, it seemed to be a promising evening.

One glance into the attractively set hall, however, told the story. The audience was very sparse. With visible disappointment, the organizer expressed their regret at having troubled Rabbi Brod.

But Rabbi Brod took it all in stride and tried to raise his hosts' spirits. "Let me tell you a story I heard from the well-known educator, Rabbi Tzvi Greenwald of Kfar Chabad. An evening for parents was organized in one of the Chabad day schools in the United States, but only a few people showed up – four, to be precise. The principal was devastated and at some point informed the Rebbe's office of the failure.

"The Rebbe's secretary, Rabbi Chodokov, responded by sending this message of comfort. 'Look' he said. 'You might plan an evening hoping for a large crowd of, say, four hundred people. Out of that impressive audience of four hundred, you might actually reach only four people in a genuine way. And so, what difference does it make if you reach those four people out of a large crowd or directly?'

"By the same token," concluded Rabbi Brod, "let the evening go on, regardless of the numbers. One can never know which individuals may be affected."

With their spirits lifted, the organizers proceeded with the program.

Many months later, Rabbi Brod participated in a "weekend with Chabad" in Jerusalem. He was scheduled to speak after the meal on Friday night, and his lecture was to be followed by an informal *farbrengen*.[9] At such weekends, it is often this informal setting that provides the relaxed and friendly atmosphere most conducive to meaningful discussion. It was hoped that a substantial group would stay for this special experience.

Unexpectedly, though, the crowd dispersed after the lecture, and only a handful remained. "People are tired," one guest commented understandingly. "Many of them have traveled a long way today."

"Some parents had to go put their children to bed," offered another.

---

9. A chassidic gathering including talks and song.

Rabbi Brod nodded. "I'm not fazed," he smiled and began the *farbrengen* by relating his experience in Rechovot, including the story he had shared with that evening's organizers.

As he concluded, one of the guests sitting right next to him spoke up. "I can vouch for that story," he affirmed, "every word of it. Rabbi Brod, you probably don't recognize me now, with my beard and chassidic garb. But I was one of those few participants in Rechovot. Like you said: 'One can never know which individual may be affected.'"

The job description – Jewish chaplain for a Melbourne, Australia, hospital – seemed like something Goldie Goldbloom (nee Feld) could handle. Visiting patients and meeting their religious needs didn't seem too tall an order.

"This could be an opportunity to involve myself in additional outreach work, and the hours would complement my morning teaching job at the kindergarten," she thought as she filled out the application.

Goldie got the job and enjoyed the different opportunities for self-expression that the two very disparate settings afforded. The kindergarten enabled her to use her teaching skills and creativity, and challenged her ability to manage a classroom. The afternoon job required communicating warmth and care to the sick. These daily demands drew out her resourcefulness and enthusiasm.

But then, there were some situations that taxed her usual zeal, like dealing with the newcomer to her kindergarten, five-year-old Laura.

"How can I get through to her?" Goldie found herself wondering.

Her students – a varied group, mostly from non-observant homes – were mainly boys with an abundance of energy. She had them pretty much under control when Laura arrived. Good, she thought, a nice little girl to complement my rowdy bunch.

Laura seemed shy and timid at first. She clung to her mother and sniffled constantly as the woman tried in vain to coax her into the circle. Finally, her mother gave her a gentle shove and said, "Do grow up, Laura! Here's your lunch. That's Miss Feld. Call her 'Miss.'" Then she was off.

Laura took one look at "Miss," began to howl, and threw her sandwich at Goldie. While Goldie was dealing with bits of cheese and tomato, Laura bit a little boy on the cheek.

"I tried everything with that girl, but she was so difficult. So I resorted to the age-old method of positive reinforcement. If Laura, let's say, was helping the janitor (i.e., giving the broom a whirl), I would snap her picture with a Polaroid camera. Then I'd hang up the photograph and say, 'Oh look, there's Laura cleaning up!' It worked wonders.

"One Friday at the Shabbos party, I took Laura's picture as she lit the candles. She looked very sweet."

But that weekend, Goldie learned later, Laura had attempted to light Shabbos candles at home. Unfortunately, her family would hear nothing of the sort, and Laura didn't come back to kindergarten on Monday. She must have been moved to another school, thought Goldie – probably one that taught Jewish thought but not Jewish practice.

Thinking about Laura had taken up a considerable amount of Goldie's time and attention. Now she found herself with more freedom to contemplate one of her afternoon challenges – visits with Sara, an eighty-year-old woman who had been hospitalized after a stroke.

"I've always had a sense of respect and regard for the

elderly," comments Goldie, "and I sincerely wanted to communicate with her."

But that proved to be impossible. Sara lay motionless and unresponsive in an isolated room. The staff seemed to assume she would eventually die there, and the room she was given, windowless and grim, was far removed from the nurses' desk.

"As a chaplain, I was supposed to brighten her day, but it wasn't easy. Impossible, in fact. I told funny stories. I tried Russian, Yiddish, Hebrew. No response. I brushed her hair. She just slipped further and further away. One day I showed her Shabbos candles. Suddenly, she moaned.

"Moaned, and squeezed my hand. This was the first sign of communication from Sara. Here it was, something that might bring life to her. I ran to ask the nurses, who told me regretfully, that she definitely could not light candles in her room.

"And so I thought and thought about Sara. Then I had an idea. I assembled photographs of Shabbos candles and made her a mobile. Some were pictures of girls lighting candles. Some were pictures of candles shining warmly by themselves. I hung it over her bed where she could see it.

"Sara truly loved that mobile. Her eyes wandered mistily over it and tears rolled down her yellowed face. I was so glad that I had managed to do something that touched her. Even though she never acknowledged my presence in any way, those tears were her quiet thanks.

"When I returned the next week, Sara wasn't there. The mobile spun forlornly in the air from the vent, but a photo had been pulled off from it. It was the one of Laura lighting her Shabbos candles. I went to the nurses' station to find out what had happened.

"'Oh, yeah,' shrugged the nurse on duty, chewing her lunch. 'That old lady was the religious type. Before she got really sick, she'd insist about some religious practices. Her daughter never related to it; she thought the old woman was just losing her mind. Funny thing, though. The old lady somehow grabbed that gizmo in there one night and was holding a picture of a little kid when she died. When her daughter showed up, she couldn't figure out how her mother had gotten a picture of her granddaughter lighting Jewish candles. She claimed the girl never lit candles, never ever.'"

> *The Rebbe Rashab, the fifth Lubavitcher Rebbe, was once asked:"What is a chassid?"*
>
> *The Rebbe replied: "A chassid is a lamplighter." Years ago, there were kerosene lanterns on every street corner. Lamplighters would trudge through the night with a long torch, going from lamp to lamp. Even in the cold and the dark, these lone figures would make their way through the night, leaving a path of light behind them. The Rebbe continued: "A chassid goes forth with a long torch. He knows the fire isn't his, but that his mission is to kindle all the lanterns."*
>
> *The questioner persisted: "And what if the lantern is found in a desert?"*
>
> *"One must go there too and kindle the lantern. . . ."*
>
> *"And if the lantern is in the sea?"*
>
> *"One has to plunge into the water and kindle the lantern."*[10]
>
> *The Rebbe has encouraged us all to be lamplighters, to kindle the spark that exists within everyone.*

It is a two-hour flight from Johannesburg to Plettenberg Bay, on the southeast coast of South Africa. But Rabbi Ari Shishler, on shlichus with his wife Naomi in Johannesburg, wasn't daunted by the commute. It was his turn

---

10. *Sefer HaSichos 5701*, p. 136ff.

at the two-week shift to sustain a daily summer *minyan* in which volunteers from Johannesburg participated. This popular bay town attracts many vacationers, among them numerous Jews who would join a *minyan* if one were available.

One morning after the services, an older fellow, who introduced himself as Sam G., asked to speak to Rabbi Shishler.

"Unlike many of the visitors here, I'm an old-timer who retired to the Bay years ago," he said. "I join the many Jews who appreciate the effort you and your fellow rabbis have invested in coming here. However, I'd like to offer a personal note of gratitude. I don't know how I can share this with the specific people involved, so I'll tell you, as a Chabad representative.

"Some years ago, before anyone began coming out here, two young *yeshivah* students arrived at my door. They introduced themselves as Chabad students and said they had come to visit Jewish people in Plettenberg Bay. We had a pleasant chat, and at one point the boys invited me to put on *tefillin*.

"I had been brought up traditionally, had had a bar mitzvah, and knew what they were asking. But I wasn't following an observant lifestyle, so, though I enjoyed our conversation, I declined. We continued talking for a while and the boys left. Before they did, though, they urged me once again to put on *tefillin*. I refused their offer.

"A few weeks later, just before Yom Kippur, I recalled the encounter and thought about it. 'It's not such a bad idea to put on *tefillin* once in a while,' I told myself. I had a pair, and decided to do it. That left me feeling good, and after Yom Kippur, I did it again. I was soon putting on *tefillin* every day.

"About six months later, it occurred to me that you're supposed to recite prayers while donning the *tefillin*, and I resolved to add them to my morning ritual. I surfed the internet for guidance and included some prayers in my service as well. Six more months went by when I came to the realization that a person really should pray more extensively. I knew I had a prayer book stored away somewhere. After some searching, I found it and began praying from the book.

"The following year, I felt the need to add some Bible study to my prayer routine. Once again, on the internet I found a site that led me to study the weekly portion. After an entire year, I had gone through the full Five Books of Moses. I decided to repeat the cycle, delving deeper into the sources and expanding my knowledge.

"A second year passed, when one day my thoughts turned to my many fellow Jews in Plettenberg Bay. The sorry reality was that most were totally assimilated, with little or no knowledge of their heritage. Their alienation nagged at me until I decided to do something about it and share the knowledge I had acquired. So it's been three years now that I teach a weekly Torah class to a group of people who would never have sought it out on their own.

"The reason I'm telling you all this is because I feel a debt to those two young men who originally planted the seed, though for all they know, they were unsuccessful. But that seed did indeed bear fruit. As I have no way of knowing who they were, and I'm unable to thank them personally, I'm thanking you instead."

Rabbi Shishler was touched as well as curious about what he had heard.

"Do you remember what year it was that those two students visited you?" he inquired.

He did.

Rabbi Ari Shishler had been one of the boys.

*I*t was mid-afternoon when Stanley Lapon went to the front door to pick up his mail. A middle-aged accountant, he lived alone; his only companions were his tropical fish.

When he opened the door, he found a cardboard box on the doorstep. At first he thought it was a medium-sized pizza that had been delivered to his home by mistake, but when he opened it and saw the letter inside, a smile came to his face – rare for that time in his life. The letter was a holiday wish from Rabbi Yisrael and Devorah Shmotkin of Chabad House, Milwaukee, Wisconsin. The box contained hand-baked matzah to be eaten at the Passover Seder.

The next afternoon, another cardboard box arrived. Recognizing the packaging, he wondered about the double gift.

"Strange," he thought, "one box was nice, but two seems a bit extravagant on the rabbi's part. I've never known Chabad House to have an inflated bank account...."

A day later, he discovered a third box of matzah.

"Huh! This sort of thing happens sometimes with government tax refunds," the accountant mused to himself. "Just my luck. Some people get money when a computer goes berserk. I get matzah."

When the fourth box of matzah arrived, Stanley was brought up short. "What *is* this? What'll I do with all these boxes? I only need one for the Seder. Perhaps the postmaster, Rabbi Shmotkin or G-d Himself is trying to tell me something...."

He concluded that the message was from the last, and decided to do exactly as Rabbi Shmotkin had done – to give the matzah to others, thereby continuing the chain of goodwill. Since he didn't know many people, he gave two of the boxes to colleagues at work – one to a Jewish woman who had married a Christian, and one to a Jewish man whose wife was not Jewish. The third box he took with him to the Seder he would be attending at his father's home, and the fourth he kept for himself.

Unfortunately, his family Seder began dismally. His stepmother was very ill and could barely sit at the table; everyone could see her time in this world was growing short. Yet when it came time to eat "the bread of affliction," the ailing woman suddenly brightened.

"Who brought this hand-baked matzah?" she asked, making a visible effort to speak.

"I did," responded Stanley.

"Thank you very much," she said. "Every day is precious to me now, and the opportunity to eat this special matzah has added meaning to the ritual. In my condition, a person desires only that which is most authentic."

The ailing woman's words changed the mood at the table, and the evening progressed in the spirit of the holiday, which is to be celebrated with joy.

"Rabbi Shmotkin was doing something right when he gave away this matzah," Stanley thought to himself.

Three days later, when he returned to the office, the man to whom he had given the matzah approached him as soon as he got in the door.

"You know," he said, "that special matzah you gave me for Passover had a rather profound effect on my wife, who isn't Jewish, or even particularly spiritual. We used to have a Seder at my house but abandoned the practice a while ago. Even so, I gave everyone some of your matzah and she was really taken by it. She couldn't believe how ancient it looked, and that such a humble food is still a part of the Jewish ritual.

"But you know what's really surprising? She made me take down our dusty Bible and read the entire story of the Exodus to her and the kids. So I guess you could say I had somewhat of a Seder after all."

As Stanley walked toward his office, the Jewish woman who had married the gentile met him in the hallway.

"I really want to thank you for that matzah you gave us for Passover. You know, every year my daughter, my husband and I go to my parents' house for a semi-Seder. It's really just a meal, because my husband doesn't relate to it at all. When our daughter opened the matzah box, she gave everyone a piece and then read the rabbi's letter aloud.

"I was astounded when my husband turned to me and said, 'It seems she really likes this religious stuff; maybe you're right in insisting she go to Hebrew Sunday school.' He had always been against it, you see.

"I don't know what changed his mind, but I think that box of matzah had something to do with it."

"When is the bus coming?" inquired one of the children who had accompanied his parents on the trip to Yosemite Park. Rabbi Yosef and Dena Levin of Chabad in Palo Alto had organized an enjoyable excursion, bringing community members together. Now they were waiting for the shuttle bus that would take them to the next stop. Some of the people had walked over to a shaded waiting area, but the rabbi preferred to wait by the road, where the bus driver could spot him more easily.

As the rabbi stood there next to the winding road, a red convertible with its hood down and music up came by. The car slowed and stopped next to him. Its two occupants were dark-skinned, with long hair, and their accent and demeanor gave them away.

"Shalom!" one of the Israelis called out. "You look like you might speak our language. We're a bit confused by the park map; maybe you can help us out."

Rabbi Levin was happy to be of assistance. The three conversed briefly, and Rabbi Levin found out that the two were brothers from the city of Rechovot in central Israel, who had been touring the States for a while. Rabbi Levin invited them to spend Shabbat at Chabad house in Palo Alto.

"Thanks, but we have plans to meet friends in San Francisco," one of the brothers replied. They were ready to be on their way.

But Rabbi Levin was not going to let two young Israelis drive off from this unexpected meeting in Yosemite Park with only directions in hand. He pulled out his wallet and handed one of them a dollar bill.

"I told you that I was from Chabad. Our Rebbe taught us that when two Jews meet, it's not a mere coincidence. Their encounter should benefit a third. In light of that directive, I would like to give you this dollar bill and request that you be my messenger. When you're back in Rechovot, please put it into the charity box at the Chabad House and give my regards to the people there. Some of them are friends of mine from back in my *yeshivah* days."

Rabbi Levin fulfills this directive with many people he meets. Beyond the immediate benefit of participating in the mitzvah of charity, it also provides an opportunity to introduce a fellow Jew to a Chabad House in his area. Usually, the person will take the dollar and place it in a pocket offhandedly, nodding in agreement. But this fellow took the mission with apparent seriousness. He rummaged around the car for an envelope and asked the rabbi to write his name on it, so he wouldn't have to rely on his memory.

The two brothers then bade the rabbi farewell, and drove off.

Several years later, Rabbi Levin was in Israel and visited his old *yeshivah* friends in Rechovot. One of them was Rabbi Mendel Gluckowsky, the rabbi of the Chabad community. Rabbi Gluckowsky was on the phone in his home office as his old friend walked in. He jumped and said animatedly into the receiver: "Do you know who just walked into my office? Rabbi Yosef Levin from California!" He promptly summoned his children and announced: "I want you to meet the Rabbi Yosef Levin from Palo Alto."

Everyone seemed to be excited by Rabbi Levin's arrival, but he couldn't understand what all the fuss was about.

"Do you remember giving someone a dollar bill at Yosemite National Park a few years ago?" Rabbi Gluckowsky asked.

Rabbi Levin knitted his brow. "I have a vague recollection of that," he replied hesitantly. "I've done it so often that I can't recall every encounter."

Rabbi Gluckowsky then told Rabbi Levin that, when the two men he had met came back to Rechovot, they were careful to complete the mission he had given them. The brothers knew of the existence of the local Chabad House, though they had not attended any of its activities. The two were hard rock musicians, not identified in the least with Judaism.

"Is the rabbi who runs the activities here?" one of them had asked the secretary.

"No, not at the moment, unfortunately. Perhaps I can help you?"

"My name is Noam David. I have an envelope for him from California."

Noam regretted that he wasn't able to deliver the message personally, but felt he had fulfilled his obligation and left.

The secretary left the envelope on his paper-laden desk, making a mental note to pass it on later. But soon he was caught up in the busy activities at Chabad House, and the envelope slipped his mind. Some time later, a young man who lives in Kfar Chabad and works at Chabad House, teaching classes and organizing outreach activities, walked in. His name is Yosef Levin.

"Oh, Yosef," the secretary said, handing him the envelope. "This envelope has your name on it."

"Who's it from?"

The secretary knit his brow in an attempt to recall. "I think his name was Noam David. Or maybe it was David Noam…I'm sorry, I don't remember."

Opening the envelope, Yosef Levin of Kfar Chabad was puzzled by its contents.

"Who is Noam David or David Noam?" he wondered. "And why is he sending me a dollar bill?"

Yosef was determined to find out. Phone book in hand, he began to call every Noam David and David Noam listed. Every call was the same: "Hello, are you by any chance the fellow who brought an envelope to Chabad House for Yosef Levin?"

Halfway down the list, he found the musician.

"Not for Yosef Levin, but from Yosef Levin!" Noam David stated, and proceeded to tell the story.

"Nothing is a coincidence," insisted Yosef Levin of Rechovot. "We were destined to meet. When can I see you?"

Thus began an acquaintance between Yosef Levin of Rechovot and Noam David, the rock musician. They spent many hours in discussion and study. In time, Noam succeeded in convincing his reluctant brother to join him. Soon, both brothers, deeply affected by the teachings of Chassidus, in-corporated Jewish content into their band's repertoire. Many of Rechovot's unaffiliated youth would gather at their club to share in music, song and inspirational Torah messages. Thus, the brothers in turn brought many people back to Judaism, including other members of their family. In time, Noam and his brother built their own families, and now both lead a fully chassidic lifestyle.

The state of Utah operates a number of residential treat-ment centers for troubled teens. Rabbi Benny Zippel, on shlichus in Salt Lake City with his wife Sharonne, frequents these schools, visiting Jewish teens and addressing their religious needs. He and his wife also maintain contact with the families, offering assistance and support.

One day a call came from a distraught mother whose daughter had run away from school and had been tracked down by the authorities. She had gotten into all kinds of trouble, and was now being held by the police. The school wasn't eager to take her back.

"Please, rabbi," the woman pleaded. "Can you help convince the police and the school to give her another chance? She's just a confused child who has made some irresponsible mistakes."

Rabbi Zippel was resolved to do his best, but he was convinced the mother could contribute as well.

"The school is an hour's drive away," he answered. "I'll make the trip there and plead her case. From your description, though, we're going to need help from Above. Perhaps you would consider extending yourself a bit to arouse the Divine blessing of success?"

"I'll make any donation you want," the mother replied. "Just tell me to which charity I should make out the check."

"That is not what I meant at all," Rabbi Zippel assured her. "I'd like to suggest that you take upon yourself the mitzvah of lighting Shabbos candles on Friday nights."

His words met with pronounced silence.

"Rabbi," the woman finally replied, "I'm prepared to pay any amount, but I'm not a hypocrite. I never light candles. Why should I suddenly start now, just because my daughter is in trouble? I don't feel comfortable doing that."

Rabbi Zippel explained the value of performing any mitzvah, regardless of the level of one's ongoing commitment to Torah, and despite the double standard that seems implicit in turning to G-d only because of urgent need.

"I know you'll do your best for us whether I light candles or not, and I appreciate that," the woman concluded. "Meanwhile, I'll think about it and call you back."

Some time later, the woman called back. "Please send me the packet of candles and the information I need." Then she added, "Have you managed to do anything for my daughter in the meantime?"

Rabbi Zippel had indeed arranged a meeting with the police and the school authorities.

"The meeting is scheduled for next week," he informed the mother. "But today is Friday, and you can start lighting candles right away. I will get you candles and instructions before Shabbos begins."

"Rabbi, I don't exactly live around the corner from you! I'm calling from California! You will have to mail me the packet and I'll light next week."

Rabbi Zippel was undaunted. "Where do you live?"

"In Calabassas."

"What's your phone number? You'll hear from someone soon."

Rabbi Zippel called his friend in California, Rabbi Moshe Bryski. He briefed him about the woman's need for candles and gave him her number.

Rabbi Bryski called.

"Hello, I am a friend of Rabbi Zippel. I have a candle-lighting kit for you. Please give me directions to your home."

The woman was caught by surprise. "You've dialed my cell. I'm not home right now," she replied, wondering at the quick response.

"Where are you?"

"I'm in a small city called Agoura Hills."

"What street are you on?"

"Canwood Road near Reyes Adobe."

"You're one hundred feet from the Chabad House where I'm located!"

Within minutes, the astonished woman had the candle-lighting kit in her hands.

*   *   *

In the winter of 2005, Rabbi Baruch Kaplan of Mayanot Institute in Jerusalem was conducting a *farbrengen* at the Chabad House of Greater Boston. Among the many things Rabbi Kaplan shared was the above story, which he had heard from Rabbi Bryski.

After the *farbrengen*, some of the students stayed to chat with the Chabad House Rabbi, Shmuel Posner.

"I enjoyed the program tonight," commented Gideon. "But all you seemed to talk about was Divine Providence. Some of the stories really sounded a little far-fetched."

A couple of days later, during Chanukah, Gideon was

speaking to a friend who was spending a few days in Toronto. He wished his friend a happy holiday and asked about menorah lighting.

"Gideon, I don't know many people here. Where in the world would I get a menorah and candles?"

Suddenly, the story came to mind.

"If I get you one, will you light?" Gideon asked.

"Hey, that's awfully nice of you to offer, but I wouldn't want you to bother and spend the money mailing it."

"Little bother, and no expense," Gideon assured.

With some information from Rabbi Posner, a shaliach in the Toronto area was contacted. That evening, a menorah-lighting kit was waiting at the hotel where Gideon's friend was staying.

"So, did Stacy agree to share her story?" Chanah asked.

"Yes, she did," replied Shiffy with a sigh of satisfaction. Shiffy and her husband, Rabbi Yosef Landa, are on shlichus in S. Louis, Missouri.

She and twenty-two other women had been working on the upcoming Chabad Women's Mid-Winter Convention for several weeks. This was the first time in twenty-five years that the convention would be held in S. Louis, and the committee was working hard to make it a memorable event. The crew of talented and dedicated women met regularly to plan the program, and many hours were spent enlisting speakers. It's always a treat to have a local woman who has become involved with Chabad represent the host-city, and the committee had deliberated about whom to ask.

A few weeks later, at the Shabbos afternoon session of the convention, Stacy was on the podium, telling her story.

"I was newly married and eagerly planning to start a family. I was young and healthy, or so I thought. A routine visit to the doctor, however, revealed an extreme condition that threatened to prevent us from having children naturally. When I heard the diagnosis I was devastated. There is no history of this disease in my family, and I had never sensed that such a problem existed. The doctors recommended an operation that might alleviate the problem but offered no guarantees. I had the surgery done and learned how to pray.

"My husband Michael and I were close to the Chabad shluchim here, and they were instrumental in our efforts to find direction and hope. We knew we needed a miracle, and sought to tap the inner resources of our souls and thus merit that gift from Above. So, when Rabbi and Mrs. Landa invited us to accompany them to New York for the wedding of a local community member, we agreed. They also informed us of the virtue of writing a letter and praying at the gravesite of the Rebbe and mentioned that this trip would be an opportunity for them to take us there.

"I'm sure you're all guessing that we were indeed blessed. You are right. We are the proud parents of a beautiful daughter, Devorah Malka. But that's not the point of my story. In preparing to speak to you today, I was a bit concerned about making public statements about personal prayers that are answered. That's because I know there are so many women whose prayers for children have not yet been answered. I wish I knew why some blessings are revealed while others are not.

"And so my intent is not to highlight our personal good fortune. What I want to share is the knowledge that our journey was not an easy one. I want to empower you to discover the ability each of you has to trust wholeheartedly in G-d, to pray and believe in miracles. I know you all possess this, because

I've 'been there' and I'm an ordinary person, no different than any of you.

"And, most importantly, never give up. When I became pregnant, the doctors told me the pregnancy would alleviate the symptoms of my condition. They were right; there was no sign of the disease at all, and we were all certain that the pregnancy had corrected the problem. But unfortunately, the condition returned after the birth. As I assessed my body, I addressed my soul as well and dug inward for more of that inner strength I mentioned earlier. I intensified my trust in Hashem, sent another letter to the Rebbe's gravesite, and took on additional adherence to G-d's laws. With much gratitude, I'm able to tell you that, as I stand here today, my pleas have been granted and we have been blessed with a second miraculous pregnancy."

The audience listened attentively to Stacy's address. Not many noticed that one woman, Callie, had gotten up and left the room. Even those who had, would not have thought twice about it. Except for Esther, a participant from Cleveland, Ohio. She had seen something that caused her to hurry out after the departing woman – a tear on her cheek. Esther caught up with Callie in the corner of the lobby. By this time more tears had begun to flow. Esther put her arms around the sobbing woman and said softly, "I know, I know…"

"How could you know?" Callie answered. "How could you know the deep pain of infertility? I'm so sorry I came to this convention! I'm originally from S. Louis, but we relocated to Seattle and got involved with Chabad there. We just moved back this past summer, and I wanted to reconnect to Chabad here. So when I found out about the convention, I was happy to participate.

"But now I regret it. Every other woman here is pregnant! And then, to top it off, this emotional talk about belief and trust and prayer from a woman who has already been blessed. It's too much for me."

Callie stopped weeping and brought herself under control. She wiped away a tear and looked apologetically at Esther.

"Why am I telling you all this? I don't even know you."

Esther took her hand compassionately.

"We may not know each other, but I know your pain," she said. "I too have not been able to have children of my own. When I saw you get up and leave, I knew why right away and wanted to lend a listening ear and an understanding heart. The truth is, the speaker is right. Just as you feel deep pain, so you can also attune yourself to your soul's capacity for deep belief. Every Jew has that capacity, especially women. Don't be sorry that you came to the convention; you have no idea how much collective strength there is in this audience. With the women's prayers and G-d's help, I bless you that you'll be back for next year's convention too, together with your baby!"

The two women walked back to the convention hall together.

A few weeks later, Vickie, another woman who had attended and was close to Shiffy, approached her.

"I was moved by Stacy's talk at the convention," she said. "My husband and I have been waiting a long time for a child. Could you instruct me in how to request a blessing from the Rebbe?"

"Of course," Shiffy replied. "Incidentally, I've heard of an infertility specialist who has recently moved to town. His name is Dr. Michael Dahan, and he has a good reputation for success. Our sages teach us to do all we can to draw down blessings from Above within the confines of our abilities. Here, let me give you his number."

In a relatively short time, Dr. Dahan was able to assist

this woman, and she gave birth to a healthy baby boy. Shortly afterward, Dr. Dahan unexpectedly left town and moved to California. He had been in S. Louis just long enough to help Vickie.

And by next year's mid-winter convention, Callie, the woman who had abruptly left the speech, was able to join women the world over in the ultimate feminine dilemma: "Should I stay at home, or go and take my baby along?"

"What have I gotten myself into?" Helen thought as she drove with her seven-year-old daughter, Elizabeth, to Parkhill School in East Croydon, London. The early morning drive gave her some time to think over the events that had led to their trip to school together that day.

Helen had been brought up in an observant home in northwest London, but as the years went by she found herself drifting away from Jewish practice. When she was eighteen, her younger brother turned thirteen and the family planned his bar mitzvah. Helen's parents decided to hold the celebration in Israel, then a fledgling country in great need of support from Jews living abroad. Shortly after the bar mitzvah, her parents decided to make *aliyah*. Helen didn't want to leave her friends, school and comfortable environment, but went along reluctantly. She stayed in Israel for a while but eventually came back to London and lived with relatives.

In time, she met a non-Jewish man and got married. Her parents condemned her act and severed all contact with her. Their extreme response hurt Helen deeply, but she was determined to live her own life.

The couple had two children, a girl and a boy. When he was only a few months old, the boy passed away. Although

Helen had distanced herself from Judaism all these years, she felt she had to provide a proper Jewish burial for her son. When she began to inquire about the details, she found that a Jewish burial would be problematic, as the boy's father was not Jewish. She was advised to contact a Reform rabbi because "they are not so particular."

The ceremony left Helen feeling a bit hollow. In her memories, a Jewish burial seemed to have more than what the Temple offered. But, as before, she continued to push all thoughts of her religion out of her mind.

Until one day in December, five years later.

That morning, she resolved to confront the uncomfortable, nagging truth that her daughter had a non-Jewish father, attended a non-Jewish school, had non-Jewish friends and knew nothing about her religion. This was not a new realization for Helen, but lately it had been tugging at her heart.

"She's picking up all sorts of things from the multi-faith group of kids in her school, and she doesn't know the first thing about her own religion," Helen thought regretfully.

She decided to tell her daughter about their Jewish heritage and instill in her a sense of identification with her people. Elizabeth accepted this new information with delight and pride. Happily, she shared the knowledge of her identity with her friends and teachers at school. In time, word reached the principal's office, and shortly afterward, he called Helen.

"Hello," the principal said. "It has come to my attention that your daughter, Elizabeth, is Jewish and seems to be proud of it. You know our school believes strongly in pluralism; we strive to ensure that all our pupils, regardless of their background, feel accepted and have an opportunity to express themselves. Now, with the holiday season beginning, I would like to invite you to speak to our students about your winter festival of Chanukah."

How could Helen refuse?

So here she was, on the way to speak to a group of children about a holiday and an identity she had left behind so many years ago.

"The irony of it all!" she mused. "But I can't afford to daydream now; I have to organize my thoughts. Goodness, it's been so many years since I've thought about Chanukah. What am I going to say? How am I supposed to explain this holiday to kids?"

Just then she spotted a red hatchback parked in a driveway. There was an impressive menorah affixed to its roof, with a bright sign wishing all 'A Happy Chanukah.'

"A menorah on a car?! In this posh area of East Croydon?! Maybe in the community where I grew up in North London – but here? Wait, this may be just what I need."

She stopped her car abruptly and, taking her daughter by the hand, walked up to the house.

Rabbi Menachem and Goldie Junik of Chabad in London didn't often hear their doorbell ringing so early in the morning.

"Uh…oh…hello. I'm really sorry to disturb you at such an hour," Helen told the surprised Juniks. "You don't know me, but I noticed your car. You look like just the kind of people who could help me. Would you have any printed material I could use to explain the meaning of this holiday to children?"

Briefly, she explained her appointment at the school.

Asking no questions, the Juniks handed her a packet of Chanukah brochures and warmly invited her and her daughter to join them later in the afternoon for tea.

"We'll do that," Helen promised with gratitude. "You've been so accommodating to a total stranger who rang your bell at this early hour. I owe you more of an explanation, but now I must be on my way so I won't be late at the school."

Helen came back for tea as she had promised, and while visiting she shared her story.

Mrs. Junik appreciated the desire to provide her young daughter with some measure of Jewish identity, but it was unclear how committed the mother was to making any real changes in her life. Casually, she informed Helen of the Sunday morning Hebrew classes for children that she taught at the synagogue.

"Oh, no. Not Sunday morning. Elizabeth goes to ballet and then to art classes."

"I give private classes in the afternoon," offered Mrs. Junik.

Helen agreed, and her daughter began coming to the Juniks' every Sunday afternoon.

One day, Helen decided to confide in the Juniks. "My greatest wish is that my daughter meet her Jewish grandparents," she said with a heavy heart. "But I know they don't want to have anything to do with me. And it's been so many years…"

"Perhaps we can help," Mrs. Junik offered gently. "Maybe if we call, introduce ourselves, and tell them of your contact with us, they'll be more receptive."

Helen shook her head. "People have tried on my behalf, but my parents are too hurt, and they're not interested in hearing anything about me. I guess it's too late to restore our relationship, but at least my daughter should know she has grandparents."

Rabbi Junik had an idea. "Let's make a tape of Elizabeth

singing some Jewish songs that she has learned and telling her grandparents about the Jewish subjects she's been studying. Maybe that will help alleviate their sorrow and soften their hard feelings."

It worked.

Some time later, Elizabeth stopped suddenly in the middle of a Hebrew lesson and said, "Mrs. Junik, do you remember how I began learning about being Jewish? It was because of your little red car with the menorah on top."

Postscript:

Helen's family moved, but kept in contact with the Juniks, who assisted her during the difficulty she later had in her marriage. She was subsequently divorced and married a Jewish man, and her daughter Elizabeth now identifies strongly with her Jewish heritage.

> Once a renowned cardiologist visited the Lubavitcher Rebbe, Rabbi Menachem Mendel Schneerson. "You should devote your attention to treating healthy people as well as the sick," the Rebbe told him.
>
> "Am I to improve on what the Almighty has done?" questioned the doctor.
>
> "Yes," responded the Rebbe. "An ordinary layman, and how much more so a doctor, should be able to improve on what the Almighty has done."
>
> "Are you asking me to make man perfect?" answered the doctor.
>
> "No," the Rebbe responded. "Making people perfect is a job for Mashiach. But everyone should try to make his life and those of the people around him a little bit better."
>
> Each of us has his or her own mission in making our

portion of the world "a little bit better." Often, our missions
are intertwined, and as one person steps forward, he takes
others with him.

"The first time we met Ari was at a fundraiser in our synagogue," recalls Rabbi Sholom Ber Rodal who, along with his wife Rochel, directs Chabad activities in Mount Olympus in Los Angeles. "He was a cousin of our friend and supporter Gary Lustgarten, who brought him along as a volunteer. Ari told us that he was going off to Berkeley to study, and we wished him well."

About a month later, Rabbi Rodal received a shocking phone call from Mr. Lustgarten. Ari had fallen off a five-story dormitory balcony and was in a coma, in critical condition.

The Rodals immediately arranged for a Chabad shaliach in the Berkeley area to visit the boy. Miraculously, Ari not only survived, but awoke from his coma. After a few months of treatment, he was transferred to a rehab facility in the Los Angeles area.

Rabbi Rodal spent time with him there and brought him Jewish books. From their conversations, he learned that Ari's parents had divorced when he was two, and his father had been given custody. When Ari was ten years old, his father decided to move to Asia to pursue a new business. Ari was upset about the move and adamantly refused to go, so his father reluctantly left him with his parents, Ari's grandparents.

Ari had remained estranged from his father and would not even take his phone calls. After repeated attempts, his father had stopped calling. It was almost ten years since Ari or his grandparents had seen or spoken with him. They were not even sure where the father was located, for his initial plans had been vague and much time had passed.

After Ari was discharged from rehab, he and his grand-mother would often join the Rodal family for Shabbos. During one Friday-night conversation, Rabbi Rodal suggested that perhaps the time had come for Ari to reconnect with his father.

To the rabbi's surprise, both Ari and his grandmother were receptive. Locating the father wouldn't be easy, however, since the only information they had was that he was "somewhere in Asia," possibly Thailand or Japan.

Rabbi Rodal was undaunted; he had a plan. Immediately after Shabbos, he sent off an e-mail message to the shluchim website. "Does anyone know a Jerry Sugar in Asia?"

The reply was quick in coming. Rabbi Yosef Chayim Kantor, the Chabad shaliach in Bangkok, responded. He not only knew of the man; Jerry Sugar was a member of his syna-gogue. When Jerry heard that Ari wanted to get in touch with him after all these years, he was ecstatic. He had often wanted to initiate contact but was afraid of further traumatizing his son.

Jerry chose to speak with Rabbi Rodal first. "Rabbi, you don't know what you've done for me," he exclaimed tearfully. "I can't believe this is happening at long last. If Ari is ready, so am I."

The father and son began to connect, hesitantly at first, by e-mail. They progressed to telephone calls and were finally reunited in an emotional meeting in Los Angeles.

Rabbi Avraham Plotkin had not imagined he would be eager to pay a *shivah* call. He and his wife Goldie had recently arrived in the Markham suburb of Toronto, and had been anxiously seeking out Jews, but although the couple was energetic and determined, they discovered that it's not easy to get started in a new area. So when a woman they didn't know knocked on their door one evening, they were only too happy to welcome her in.

"I live nearby," the woman had said, "and I noticed that you've moved into the neighborhood. From your looks, I assume you're a rabbi. Well, there's a family who lives four doors from here; a relative of theirs has passed away. The family is observing the customary week of mourning, but it seems there is no one to conduct the services. You could be of assistance there."

Rabbi Plotkin took the address and went off right away to his first local assignment. When he arrived at the house and introduced himself, one of the mourners jumped up in surprise.

"Oh my goodness, a rabbi! Just what we need!" she exclaimed. "And you say you're from Chabad? That's wonderful!"

Rabbi Plotkin was touched by the warm greeting but wondered why he merited such an enthusiastic welcome.

"I would like to offer my condolences and am here to offer any help I can," he said.

"Oh! It's so thoughtful of Rabbi Moshe to have notified you and equally kind of you to have come," the woman said gratefully.

"Rabbi Moshe?" Rabbi Plotkin asked, puzzled. "Notified me? Moshe who? From where?"

Now it was the woman's turn to look confused. "Moshe! You know, Rabbi Moshe Denberg, that wonderful young man from Chabad in Hong Kong."

Soon the story unfolded.

The woman, Sandra Yuk, and her husband had been living in Hong Kong when her mother had fallen ill and passed away. The family decided to bury her in Toronto, where she had lived with her other daughter, Linda Chodos. Sandra was concerned that the proper procedures for the burial and the *shivah* week be observed. Shortly before leaving Hong Kong, in the midst of busy arrangements, she had shared her concerns with Moshe Denberg, who was working for the shluchim there, Rabbi Mordechai and Goldie Avtzon. He had calmed her and told her of a rabbi in Toronto to whom she could turn. In the rush, there was no time to look up the man's address and phone number, so Rabbi Moshe had written the name on a piece of paper.

"When you arrive you'll be able to find his number easily," he assured her.

Sandra thanked him and departed. But when they arrived in Toronto, she and her husband discovered that arrangements had already been made for the burial. The crumpled piece of paper lay forgotten at the bottom of her purse.

"Now that the burial is over and we're sitting *shivah*, I realized how uplifting it would be to conduct proper services, and pay due respect to my deceased mother," Sandra confided. "I'm so happy that you've come to help with that. And I naturally assumed it was Rabbi Moshe Denberg who notified you," she concluded.

Well, not exactly, but when Sandra dug the crumpled piece of paper out of her purse, the name written on it was indeed Rabbi Avraham Plotkin.

"*T*here were times when I had wondered if it was worth the effort," reflected Rabbi Yisroel Schanowitz, on shlichus with his wife, Shternie, in Summerlin, Nevada. "The issue isn't my personal convenience, of course; it's the nagging thought that maybe my time could have been used more effectively."

Rabbi Schanowitz was referring to his practice of traveling to prisons in the outlying area to make sure that no Jewish prisoners would be neglected. But the trips were often futile, as there were no Jews to visit. And there was an additional problem, highlighted in a recent court case involving prisoners battling for their "Jewish rights." This had led to the disclosure of a fraudulent claim; one of the prisoners involved wasn't Jewish at all. So even if someone was listed on a warden's list as Jewish, the rabbi often felt uncertain about his true identity.

On one such visit, Rabbi Schanowitz was walking out of a prison compound when a fellow coming in stopped him. The man seemed surprised to encounter a rabbi in such a place.

"What brings you here?" asked the man.

Rabbi Schanowitz introduced himself and briefly explained his mission. "And what do you do here?" he inquired in return.

"I am B.L., the prison doctor," the man replied. "It's interesting that I should run into a rabbi out here. I've been thinking about attending synagogue on Friday night. Do you know of a place?"

Rabbi Schanowitz gave him the address of the Chabad House and invited him to attend services and join in the Shabbos meal.

Dr. L. began attending every Friday night but politely refused to join in the meal. He kept his distance, saying he was not interested in any further involvement in organized religion. All the Schanowitzs could learn about him was that he had recently lost his wife.

A few months later, in a brief conversation, Dr. L. told the rabbi that he was acquainted with another Chabad rabbi in Florida.

"My grandfather attended a Chabad synagogue when he

lived in Florida. That rabbi maintained mail contact with me for years. During the time I lived in Ely, Nevada, where there is no Jewish community, the mail from Florida was a gentle reminder of my grandfather," he related.

"What's that rabbi's name?" Rabbi Schanowitz inquired.

"Rabbi Sholom Blank," was the reply.

"Why, he's my father-in-law!" exclaimed Rabbi Schanowitz.

This revelation created a bond that brought Dr. L. closer to the Schanowitzs, and he took an active interest in Chabad activities.

Mr. and Mrs. Lerman were planning to relocate from Long Island, New York, to Stamford, Connecticut. They had had contact with Chabad on Long Island and were referred to the shluchim in Stamford, Rabbi Moshe and Leah Shemtov. Mrs. Lerman called to inquire about the Jewish community there.

Introducing herself, she then began to recount something of her family history.

"My husband isn't Jewish. As our three children were growing up, though, I decided they should identify in some way with their Jewish heritage and began to teach them on my own. I didn't really have a formal Jewish education myself, but when I was a youngster in Brooklyn, I had attended a Release Hour program. This was a weekly hour of Jewish education organized in public schools by Chabad.

"One year, when I was in the third grade, we had the greatest teacher. We liked her classes so much that, when she suggested we meet more than once a week, a group of us readily agreed. We met for an extra hour each week in different children's homes and really loved it. Our teacher met our parents and together they organized a variety of events; we felt like a special club. Our teacher made each of us a colorful notebook, in which we wrote, colored and pasted all kinds of things about the holidays and commandments.

"Would you believe that that was over thirty years ago, but I still have the notebook! Now I'm using it to teach my children about being Jewish."

Leah was intrigued by Mrs. Lerman's story. It didn't surprise her to hear of the teacher's dedication; Jewish education has always been one of Chabad's central efforts. But she was curious.

"Do you remember the teacher's name?"

"As a matter of fact I do," Mrs. Lerman responded. "I lost touch with her but never forgot her name. It was an odd-sounding name to us kids – Mashi Popack."

Leah was astounded.

"Well, her married name is Lipskar," she told Mrs. Lerman, "and she's been living as a Chabad emissary in Johannesburg, South Africa, for the past twenty-seven years. I would know; she's my mother!"

*T*he Furman family had decided it was time to find a more dynamic synagogue than the one their neighborhood offered. Their home was a traditional one, and they wanted to be connected with an active center of Jewish life. Their search led them to Chabad of Pasadena, which is directed by Rabbi Chaim and Chanie Hanoka and Rabbi Yisroel and Chanie Pinson.

The first time the Furmans attended services, Erica found

her way to the women's gallery and looked around. She chose a seat on the side and focused her attention on the prayer book.

"I was new," recalls Erica. "I didn't know anybody, and I wasn't familiar with the services there."

But newcomers at Chabad Pasadena are not left to themselves for long. Especially not on a Shabbos when Chanie Pinson's mother, Mrs. Bina Hanoka, is visiting from Boston. She doesn't come that often, but when she does she naturally joins her children in their outreach efforts. When she arrived at the synagogue, this friendly, sensitive woman noticed Erica and sat down next to her.

"She put me at ease, extending a warm welcome and helping me follow the service. Later we conversed, and she took a genuine interest in who I was and how she could help ease our arrival. We got to the inevitable 'Jewish geography' thing, and I told her I had grown up in Flushing, New York.

'Really?' she replied. 'I taught in a Hebrew school there long ago, but I don't remember its name.'

"'The only Hebrew school I know of is called Garden Jewish Center,' I answered, adding that I had attended the school as a child, and recalled one particular teacher who stood out in my mind, and whose enthusiasm and dedication had stayed with me for years.

"'Who was the principal then?' inquired Mrs. Hanoka.

"'Funny I should remember, it was such a long time ago. His name was Walter Orenstein.'

"'He was my boss!' Mrs. Hanoka exclaimed.

"I looked at this friendly woman more intently, and suddenly had a flash of recognition.

"'Ms. Hertzberg?' I blurted out.

"'Aidel (my Hebrew name)?' she responded, equally surprised."

This warm beginning led to an ongoing relationship with the Furmans, who have become true friends of Chabad.

> *It is written:*[11] *"Educate a child according to his way; even when he grows old, he will not depart from it." The Rebbe explained this teaching by an analogy. When one damages or improves a grown plant, the effect is often localized. In contrast, damage to a seed has an effect on the entire plant that grows. And in a positive sense, the care and attention lavished over a sapling bears fruit as it develops into a flourishing tree.*

*R*abbi Y'chiah and Bat Sheva Lihany of Grenoble, France, relate that their search for a place to locate their school had been underway for quite a while. A desirable property in a central location finally became available, but there were many eager potential buyers.

Eventually, the owner decided to sell it to Chabad. The grateful Lihanys could not believe their good fortune. Everyone wanted to know what caused him to overlook the many offers that had been made by prominent organizations and businesses, offers that would have given him a sizable and assured profit.

"When I asked these potential buyers why they were interested in the building," he explained, "they told me they needed a school building to educate youth. In the business world, one can never be totally certain about the honesty of the people with whom one is doing business. These individuals work with souls; I trust their integrity."

Indeed, thanks to that trust, he extended the Lihanys a long term, comfortable loan for the purchase.

---

11. Proverbs 22:6.

When Rabbi Meir and Sarit Brook attempted to open a Jewish school in their shlichus city of Baku, Azerbaidzhan, they encountered a brick wall. Unfortunately, it wasn't the wall of the building they had in mind. Their first challenge came from the Ministry of Education in Baku.

"Absolutely not!" exclaimed the representative. "See here, Rabbi. We appreciate and try to accommodate the forty thousand Jews that live in this country. But you can read the map as well as I. This is a secular Muslim country. Neighboring on fundamentalist Iran, we have to be very sensitive to cultural factions. If we allow a separate school for the Jews, we will have to allow the same for the religious Muslims, the Iranian minority, and other groups that are part of our population. Private schooling is often the first step towards factional organization. In this part of the world, if we want to protect our country from extremists, we have to be very careful."

"But the Jews are a totally different type of group," Rabbi Brook insisted. "We are honorable citizens that have no political or national aspirations here. All we desire is to educate our children in our traditions, which include loyalty to the local government."

"I agree with you on that," replied the official. "Precisely, because we respect our Jewish citizens, we are concerned with your welfare. Singling you out with a private school will only cause unnecessary tension and target you for possible attack."

But Rabbi Brook was adamant. "We are grateful for the government's sympathetic approach. However, Jews have never let worry about an unknown future become an obstacle that deters them from investing in Jewish education. We feel strongly about going ahead with our plans."

The official was understanding but unyielding. Finally he stated, "In any case, this is not a matter of concern to the

Ministry of Education only. In order to open a school, before obtaining a license from our department, one must obtain a registration permit from the Ministry of Justice. Go speak to them first, and if they grant you the permit, come back to us."

But the Ministry of Justice insisted that the first step was to obtain the license from the Ministry of Education... Eventually, Rabbi Brook was advised to first prepare a school building lawfully acceptable and properly equipped, show a list of registered students and qualified teachers, present a curriculum and prove operational capability. When all that was done, he could come again to plead his case.

Evidently, the officials underestimated the energy, determination and dedication of the shluchim and assumed that Rabbi Brook would not be back for a long time. They were surprised to see him back soon afterwards. His work was thorough, and he was promised the necessary permits from both the Justice and Education departments. With the first day of school quickly approaching, Rabbi Brook decided to open the school despite the fact that he did not have the permits in hand.

For the first time in modern history, eighty Jewish children were studying Torah in a Jewish school in Baku. On a regular basis, officials from both the Ministries of Education and Justice visited the school to assess its program, assuming that the other office had granted the permits.... For seven successful school months, no official complaint was issued.

Then, one day, an official arrived and demanded that the school be closed. Rabbi Brook tried to reject the ruling on grounds of discrimination against Jews, which would not be in the government's interest.

"Oh no," the official informed him. "The grounds for the ruling are unpaid employee taxes. None of your employees have reported the income they earn from working in your school."

"But I cannot file those forms without the permit, and I am still waiting for the government to fulfill its promises to me," he explained apologizing.

The official shrugged sympathetically and left.

Rabbi Brook attempted to arrange a meeting with the president of Azerbaizhan, Mr. Heidar Aliyev; however, the president had recently suffered a heart attack and was in the United States for recuperation.

Soon afterwards, Rabbi Brook was summoned to the vice minister of Education. "I have orders for you to close the school. If you refuse, I will have to report you to the police. I would certainly not like to have to do that. I have intervened on your behalf until now, asking for time, but I can no longer assure you that assistance. You must sign this order of compliance."

"I am not in a position to make this decision on my own," Rabbi Brook replied. "I must seek the advice of the chief rabbi of the c.i.s., Rabbi Berel Lazar."

"Then call him right now from my office!" the minister ordered.

At that moment Rabbi Lazar was on a flight and could not be reached.

With a heavy heart, Rabbi Brook signed the form. Two hours later, he contacted Rabbi Lazar and informed him of the events. Rabbi Lazar was aggravated and sought the help of the philanthropist, Mr. Lev Leviev, whose dedication to Jewish education is legendary, world wide and especially in the c.i.s.

He appealed to him to visit Baku and assess the situation on site. Mr. Leviev arrived and was impressed with the diligence and successes of eighty happy schoolchildren. Meanwhile, the president had returned to Azerbaidzan and Mr. Leviev requested an audience. Mr. Leviev addressed the president, recalling his position of second in command during the

Communist rule. "Your governing capabilities and achievements are well known and applauded by the public. The Jewish community in particular appreciates all you have done to promote your citizens' welfare. As education is of prime importance, the community would greatly appreciate your assistance in enabling them to maintain their school."

"What exactly is the problem?" the president inquired.

Rabbi Brook explained.

President Aliyev queried the ministers: "Why all the hassle? I want the Jewish population in Azerbaijan to enjoy peace and security in our country. There is no reason that these respectable citizens should not have their own school."

In two days, Rabbi Brook had the permits in hand. Three weeks later, the ailing president died. When his son, Ilham Aliyev, gained his deceased father's position, the Jewish community was concerned about possible changes. But government officials assured them that the son would maintain his father's approach.

A year later, Mr. Leviev met with President Ilham Aliyev. "I am fond of the Jewish people and regard them as my brothers," he announced. "As a gesture of goodwill, I am granting Chabad a 15,000 square meter plot of land on which to develop their institutions."

*R*abbi Zalman and Mimi Zaklas decided to open a branch of the Or-Avner network of Jewish schools in Novosibirsk, Siberia. Since this would be the first time a Jewish school had ever been opened in that region, they had some doubts about registration. The local Jews were still intimidated by the past seventy years of Communist rule. Enrolling one's children in an overtly Jewish institution was a very public step, and there was still an unspoken rule that one should conceal one's Jewishness as much as possible.

To counteract this, Rabbi Zaklas invested much time, effort and funding in advertising the future school. Hearing about it on radio and television and reading about it in the newspaper would help people perceive the facility as a reality, and would alleviate fear and apprehension. The school was described as a modern educational facility, affording its students busing, hot lunches and a superb education.

Much to the Zaklases' surprise, the response was over-whelming. Shortly after the publicity campaign began, the phone rang with many inquiries. These, unfortunately, were interspersed with other, unpleasant calls with clear anti-Semitic undertones.

"So?" hissed one caller, "you Jews are so wealthy that you're controlling the local media and can afford to advertise your school even more than Coca Cola advertises its drinks!"

But all in all, the Zaklases were very pleased with the enrollment process, and preparations for the school went ahead as planned.

One morning, when Rabbi Zaklas arrived at his office, he was taken aback by the chaotic scene that met him. Scores of grim-looking policemen accompanied by large dogs filled the area.

"What's going on?" he asked apprehensively.

His assistant briefed him. "A woman called early this morning and told us a bomb has been planted in the building! I immediately called the police, and now they're searching every inch of the place."

It soon became clear, however, that the call was a hoax. Rabbi Zaklas and his assistant made their way inside. At the doorway, the rabbi encountered a policeman reading with interest the large sign above the entrance that advertised the future school.

"What's this all about?" he inquired.

Rabbi Zaklas explained their plans for the school.

"Why, that sounds very interesting," exclaimed the policeman. "Both my wife and I are Jewish, you see, and we'd be delighted for our children to have a Jewish education. Can I have more details?"

One Yom Kippur, the Baal Shem Tov was praying together with his disciples in a small Polish village. Through his spiritual vision, the Baal Shem Tov had perceived that harsh heavenly verdicts had been decreed against the Jewish people. He and his students were crying to G-d from the depths of their hearts, imploring that He rescind these decrees.

Emotions ran deep among the congregants, and everyone opened his heart in sincere prayer.

Among them was a simple shepherd boy. He did not know how to read; indeed, he could barely say the letters of the Hebrew alphabet. As the intensity of feeling in the synagogue began to mount, he also wanted to pray. He opened the prayer book to the first page and began to recite the names of the letters: alef, beis, veis, reading the entire alphabet. He then cried out: "This is all I can do. G-d, You know how the prayers should be pronounced. Please, arrange the letters to form the proper words."

This simple, genuine prayer resounded powerfully within the Heavenly Court. G-d rescinded all the harsh decrees and granted the Jews blessing and good fortune.

Fast forward a couple of hundred years: In the first year after perestroika became a reality, an American rabbi was leading the Kol Nidrei services in the main synagogue of Kiev on the eve of Yom Kippur.

Announcements of the services had been posted all over the city and Jews responded eagerly. Old men and women who remembered accompanying their parents to shul as children, young families who wanted a taste of their heritage after more than a half-century of Soviet persecution, and youth in their teens who barely knew they were Jewish, flocked to the synagogue.

The cantor chanted Kol Nidrei. The moving melody stirred the hearts of all those who had come. But as the service proceeded, the rabbi sensed that the congregation was having difficulty remaining focused on the long service. After all, most of the people had never been in a synagogue in their lives; none of them knew how to pray. Despite the best intentions, Hebrew-Russian prayerbooks, and explanations in Russian, he realized that there was a need for a break.

After the Amidah prayer, he ascended to the lectern and told the above story. As he paused to let the story impact his listeners, a voice called out: "Alef." And thousands of voices thundered back, "Alef." The voice continued: "Beis," and the thousands responded, "Beis." They continued to pronounce every letter in the Hebrew alphabet, and then they began to file out of the synagogue. They had recited their prayers.

"Yes," insisted Robin Dixon of the *Los Angeles Times*, "I want to go to the city of Lubavitch. And no, the seven-hour drive from Moscow is not a deterrent."

Rabbi Avraham Berkowitz was impressed by Ms. Dixon's determination. As executive director of the local Federation of Jewish Communities, and shaliach in Moscow, with his wife Leah, he was the right person for this journalist to have contacted. She had called saying that her paper, whose stories are often syndicated, was interested in doing a feature piece on the revival of Jewish life in Russia.

"My preliminary research led me to Chabad," she had said. "It seems that yours is the most dominant group in Jewish life in Russia today. Its dedication and success intrigued me, and after I discovered that it all began in the small town of Lubavitch, on the border of Belarus, hundreds of years ago, I decided that a visit to the town could provide the backdrop for my story."

Rabbi Berkowitz didn't want to dampen her interest, but he had his doubts. What was there to see in that tiny, backward village, whose roads aren't even paved? The only Jewish presence in the town these days are people who come to pray at the gravesites of the Lubavitch Rebbes buried there. What could he show this journalist, other than the small museum adjacent to the graves?

As he pondered the matter, Rabbi Berkowitz had an idea. It was the summer of 2001. In the spring of that year, some of the hundreds of Lubavitch *yeshivah* students who come to Russia to arrange Pesach Seders had made contact with Jewish children in the area. The students were stationed in Smolensk, close to Lubavitch, and in the summer they set up a camp in a Lubavitch public school. That camp would be an ideal place for Ms. Dixon to witness the rejuvenation of Jewish life.

The trip was planned. When the car came to pick up Rabbi Berkowitz, he joined the photographer and a local Russian who worked for the *Los Angeles Times* as a translator and researcher. Rabbi Berkowitz inquired, in the course of conversation, about their religious ties; both said they were gentile. The translator introduced himself as Yasha Ryzhak, a member of the Russian Orthodox Church.

Aware of the story's potentially wide audience and of the long drive ahead, Rabbi Berkowitz began explaining the history, philosophy and activity of Chabad. He expounded on the origin of the movement in the town of Lubavitch, whose very name means "the city of brotherly love." As he spoke, Ms. Dixon took notes and Yasha asked many questions. Something about his inquiries seemed to be beyond normal curiosity.

At one point, Yasha suddenly declared, "I really should call my grandmother. We'll soon be approaching Smolensk; my family originates there. I've never traveled to this region before, and I'd like to see the place."

After spending fifteen minutes on the phone with his grandmother, he turned to Rabbi Berkowitz with an expression of wonder mixed with confusion.

"Rabbi," he said slowly, "my grandmother just told me something I had never known. When she heard I was traveling to Lubavitch, she became very excited and told me that, during the war, her family members had forged their identity papers and changed their names. They were of chassidic origin; the men had studied at the *yeshivah* in Lubavitch. Her great-grandfather's name was Zalman Rivkin, after the rabbi who founded the movement."

Rabbi Berkowitz was amazed.

"Is this your maternal or paternal grandmother?" he asked deliberately.

"She's my mother's mother."

"Then, Yasha, according to Jewish law, you are a Jew!" Rabbi Berkowitz declared. This information caught Yasha totally unprepared. An extended conversation ensued over the remainder of the drive. Yasha listened intently but found it difficult to relate to his newly found identity.

Later, the visitors encountered the camp children and were moved by the ease with which these youngsters, who had no previous Jewish education, absorbed the concepts they were learning, and by the pride they took in their religion.

In the small museum, Rabbi Berkowitz pointed to a striking wall hanging depicting the chassidim who had studied in the town, one of whom was wearing *tefillin*.

"This is probably what your grandfather looked like, Yasha. Every day, he put on his own pair of *tefillin*, just as you see portrayed here."

"I hear what you're saying," Yasha responded, "but I'm not Jewish."

"According to Jewish law, you are," Rabbi Berkowitz reminded him. "Would you like to put on *tefillin*, if only to honor the memory of your grandfather?"

After some contemplation, Yasha agreed.

"How strange," he murmured as he unwound the straps. "Suddenly, I feel I'm a Jew!"

Inspired by the visit and by the extensive interviews she had conducted, Ms. Dixon wrote an impressive feature story, which was set to run on September 12, 2001. The terrible events of September 11, however, pushed aside all other news for weeks thereafter. Ms. Dixon regretfully informed Rabbi Berkowitz that, since it was a time-sensitive story, with the summer camp as one of its highlights, the paper had filed it for a later appropriate date. She apologized for having taken so much of his time for an article that would remain temporarily unpublished.

But Rabbi Berkowitz wasn't disappointed. As far as he was concerned, it was a higher authority that had ordained the long trip to Lubavitch, and its effects were becoming clear even without the publicity of the influential newspaper. Yasha (now Yakov) Ryzhak delved into his newly-discovered Judaism with zeal and today is a proud member of the Chabad community of Moscow.

*R*abbi Shmuel Kaminetzki and his wife Chanah began their shlichus in Dnepropetrovsk, Ukraine, with a strong feeling of commitment and determination. After all, Lubavitch people throughout the world feel a connection to this city because it is where the Rebbe spent his early childhood while his father, Rabbi Levi Yitzchak Shneerson, served as chief rabbi.

The Kaminetzkis' goal was to bring Jewish life back to this city, but that was no simple feat. They arrived in Dnepropetrovsk before *perestroika* had become a full-blown reality, and the challenges they faced were as numerous as the undercover KGB officers who still surveyed the city. Long-ingrained fear and suspicion were everyone's constant companion; people concealed their Jewish identity. The Kaminetzkis knew Jews who would cross the street when they approached, because they were afraid to be seen associating with them.

Newcomers, visitors and tourists were a rare sight in Dnepropetrovsk. The town was "off limits", and for good reason as far as the Russians were concerned; it was the site of the world's largest Scud missile plant. No wonder this city of one-and-a-half million did not even appear on the maps in those days.

In their search for a structure to use as a base, the couple came upon a dilapidated synagogue that was locked except for a short while each Shabbos, when a handful of elderly Jews would quietly come and go.

They chose to begin there. Renovating the building as best they could, they established a *yeshivah*, "importing" students from New York. The students committed themselves for a set period of time, and this brought a small stream of young men to study and assist in outreach to the community.

Two of those students, Motti Korf and Uri Labor, decided to stay on beyond their commitment, to explore commercial opportunities in the city, which was just opening up to Western-style business after a seventy-year hibernation during the Communist regime. They joined the rabbi and his wife in working to help local Jews to feel at home in the synagogue, themselves included.

As the High Holy Days drew near, plans were discussed. They all felt that the *minyan* should be as similar as possible to what they had experienced at home. To that end, they resolved to explain and implement all the relevant Jewish customs and practices.

In the last hours of Yom Kippur, the congregation was briefed about the custom of bidding for the honor of opening the ark before the *Neilah* services. That act was a good sign, the rabbi explained, for opening the ark opens up a channel of abundant blessings for the new year.

The congregation watched with interest as the two young men competed in the bidding. Only a few noticed the newcomer who had just walked in. The man observed the scene with a perplexed look and walked up to the rabbi.

"Hello, I am Victor Pinchuk," he introduced himself. "My mother always told me about my Jewish heritage, so I decided to come to the synagogue today. I didn't have a spare moment until now. But what's going on here? Is this a place of prayer or of business?"

Rabbi Kaminetzki shook Mr. Pinchuk's hand warmly. He would have been equally cordial to anyone, but was particularly pleased by his arrival, as he was aware that the newcomer had close ties to the country's president. As of yet, Victor had not attended any of the Chabad activities, and his presence was a pleasant surprise.

Rabbi Kaminetzki took the opportunity to explain briefly about the Chabad movement and its special connection to the city of the Rebbe's birthplace. He then moved on to the custom of bidding for the privilege of opening the ark.

"You say it's like creating an opening for personal blessings?" Victor responded enthusiastically. "I like that idea. I'm joining the bidding!"

So what had begun as a modest contest between two young businessmen turned into a serious competition. The boys realized Victor's sincere intentions, and risked their own meager assets in raising the amount. Amazed at their own boldness, they stopped at $40,000, the sum total of their assets! Victor pledged $41,000, to the congregation's gratitude, and to the boys' vast relief. This boost to the synagogue funds would greatly benefit the community. That Yom Kippur marked the beginning of an ongoing friendship between Victor and the Kaminetzkis.

Before Yom Kippur the following year, Victor called. "What will this year's schedule for the holiday be?"

"Same as last," responded the rabbi.

"And the bidding?"

"Hopefully, it will take place as well."

"Rabbi, I'd like to propose a pre-date bid. I'll offer $100,000 for the merit and avoid the discomfort of outbidding anyone else."

The offer was accepted for that year, and became an annual commitment.

As they became more closely acquainted with him, the Kaminetzkis learned that Victor had a warm heart, an ardent soul and a flourishing international business. And yet, despite his extensive dealings, he was sensitive first to the needs of the individual and generous to all. He understood Chabad's special connection to Dnepropetrovsk and identified wholeheartedly with the Rebbe and the shluchim.

In time, Victor became a member of the Ukrainian government, and his family moved to Kiev. Nonetheless, every Yom Kippur he would join the congregation in Dnepropetrovsk. Shortly before Yom Kippur of 2002, Rabbi Kaminetzki felt that Victor had advanced enough in his commitment to Judaism for the rabbi to broach the subject of further adherence to the mitzvos.

"This year," he urged Victor, "try to arrive from Kiev before the onset of the holiday. You can stay overnight at your mother's house here in Dnepropetrovsk and participate in the services in a way more befitting this holiest day of the year."

Victor agreed with the rabbi. He purchased a pair of non-leather shoes and resolved to adhere to the law. That was the first Yom Kippur that he observed properly, and he fulfilled his cherished duty of opening the ark for *Neilah* with a sense of inner joy and satisfaction.

"You are certainly deserving of an abundance of blessings from above, Victor," Rabbi Kaminetzki said as he bid him farewell after the holiday. "May G-d shower you with additional blessings, just as you have extended yourself this year in observing Yom Kippur in a more meticulous manner."

Two weeks later, in the last week of October 2002, Mrs. Pinchuk asked her husband to accompany her to the Palace of Culture of the Podshibnikoviy Zavod in Moscow. The hit Russian musical *Nord-Ost* [North-East] was playing, and she wanted to attend. Victor accommodated his wife, and the two made the trip from Kiev.

As they sat in the theater, however, Victor suddenly felt they must leave immediately. It was as if an inner voice were beckoning him to the exit. He motioned to his wife. Puzzled as to what had come over her husband, Mrs. Pinchuk nonetheless followed him out.

"I don't really know what it was," Victor admitted once they were outside, "but I had the distinct sense we had to get out of there. Let's go have some dinner now."

After their meal, Victor's wife requested that they return to the theater. "It's just about the end of intermission," she said, looking at her watch. "Let's go back for the second half of the show."

Victor could see no logical reason to disagree.

The couple made their way back to the theater and settled into their seats just in time for the second half. But no sooner had the show resumed than Victor once again felt compelled to leave. This time it seemed even more urgent than before, and was accompanied by a claustrophobic sensation. This sensation was so overwhelming that he took his wife by the hand and told her they must leave immediately. With Victor leading the way, the two made their exit.

"We're going home," Victor said adamantly. On the flight back to Kiev shortly afterward, they heard of the dreadful Chechnian terrorist attack at the theater they had just left.

Late that night, Victor called Rabbi Kaminetzki, who had already heard the news. The President of Ukraine had offered a public prayer of gratitude to the Almighty for the Pinchuks' narrow escape.

"I must do something to express my thanks to G-d for directing me out of that theater," said Victor emotionally. "That inner voice that led us out came from somewhere higher than myself. Maybe it was because of those extra blessings you wished upon me this past Yom Kippur."

"Victor," Rabbi Kaminetzki replied earnestly, "you are already doing much good and are deserving of many blessings.

Your continuous support of Jewish life and generous promotion of Jewish identity have certainly earned you G-d's ongoing protection."

"Thank you for the kind words, rabbi, but I really feel an obligation to do something in gratitude," he insisted. "It is very late now and I don't want to keep you any longer, but I'm awaiting your suggestion about how to express my thanks."

Victor called back a number of times, urging the rabbi for a response. It was during one of these calls that Chanah Kaminetzki mentioned that the Chabad kindergarten was in a tiny facility and had a long waiting list of applicants.

"Perfect!" exclaimed Victor. "I will fund a new kindergarten and equip it with all that is necessary. It will be called 'The Zindlicht Building,' my mother's maiden name."

"Most appropriate," replied Mrs. Kaminetzki warmly, "*Zindlicht* in Yiddish means 'lighting a candle,' and it is the purity and innocence of children that brings light into the world." Later Victor also discovered that his Hebrew birthday falls on "the candle-lighting holiday" of Chanukah.

"Siberia?!" Mimi Zaklas exclaimed to her husband Zalman. Married just six months, the couple was seeking a place to go on shlichus.

"I know what you mean," Zalman answered with a smile. "For me too, the name alone gives me the chills! I grew up hearing stories of my zayde, Rabbi Moshe Vishedsky, who spent seven years at hard labor in Siberia. But maybe just because of that, I felt intrigued when Rabbi Lazar, the Chief Rabbi of c.i.s., suggested we consider it. He's offered us tickets to explore the option. We won't be committing ourselves to anything right now, nothing more than a two-week pilot tour."

"Of course I'm willing to go explore the option," agreed Mimi. "I have to admit, though, that it's the least likely place I imagined myself going on shlichus. So when do we leave? I can't wait to tell my mother that we're going on a 'honeymoon' to Siberia!"

So the young couple set out for Novosibirsk, equipped with warm coats and lukewarm expectations. They arrived around Purim and began to seek out the Jewish community.

"We discovered, unfortunately, that the low temperatures were reflected in a sad lack of spiritual warmth. The shul, the Novosibirsk Synagogue, was one tiny room in an old rickety building that was on the verge of collapse. It was attended by a handful of elderly Jews who gathered once every few weeks.

"We were adamant to do something for the community then and there, regardless of our ultimate decision about returning, so we organized Shabbos services in a more spacious apartment and invited people to join us. It was exhilarating, joining the local people in singing the Lubavitcher melodies with Russian words that we had been taught as kids.

"After Shabbos, I went to the shul to return the prayer books I had borrowed for the services. Nothing, except perhaps the history I had learned in school, could have prepared me for what met my eyes. Only one word I know can adequately describe the scene: pogrom.

"I stood there in shock and tears, viewing the total desecration of a Jewish place of worship. The Torah scrolls had been ripped apart and trampled. Prayer books were torn to shreds, the pages flung about everywhere. What was left of the shul's rickety reader's platform and furniture was in shards. Menacing, degrading graffiti were scrawled on the walls, which had been branded with huge swastikas.

"My feelings fluctuated between gloom and anger. I did

the best I could to collect the holy parchments and books and then went quickly to the home of the community leader."

Though equally appalled, the local man shook his head in resignation.

"It's not the first time," he admitted sadly. "There's not much we can do."

Other members of the community echoed his words and submissively set about cleaning up and calculating the damage. But Zalman Zaklas was not willing to accept the situation as unalterable. He placed a call to Rabbi Berel Lazar in Moscow and described what had happened.

"You're right," Rabbi Lazar declared. "We should make a public issue of this and not let it go by in silence. You contact the local press, and I'll arrange for national and international coverage. We'll let it be known that pogroms are not to be tolerated in the modern-day c.i.s."

The following morning, Novosibirsk woke up to newspaper and television crews crowding the tiny *shul*.

"We'll conduct an interview with you standing in front of the destruction," one of the reporters directed Rabbi Zaklas. He positioned him and began the interview on the spot.

"So you're the rabbi of the Jewish community here?" he asked.

Zalman had no time to think. The press agent was totally unaware that, what for him was a simple piece of information, required a life-altering decision for the young man. But there was only one answer. Rabbi Zaklas surprised himself at the matter-of-fact tone of his reply.

"Yes, I am the rabbi of the Jewish community of Novosibirsk."

"Well, what is your reaction to this terrible act?" the reporter continued. Once again, the newsman couldn't know that

Rabbi Zaklas was not only answering him but committing himself to a shlichus in Siberia.

"The world must know that we will not tolerate anything of this sort! The Jewish community of Novosibirsk will not be intimidated by hoodlums. On the contrary, we will build a new synagogue that will stand as a symbol of strength and bolster community activities so that Jewish life will flourish here."

Rabbi Zalman and Miriam Zaklas had made their decision.

If they had any lingering doubts, these were dissolved by the headlines in the papers and by the television news reports mentioning Rabbi Zaklas's rabbinic position. Calls from numerous family members and well-wishers from around the world who had learned of their new position via the media gave them no room for second thoughts.

* * *

"Our first activity as shluchim actually began on the plane bringing us to Novosibirsk," recalls Rabbi Zaklas. "It, too, brought unexpected publicity. I just did what any Chabad person would have done. I had no idea of the outcome until a friend of mine from Israel, Shmuel Peles, called me sometime after we had arrived to begin our shlichus."

"Zalman, let me tell you something you might find interesting," Shmuel began. "I've just returned from an important event that took place in the International Convention Center in Jerusalem. It was a conference hosted by the Foreign Ministry for the purpose of encouraging Israeli and Russian business ties. All the country's elite was there, from the prime minister to the noted businessman and philanthropist, Mr. Lev Leviev, and many others.

"Between sessions, there was live music. But then one

of the musicians took the microphone and began speaking. Everyone's attention was captured by his unexpected words, which were definitely not on the program.

"'This event is in promotion of Israeli-Russian business ties,' the musician said. 'Although it's probably not my place to address you, I'd like to share an incident with you that highlights another aspect of such ties. It may even be appropriate, since it's about business, albeit the business of the soul.

"'Some time ago, a fellow musician, who's with me here today, and I were invited to accompany performer Yisrael Parnes on a trip to Novosibirsk, where we were scheduled to entertain the Jewish community. We were told that, for the past fifty years, this annual concert was the only event that brought the Jews of Novosibirsk together in open proclamation of their Jewishness.

"'On the plane, a fellow passenger introduced himself as Rabbi Zaklas and invited us to put on *tefillin*. Now, my friend and I are not exactly predisposed to Jewish observance. But the rabbi was not put off by our initial lack of interest. He spent quite some time explaining the value of putting on *tefillin*, and eventually my friend agreed. But not me. I'm a fifty-two-year-old nonbeliever, and I wouldn't budge. But my friend joined ranks with the rabbi, and their arguments finally convinced me.

"'As I donned the *tefillin*, I suddenly felt moved to tears. I mentioned that we had recently held a bar mitzvah ceremony for our son, but I myself never had one. When Rabbi Zaklas heard this, he exclaimed that we should mark the occasion right there on the plane. After all, the music could be readily provided! And so, there we were, celebrating my bar mitzvah, with other passengers joining in the singing.

"'I would like to use this opportunity to thank the shluchim of the Lubavitcher Rebbe, and Mr. Lev Leviev, who do so much to strengthen the multi-faceted contacts between Russia and Israel.'"

"What a glorious past this community must have had!" Rabbi Mendel and Sarah Pewzner thought sadly as they gazed at the once-proud Great Synagogue of S. Petersburg, Russia.

The massive structure, which boasted over one thousand seats, stood in decay, a haunting testimony to a Jewish lifestyle long vanished.

"Never mind the past," the couple said to one another in determination. "We've come here on shlichus to build a future. We'll bring Jewish life back to this city, and one day, with G-d's help, this magnificent place will flourish again."

For the meantime, though, the present seemed anchored more to the past than to the future. To realize their goal of restoring Jewish worship in the city, the Pewzners needed a site. Adjacent to the grand old synagogue was a smaller sanctuary in similar condition. After much effort, they managed to clear the rubble and make the smaller building suitable for use. As they labored to expose the beams of the building, they strove to reawaken the Jewish consciousness that lay concealed in that city.

Step by step, Rabbi and Mrs. Pewzner began building a community. It was slow going, for much in Russia moved slowly in those days. Communication was primitive; even a simple fax machine was considered a luxury. The Pewzners had to travel to post offices and the like when they needed such amenities.

One day, Rabbi Pewzner went out to Nevsky Avenue, a main boulevard, to send a fax. On his way home, he passed the

Grand Hotel Europa. Due to its cosmopolitan clientele, the hotel sold goods that could not be obtained elsewhere. Rabbi Pewzner went inside to make a purchase. As he walked through the lobby, a stately looking couple approached him.

"You must be from Chabad?" the man inquired.

Rabbi Pewzner nodded, taken a bit by surprise. Yes, he supposed he did look Jewish, but who in S. Petersburg would have the insight to identify a Chabad chassid in particular?

"Don't be surprised," the man smiled. "I could tell by your hat and the way your *tzitzis* hang out! You see, I'm very familiar with Chabad in my country, Brazil. I've also had an audience with the Rebbe."

The man held out his hand.

"Pleased to meet you," he said. "My name is Edmund Safra, and this is my wife, Lilly."

Rabbi Pewzner felt fortunate to have met this famous Jewish banker and philanthropist, right here in his city. The two men spoke for a while and resolved to meet again for *minchah*. Mr. Safra participated in the service and expressed his pleasure at the opportunity to pray with a *minyan* in S. Petersburg. After the services ended, he reached into his pocket for a pen to jot down the Pewzners' phone number.

Then, laughing, he took his hand back out.

"Empty pockets!" he exclaimed. "I don't carry any cash; I don't even have anything to put in the *tzedakah* box," he explained. "The only cash I always carry, but will not part with, is the dollar I received from the Rebbe, along with his revered blessings. His blessings have brought much good fortune to me, and I appreciate all that the Rebbe has done for world Jewry. I'm especially impressed with his vision in sending people like you all over to revive and sustain Judaism. I'd like to hear more about your work here."

While Rabbi Pewzner and Edmund Safra were conversing, Mrs. Safra walked about the old synagogue, expressing dismay at the building's still miserable condition. Mr. Safra promptly pledged to undertake the complete renovation of the small synagogue and to make monthly contributions toward establishing Jewish education in the city.

Needless to say, the Pewzners were overjoyed by this turn of events and saw to it that the Safras' donations paid high spiritual dividends. The small synagogue was renovated handsomely and attracted many newcomers. A Jewish school was opened.

Three years later, Edmund and Lilly Safra revisited S. Petersburg, and were delighted with the progress that had been made. As they marveled at the restored synagogue, Mr. Safra's eyes moved to the adjacent structure.

"That large synagogue must have been a magnificent building once," he mused aloud. "I wonder what it would cost to restore it."

Rabbi Pewzner made a point of finding out. Once again, the Safras generously pledged to foot the bill. It was a formidable undertaking, but today the Grand Choral Synagogue, Beit Edmund Safra, has indeed reclaimed its glorious past.

"Our first Simchas Torah in Bishkek, Krighiztan, was a truly illuminating experience, even though we had no light!" recall Rabbi Arye and Rivka Raichman, who are on shlichus in this distant country bordering China.

"We were moved by the obvious desire of the local Jews to connect with their Judaism," relates Rabbi Raichman. "Close to one hundred people showed up for the High Holy Days, and for lack of space in the old synagogue, they took turns entering and participating in the services. We knew there was much less awareness of Sukkos and Simchas Torah, so we publicized the upcoming holidays and invited people to join us.

"A substantial number showed up on the eve of Simchas Torah, and I outlined the events of the evening. Just as the time came to begin the dancing, which we had highlighted in our description of the holiday, a blackout occurred. There we were, Torah scrolls in our arms, ready to burst into song, when we were engulfed in darkness. I was beside myself, wondering how to proceed. But the locals didn't seem fazed at all. They explained that the municipality didn't have the funds to accommodate the growing need for electricity.

"'It'll go on again sooner or later,' a voice was heard in the dark. 'Let's go home and come back in a while.'

"But the people wouldn't hear of it. 'We've come here to celebrate our first real Simchas Torah in years,' they protested. 'We're not going anywhere!'

"A few candles had been lit in the synagogue, as was customary, at the front of the room near the cantor's stand. Someone brought them to the center of the room. People began to sing, and we celebrated in Bishkek like they had done before Communist rule, with joyous singing and dancing.

"Even in the dim light I could make out the tears that flowed along with the festive happiness. 'How similar, yet how different!' one elderly man exclaimed. 'For so many years of Communist rule, we desperately tried to celebrate our religion, but had to do so under cover of darkness. Now here we are – true, there's no light, but the joy of openly expressing our Judaism illuminates the heart!'"

> The Hebrew term *teshuvah* is usually translated as "repentance." The literal translation of the term, however, is "return."

Repentance implies a reversal of one's conduct — a recognition of past shortcomings, and a firm resolution to change
in the future. The two are interrelated; the awareness of our
inadequacies impels us to reorient.

The concept of *teshuvah* as "return" emphasizes the
fundamental spiritual potential of every person. Chassidic
thought teaches that within each of us resides a Divine soul, a
spark of G-d.[12] This infinite G-dly potential represents the
core of our souls, our genuine "I."

From this perspective, sin and evil are superficial elements
that can never affect our fundamental nature. *Teshuvah* means
rediscovering our true selves, establishing contact with this
G-dly inner potential and making it the dominant influence
in our lives. Seen in this light, our motivation to do *teshuvah*
is not an awareness of our failings, but rather a sensitivity to
this infinite potential within our souls.

"*I* was in the midst of teaching a class," relates Rabbi
Shabtai Slavaticki, who, together with his wife Richa,
runs the Chabad house in Antwerp, Belgium, "when
a young man in his mid-twenties arrived at the doorway
unannounced. He apologized and asked if he could interrupt
for just a minute. I excused myself and stepped out to where
he and a female companion were waiting. They looked like
'New Agers' but that didn't conceal the man's markedly Jewish
face.

"'I've heard this is a place where one can come and study
about Judaism,' the man said. 'I was also told that one can
board here for a while. I just wanted to get a quick glimpse of
the place and of who teaches here. I'll be back when I'm ready
to begin. Is that o.k.?'"

---

12. Cf. *Tanya*, ch. 2.

Rabbi Slavaticki nodded in assent. The visitors bid him farewell and left as suddenly as they had come. Rabbi Slavaticki hurried back inside to resume his class.

Some time later, the young man returned, introducing himself as Eitan. He was shown a room at Chabad House where he could stay. Surprisingly, he announced that he was ready to begin learning as soon as he unpacked his belongings. A few minutes later, he was seated at the table awaiting the first lesson. Rabbi Slavaticki took this alacrity as a sign of eagerness; to his surprise, though, Eitan seemed to be a rather passive student, sitting silently with a detached demeanor.

"Perhaps he's just getting oriented and will warm up after a while," he thought.

The next morning the rabbi prefaced his session with an invitation to put on *tefillin*.

"No." Eitan refused. "My goal in coming here is only to study."

Yet, when they sat down to study, he seemed aloof and lacked interest. This puzzling behavior did not deter Rabbi Slavaticki, and he maintained his calm and friendliness throughout the classes. Everything became clear a few days later when Eitan requested a private talk with the rabbi.

"I owe you an apology," he said earnestly. "I've been taking advantage of your generosity in giving of your time, effort and hospitality. Please bear with me as I start from the beginning and explain. I'm originally from Israel and have always associated myself with the secular-leftist ideology there. After my studies in sociology at the Technion in Haifa, I felt the need to explore different philosophies and reach the universal truth of existence.

"My search led me to a master guru who resides in India. I followed his teaching in the hope of being accepted to his inner circle of disciples. The last step toward this goal was a personal encounter with the master, during which one would express one's commitment, and, one would take on a new name, symbolizing a new orientation towards life.

"I approached the guru with great expectation and satisfaction at reaching my goal. He inquired where I was from. When I told him that I was from Israel, he demanded to know if I felt that I had totally severed my ties to Judaism. In all honesty, I had to admit that I still maintained some feelings for my religion. To you, rabbi, I can confess that at one point in my journeys I felt the need to communicate with a profound person of the Jewish religion. I had heard of the Lubavitch Rebbe and decided that he was a person of stature. I wrote a letter to the Rebbe expressing my contemplations, but I never actually sent it. I kept it with me in my knapsack.

"The guru wasn't satisfied with my answer. He instructed me to travel to Holland, where my companion is from, and investigate my religion. He assured me that I would be disillusioned with my findings. That experience would 'cleanse' me, and I would then be able to take on a new identity under his guidance.

"I followed his instructions and began my search. I visited synagogues in Holland, asking where I could learn about Jewish philosophy. It was suggested that I travel to nearby Antwerp, where the Chabad House would provide classes and accommodations. That's when I arrived and first met you. But you see, I had an agenda and attempted to block myself from internalizing anything you taught. All I wanted to do was follow the instructions of my guru.

"Yet what I was hearing penetrated my heart with its pure truth. I felt that I was finally exposed to the real thing, something that could give my life meaning and significance.

Please accept my apologies for having deceived you. Now I sincerely request the opportunity to learn Torah."

Rabbi Slavaticki heeded Eitan's request wholeheartedly and the two spent many hours of study together. Eitan took to the classes seriously, but was not ready for a commitment to fulfill mitzvos. Even after substantial study, he felt unsure. Once more he confided in Rabbi Slavaticki.

"I've decided to take 'time out.' Although I sense that I'm going in the right direction, I need to be sure my enthusiasm is genuinely coming from within and not merely inspired by the environment here. I am going back to Holland for a while, to see if the desire to connect with Judaism is generated from the real me, without external influence."

With that Eitan departed. Rabbi Slavaticki knew he must be patient, but the weeks turned into a month and more, and no word from Eitan. The High Holidays came and Rabbi Slavaticki found himself immersed in prayer on Rosh HaShanah. As he uttered the verse, "May all creations know that You are their Creator..." his thoughts were with Eitan. He added a silent prayer that Eitan, too, would recognize the ultimate truth.

Just then, he felt a hand on his shoulder. Stirred from his intensive prayer, he looked up. It was Eitan. In total amazement, Rabbi Slavaticki embraced him and offered him a seat nearby.

After the services, Eitan related the following account.

"I began my morning as I do every day, with meditation. In the stillness of the moment, it suddenly dawned on me with total clarity that indeed there is a G-d and that His Torah is true. From some long forgotten memory, I remembered that this was the High Holiday season. I went to check the calendar and realized it was Rosh HaShanah. I knew that I had to be here in the synagogue. But I also knew that one should not travel on this holy day. Aware that this moment of recognition of the truth could slip by, I concluded that it was a matter of danger to the preservation of my soul, so I took a train and here I am. Do you think G-d will forgive me?"

It was his first day on campus at San Diego State University, and Rabbi Moishe Leider, who had just arrived on shlichus with his wife Sura, felt almost like a freshman himself. At lunchtime, students of all types, nationalities and color poured out of the buildings and onto the main square where he had set up his table.

Soon a fellow approached Rabbi Leider's stand. His striking face did look Jewish, although he was wearing a long American Indian shirt and moccasins.

"Are you a rabbi?" he inquired.

"Yes, I am. How can I help you?"

"My name is Dean, and I'd like to learn about Judaism."

Rabbi Leider answered, "Pleased to meet you, Dean. My name is Moishe Leider, and that's just why I'm here! When can we get together?"

"How about Sunday?"

"Well, I teach at the Hebrew school on Sunday mornings. The school's about a forty-five minute drive from here, in a new area called Rancho Penesquitos. We can meet as soon as I get back, if you like."

The young man thought for a moment. "Actually, I wouldn't mind going along with you to your teaching session, if that's okay with you."

Rabbi Leider wasn't sure why he would want to do that, but consented with no hesitation. He wrote down his home address and handed it over.

"Please be at my house at 9:00 a.m. Sunday morning. I'm looking forward to talking."

The two parted and the rabbi carried on with his efforts on campus.

On Sunday, Dean showed up on time, and they left for Penesquitos. During the ride, Rabbi Leider learned a little about his passenger.

Dean was a thoughtful young man with a strong sense of spiritual values, who had long realized the importance of living a more meaningful life. His family had moved from New York to California when he was fourteen.

"Moving from coast to coast sharpened my sense of observation," he said. "Back east, people were obsessed with pursuing another dollar. Here in the west, they're obsessed with pursuing another pleasure. It all seems so superficial; there must be more to the American dream than that."

A serious car accident at the age of sixteen had been the clincher. "After coming so close to death, I felt that I had to find more depth to my life."

Dean's search had led him in various directions, including a study of the natural healing practiced by the Sioux Indians in the backlands of South Dakota, and from there to the Hopi Indian reservation in Arizona. Periodically, the groups he encountered would mention the spiritual essence of the Jewish people.

"That was a revelation to me," he admitted. "I was spiritually oriented but didn't think much of my Jewishness. And yet, I was reminded of it constantly by other people marveling at what they called 'the phenomenon of the Jews.'

"Then I spent a few days with the chief of the Hopi Indians, White Bear Fredricks. I learned much from this exceptional spiritual man and planned to stay on at the reservation to seek more understanding. To my surprise, Chief White Bear objected. He told me that every individual is born into a people, and should live his life as part of that people. 'Go to the Jews,' he advised. I was shaken. Here was a place where I felt I was finally finding guidance and direction, and I was being told to search elsewhere. Besides, I knew very little about my religion.

"But I heeded his advice and left the reservation. I went back to California and settled in my own apartment, visiting my parents from time to time. Shortly afterwards, I got a phone call from an old friend, Ira Nasi. Ira and I had gotten along well when we lived in New York but hadn't spoken in four years; he didn't know my new number. That he should have called right when I was visiting my parents' home was uncanny.

"After we spoke for a bit, catching up, Ira told me he was studying at San Diego State. 'I remember you always thought a lot about religion,' he said. 'Would you like to sit in on one of my Judaism classes? The professor is an interesting guy.'

"My parents encouraged me to go. They had always been uncomfortable with my personal quest and really wanted me to become more mainstream, go to college, and get on with my life. So I met Ira and attended the class.

"It was disappointing and frustrating. The professor spoke about some of the most important events in Jewish history, but in a joking sort of way. Even though I didn't know much about the subject, Judaism is no joke to me, especially since I was being told to 'join the ranks' and had become serious about exploring my heritage.

"I came out of that class longing for something real, and there, in front of my eyes, stood an authentic-looking rabbi!"

Much later, Dean told Rabbi Leider why he had asked to join him at the Hebrew school.

"I was looking for the truth and wanted to learn it from someone genuine. Children are honest and truthful. I wanted to see if you were successfully communicating G-d's word to children, because anyone who can do that is probably living by His word. That person would be a good teacher for me."

Dean was impressed by Rabbi Leider's rapport with the children. Today David (Dean) Levitan, his wife, Bassie, and their children live full chassidic lives.

While on shlichus at Rutgers College, New Jersey, Chaim and Rivkie Grossbaum extended themselves generously to the students. One night, at 1:00 a.m. to be exact, Rabbi Grossbaum called a certain student to invite him for Shabbos. To his dismay, he realized too late that he had accidentally dialed the student's home number rather than his dorm, as he had intended.

He apologized profusely.

"Please don't worry about it," the parents assured him. "But we would like to know why you tried to call our son in the middle of the night. Don't rabbis have hours?"

"In my job," Rabbi Grossbaum explained, "we do what is most effective. Students are difficult to contact throughout the day, so I have no choice but to call them at this hour. It's the best time to reach them."

The parents later shared this phone encounter with an acquaintance. He was so impressed with Rabbi Grossbaum's dedication that he contacted him and expressed his desire to support his work.

A family of five balanced precariously on a motorcycle, navigating the overcrowded lanes shared by elephants with license plates and red lights on their rear ends, weaving past outdoor eateries frying all kinds of creatures....

Such is the setting in which Rabbi Yosef Chaim and Nechama Kantor pursue Chabad activities in Bangkok, Thailand. Chabad provides a Jewish haven there for the throngs of backpackers, business people, and tourists who flow through this exotic country.

Shabbos at Chabad House is the place to go, and the generous meals and inspiring talks keep body and soul attuned to Judaism in this Far Eastern supermarket of self- exploration and spiritual journeys.

Once, at the Shabbos day meal, Mrs. Kantor was relating a story she had heard from Reb Pesach Nussbaum of Montreal, a student of her father, Rabbi Zalman Shmukler.

Reb Pesach worked for a computer company and was asked to travel to Taiwan on a business deal. He debated, because the trip was scheduled for the last weekend in the month of Elul. That Saturday night would be the first recital of the *Selichos* prayers, and he wanted to be with his community. But the offer was financially attractive and he had a growing family. After some deliberation, he decided in favor of the trip.

He arrived in Taiwan only to find that the deal had fallen through at the last moment, and all his appointments had been cancelled. His company informed him that he would be duly compensated, but this was of little consolation; he still had to stay in Taiwan for the weekend. Although he had come to terms with making the taxing trip and with having to miss Saturday night *Selichos* services, now it all seemed like so much wasted effort.

Over Shabbos, he met other Jewish businessmen staying

in the same hotel. He convinced a number of them to join him in the *Selichos* services at midnight on Saturday, as is customary. Reb Pesach promised to lead them as cantor. But then, to his dismay, he could not find the *Selichos* prayer book he was sure he had packed. He decided to lead the *minyan* using the abbreviated *Selichos* services printed in the daily prayer book. In any case, the rest of the *minyan* was not well versed in these seasonal prayers, so in such circumstances, he decided it would be the most acceptable alternative.

What he could not put into words for lack of text, Reb Pesach made up for in devotion. The absence of a community or an appropriate prayer book, the upcoming High Holy Days, and the futility of the trip all found expression in heartfelt prayer.

The participants were uplifted by the experience, and Reb Pesach sensed their mood. He set a table with all his remaining kosher food, and led a lively *farbrengen* until the wee hours of the night.

When he awoke the next morning, Reb Pesach found a fax that had been slipped under his door. It was from Neil, a young man who had attended the service the night before. The fax was time-stamped 6 a.m. Neil wrote that the intensity of the prayers had ignited his soul, and that he had committed himself to set out on the road to self-discovery.

Mrs. Kantor paused for a moment. She was about to conclude the tale, as she had many times before, by stressing the role of Divine Providence, and how Reb Pesach Nussbaum had discovered a significant purpose for his seemingly futile trip.

But as she paused, one of the Shabbos guests began to speak.

"Excuse me for interrupting," he requested. "My Hebrew name is Nachshon and, if you don't mind, I'd like to tell my story."

All eyes turned to the speaker in curiosity.

"I was brought up with very little knowledge of Judaism and every so often wondered about its validity. In my work for a non-governmental organization, I travel extensively. Once, before a long trip to the Orient, I purchased a copy of *The Chosen*, by Chaim Potok, in an attempt to investigate Judaism. I was fascinated with Potok's description of prayer as a devout experience. I had been to Jewish temples before, but the prayers there somehow always seemed to lack the depth and vitality I imagined they should have. I concluded that the author was describing something from the past, something that simply hadn't survived to modern times.

"These thoughts were in the back of my mind as I went about my business in Taiwan. I knew from previous trips that Jewish businessmen often stayed at the Ritz, and I decided to join the Shabbos services there, if only to reconfirm my conclusions. As I had expected, the prayers seemed devoid of the intense feeling described in the book, and I felt justified in my observations.

"For some reason, I decided to go back the following week. This time, though, the rabbi who had led the services wasn't there. In his place was a devout-looking man whose prayers were alive with feeling. I was mesmerized. 'Perhaps I was wrong after all,' I thought to myself. 'Maybe Jewish prayer really isn't a thing of the past.' And then there were these special prayers late at night, in preparation for the upcoming High Holy Days. I was very touched by the rabbi's intense prayer, and decided to send him a note acknowledging his contribution to my spiritual search.

"That night marked the beginning of my journey back to Judaism.

"Rebbetzin, I'm very sorry to have interrupted you. But you see, it's my story that you have been telling."

*L*ife had not been easy for Barbara. She had grown up in an abusive home, married young and divorced soon afterward. Now she was left to raise her small son alone. In her emotional and financial need, she succumbed to the attempts of missionaries to take her and her son under their wing. There was a price to pay, of course, but she felt that in her situation, allegiance to Judaism was not a priority. So mother and son converted to Christianity in exchange for care and assistance. They settled into their new community in Seabrook, New Hampshire, and joined the local church.

In time, one of Barbara's friends from the church, who knew of her Jewish origins, began asking about Judaism. She was curious and wanted to compare the two religions.

"I'm sorry," Barbara replied honestly, "but I wasn't brought up in a religious home and don't really know much about it. But I know there are temples for Jewish people, so maybe that's where you could find out more."

Barbara wasn't particularly interested in pursuing the topic, but her friend asked her to come along to a temple with her one Saturday.

"Just this once," the friend insisted. "I really want to go, but I'd feel uncomfortable there on my own."

Reluctantly, Barbara consented. The nearest temple was located in the bordering state of Massachusetts. And so that is where the two women found themselves one Saturday morning.

At the end of the service, the rabbi gave a short sermon. Short as it was, it struck a chord in Barbara's heart. "I've never heard such poignant words about the soul," she thought to herself. In her youth, she had occasionally been to temple, but did not recall any sermons that sounded like this one. She was so moved by what she had heard about the infinite quality and strength of the Jewish soul that she decided to speak with the rabbi.

She approached him. "I would like to ask about some of the concepts you mentioned, rabbi. But first, I would like to compliment you. It's no wonder you have your position here as congregational leader."

"Thank you for the kind words," he replied, smiling. "But I'm not actually a rabbi. I'm filling in for the rabbi, who is on sabbatical in Israel. He asked me to deliver the sermon on Saturdays during the year he is away."

"Not a rabbi?" Barbara wondered. "Then where did you gain your knowledge?"

Rather than answer her question directly, the man said only: "How about if you come back next week and we'll talk then?" Barbara nodded and left.

* * *

Where indeed had he gained the knowledge to deliver such a short, but moving sermon? The man's name was Dean S., and his learning had begun not long after Rabbi Asher and Faigy Bronstein arrived in Andover, Massachusetts. One day they received a call from a representative of the Merrimack Valley Jewish Federation.

"Welcome to town, Rabbi Bronstein," the caller said, sounding friendly and inviting. "The Federation is planning an 'Israel Day' in Andover. Would you like Chabad to have a booth on the exhibition grounds?"

"Certainly," replied Rabbi Bronstein eagerly, "Thanks very much for asking us."

The arrangements were made, and the Chabad *tefillin* booth commanded an attractive spot at the fair. Among the passersby that Rabbi Bronstein attempted to interest in putting on *tefillin* was a fellow who introduced himself as Dean S.

"I go to temple every Saturday morning and listen to the rabbi's sermon," Dean proclaimed earnestly, "but I've never heard about – what is it you call these things – *tefillin?*"

With Rabbi Bronstein's guidance, Dean put on *tefillin* for the first time in his life. The two chatted for a while, and Dean seemed interested in learning more about Judaism. They agreed to stay in touch, and exchanged telephone numbers.

But Dean didn't call, and Rabbi Bronstein's messages went unanswered for six weeks.

Then one day Dean called back. "I'm sorry, rabbi," he apologized. "My wife is not keen on my interest in Judaism, so your messages never got to me. Today was the first time I learned of your calls."

Dean and the rabbi set up a Sunday class, and he began to learn the teachings of Chabad. About five months later, the rabbi of Dean's temple requested that he deliver the sermons on Saturday during his absence. Of all the congregants, he regarded Dean as the most knowledgeable.

Thus, unbeknownst to the temple rabbi, the weekly sermons contained many chassidic insights. Dean was hesitant to disclose the source of his material, because he was concerned that some of the congregants might not identify with these teachings if they knew that they came from black-coated rabbis. And so when Barbara addressed him, he wanted to be sure her interest was sincere.

Barbara indeed returned the following week, and this time, after the sermon, Dean told her about Chabad. "I really connect with the things you said," Barbara confessed. "I'd like to find out more about Chabad."

Barbara spent the next Shabbos at the Bronsteins, and this marked the beginning of her journey back to Judaism. Today she and her son lead a complete Torah lifestyle; Dean and his family do as well.

"Hello, may I speak to Chief Rabbi Jacobs?" said the voice over the phone.

"Certainly. Who shall I say is calling?" inquired the secretary at the office of the Inter-Provincial Chief Rabbinate for the Netherlands.

There was a short hesitation before the caller responded: "Just say it is Mr. Van Dam. He doesn't know me."

Rabbi Binyamin Jacobs took the phone.

"Rabbi, my name is actually not Van Dam, but I prefer to remain anonymous. I'm not searching for spiritual guidance, as I'm not observant. The issue I would like to discuss is purely humanitarian.

"I'm an elderly man and am thinking about writing a will. My wife passed away, and we never had any children. We both endured the Holocaust and experienced hunger and suffering first-hand. I am a man of means and would like to leave money to an organization that helps people in need of care, friendship and subsistence. Can you direct me to one that addresses these causes?"

Rabbi Jacobs thought seriously about the matter and suggested Chabad of Holland, since its objectives fit those that "Mr. Van Dam" described. The caller thanked him. He said he would consider the suggestion and would contact him if he chose to pursue it further.

A week later the elderly gentleman called again.

"Rabbi Jacobs, I have decided to follow your suggestion, and have included Chabad of Holland in my will.

"You're probably wondering who I am and why I chose to consult with you on this matter. After all, there are other rabbis in Holland, and you don't know me. Well, I will tell you. We have indeed met on a few occasions. This goes back many years, but I will begin with my most recent encounter with your Chief Rabbinate, yourself and your family.

"As you know, the city hosted a fascinating exhibition of Jewish life in Holland in honor of the 275th anniversary of the Amersfoort synagogue. Visitors there were presented with headphones offering explanations of the displays. I enjoyed the exhibition and was very impressed with the narratives; they were clear and engaging. I learned from the credits that it is your son, Yanki, with his pleasant voice and excellent delivery, who is to be thanked for that.

"It was highly enjoyable to encounter two generations in a family of local rabbis featured there, for I came across photographs of you as well, officiating at weddings and other Jewish events.

"Then I recalled that I had often observed you and your family, some thirty years ago, on your daily drives from Amersfoort into Amsterdam, apparently taking your children to school. Perhaps it was my war-torn youth, or maybe it was my own childlessness that drew me to notice the van full of exuberant, observant Jewish children.

"And then, of course, there was the eulogy you delivered at my mother's funeral, twenty-six years ago. Her name was Mrs. Waterman. Do you remember?"

In fact, Rabbi Jacobs, who had been listening attentively, remembered the woman very well. She had served as the matron of a prominent Jewish home for seniors in Den Dolder, where his own grandparents had resided. He had been a child then, but he remembered the night his family received an urgent call; his grandfather had suffered a heart attack. Mrs. Waterman, known for her compassion and dedication, had come running in the middle of the night. The vision of this kind woman attending to his grandfather as he breathed his last was engraved on the Chief Rabbi's mind. He had not seen nor had any contact with her for thirty years when he was called, now a prominent rabbi, to officiate at her funeral. Recalling his memories of Mrs. Waterman from his youth, he had eulogized her exemplary character.

The caller, whom he could now identify as Mr. Waterman, was telling him how moved he had been by the poignant eulogy.

"For all these reasons," Mr. Waterman concluded, "when I was searching for a rabbi with whom to discuss my will, I decided to call you."

Rabbi Jacobs was touched. He wanted to reach out and perhaps draw this soul a little closer to his religion. It's never too late to start, he thought, and proposed a learning session with Mr. Waterman at his convenience. Mr. Waterman was willing to meet once every six weeks. This arrangement continued for the next three years. Their periodic meetings included participating in a Seder at the Jacobs' home, where the rabbi and his wife Blouma – a full partner in his work – graciously hosted a table full of guests of a variety of ages and backgrounds. Inspired by this experience, Mr. Waterman pledged monthly contributions toward Jewish education in Holland.

Although they had grown better acquainted, Mr. Waterman was a private person and Rabbi Jacobs was not the nosey type. All he could learn about the man was that he

grasped Jewish concepts well, his grandfather had been observant, and he himself held a high position in one of Holland's
top pharmaceutical companies.

One day, Rabbi Jacobs heard that Mr. Waterman had been
hospitalized. When he arrived to pay him a visit, a woman was
just leaving the room. Mr. Waterman bid her farewell as he
welcomed the rabbi.

"I'm so glad you came; there's something I need to discuss
with you," he said. "In truth, it is not I but the woman who
just left who has prompted this conversation. She is a friend of
mine and we often spend time together. A while ago, we were
strolling in her hometown of Zaltbommel and passed an old
Jewish cemetery. I had told her previously of my relationship
with you and, coming to that site, my friend, who is not Jewish,
inquired if we had discussed burial plans.

"I told her we had not. She urged me to do so, as it was my
responsibility to my religion. I responded that there was nothing I could do; I had already purchased a plot in a non-Jewish
cemetery. But she insisted I discuss the matter with you.

"You see, when my wife died, she was buried in a non-
Jewish cemetery, at her request. I had tried to persuade her
otherwise, but after the Holocaust, she lost all sense of her
Jewish origins. She was a wonderful woman and we had a
good marriage, and so I was unwilling to ignore her wishes. I,
of course, want to be buried next to her, and since I know one
cannot relocate graves, I am bound to my plot in the non-Jewish
cemetery. Because there is nothing I can do about it, I would
not have brought this up but for my friend's prodding."

Rabbi Jacobs marveled at the unfolding of events that
would eventually enable a proper Jewish burial for Mr. Waterman
and his wife. He explained that, in certain circumstances, with

proper rabbinical guidance, it is possible to re-inter a Jew. Mr. Waterman was overjoyed.

"I know that deep in her soul this is what my wife would have wanted, but the Holocaust left scars so deep that she was afraid to be buried in a Jewish cemetery."

Once a state senator from New York asked for yechidus, (a private meeting) with the Rebbe. Over an hour later, he came out moved. "I hadn't realized what a great man your Rebbe is," he told Rabbi Leibel Groner, the Rebbe's secretary.

The senator explained that he had sought the Rebbe's counsel concerning a personal issue. After the Rebbe had advised him with regard to these matters, he asked if he could request a favor from the senator.

"'Here it comes,' I thought to myself," he told Rabbi Groner, "'just like all the others, he's also looking for the pay-off.'

"But what did the Rebbe ask me?

"'There is a growing community in Chinatown,' the Rebbe said. 'These people are quiet, reserved, hardworking and law-abiding, the type of citizens most countries would treasure. But because Americans are so outgoing and the Chinese are, by nature, more reserved, they are often overlooked by government programs. As a state-senator from New York, I suggest that you concern yourself with their needs.'

"I was overwhelmed. The Rebbe has a community of thousands in New York and institutions all over the country that could benefit from government programs. I am in a position to help secure funding for them, but the Rebbe didn't ask about that. He was concerned with Chinatown. I don't think he has ever been there, and I'm certain that most people there

don't know who he is, but he cares about them. Now that's a true leader!"

The Rebbe did not merely manifest an unbounded concern for the welfare of all mankind, he provided us with teachings that motivate and enable us to share this mind-set. Though he obviously directed the majority of his efforts towards Jews, he also spoke of the contribution the gentiles could make to perfect the world, heralding the age when all the nations will "call upon the name of G-d and serve Him with a single purpose."[13]

"These kind of calls are out of my league," thought Professor Leon Zelman, chairman of the Jewish Welcome Service in Vienna, receiver in hand, as he contemplated how to respond. "I'll pass it on to my friend Rabbi Jacob Biderman from Chabad. Let him deal with it."

The phone call was indeed somewhat out of the ordinary. At the other end of the line was an elderly gentleman with a shaky voice, who introduced himself as Hans D.

"Hans D.?!" Rabbi Biderman thought in surprise. "He's the famous publisher and chief editor of the *Kronen* daily newspaper that claims to have three million readers out of a population of seven million. People say he's the most powerful person in Austria. What could he want?"

Rabbi Biderman could never have imagined what was coming.

"Rabbi, I'd like to make an appointment with you. There's an issue that is weighing heavily on my conscience. When can we meet?"

---

13. *Zephaniah* 3:9; quoted by Maimonides in the *Mishneh Torah, Hilchos Melachim* 12:5.

The next day, Mr. Hans D., whom some wags call the "emperor of Austria," was sitting in the modest office of Rabbi Biderman's synagogue.

"As you know," he explained, "one of my editors, Ernst N., has written some editorials with audible anti-Semitic overtones. I should have kept such material out of print, but I wasn't sensitive enough at the time and let them run. I am here to seek atonement and to find a way to amend that wrong and the damage it did. What would you advise?"

Rabbi Biderman's first response was to suggest that the media mogul seek the services of the clergy of his own religion, but the man insisted that he wanted the advice of a rabbi.

"I wasn't at all prepared for such a request," recalled Rabbi Biderman. He wondered what he should say to the troubled man. Then suddenly it dawned on him. Chabad was struggling with a certain matter, and this man might be part of the solution.

It had all begun with an unexpected revelation about a valuable plot of land within the city's Central Augarten Park. A municipal clerk had disclosed to some Chabad members that, before World War II, a sanatorium for Jewish children had stood on six acres now enclosed within the grounds of the public park. "It would be appropriate to return the site to its original purpose," the clerk had said.

At that time, the Lauder Chabad School, with over four hundred pupils studying in scattered, substandard apartments, was looking desperately for a site for their center. That lot would be a heaven-sent gift. It had space enough for a school, a synagogue and a community hall. And the location was perfect – right in the heart of the Jewish neighborhood, yet within the park – ideal surroundings for children. Moreover, it would be a meaningful way to pay homage to the children from the sanatorium who had been murdered in the Holocaust.

Unobtrusively, Rabbi Biderman had begun negotiations with the mayor and municipal officials. When word of it got out, though, there was an uproar. Rival newspapers and TV stations joined forces. City officials who usually opposed one another made joint statements, and competing civil organizations became allies in denouncing the proposal.

"Protect our park from construction" and similar headlines were in all the papers and posted on trees in the park. Petitions were signed and demonstrations were held. In the face of such opposition, the Chabad team reluctantly saw their case to be as good as lost.

And now, so unexpectedly, this meeting with Hans D.! Just that morning, Rabbi Biderman had written a letter to be read at the Rebbe's gravesite requesting a blessing for this apparently no-win situation. Suddenly, everything fell into place. What a perfect way for Mr. Hans D. to make good the *Kronen*'s misdeed: The paper could throw its weight behind this worthy cause, granting Jewish children the opportunity to learn and grow in proper surroundings, and empower the Jewish community to flourish.

Mr. Hans D. listened intently.

That week, the issue hit the front pages again. But this time, the headlines carried a different message. "Children and trees belong together" stated the influential *Kronen* paper in large print. "Let children play in the park" read another headline. The headlines were supported by convincing editorials and persuasive articles in favor of the Chabad school. At the same time, the principal of the high school, Rabbi Dov Gruzman, the principal of the elementary school, Edla Biderman, and the director of the kindergarten, Chani Eidelman, organized a petition signed by parents, students and friends.

All these efforts caused a shift in the public and political arena. Television stations, other newspapers and politicians now dared to come out in favor of the project. Finally, the mayor himself publicly declared his support, and the city council adopted the proposal unanimously.

So it came to be that the meticulously designed Lauder Chabad Campus graces the beautiful grounds of Central Augarten Park, with children and trees thriving side by side in peaceful harmony.

"*H*ello, may I speak to Mrs. Myers?"

"This is she," responded Chanie Myers, who, together with her husband, Rabbi Baruch Myers, and their ten children, run Chabad activities in Bratislava, Slovakia.

The caller was Mr. Petr Toth, from the Dom Kultúry Ružinov Cultural Center. The center was planning its annual three-day community seminar, which attracts thousands of people. This year, the central theme was to be "Focus on Physical and Emotional Health," and Mr. Toth was inviting Mrs. Myers to speak on the significance and benefits of raising a large family. The objective was to encourage couples to have more children.

"I'm not a public health professional," Mrs. Myers thought to herself with a chuckle, "but I am probably the most experienced Jewish mother in the country!" She was willing to accept the invitation, but was curious.

"How did you get my name?" she inquired.

"A friend of mine by the name of Jaroslav Novak recommended you," Mr. Toth replied. "He said you would probably be a good speaker for our program."

"Novak?" Mrs. Myers mused out loud. "I don't recall an acquaintance by that name, and I wonder how he would know me as a speaker. I only speak to female audiences."

"Well, actually, he doesn't know you personally," Mr. Toth explained. "He's heard your name mentioned by his priest. In his Sunday sermons, the priest often quotes from interviews you've given in Slovenka, Rodina and Infinity women's magazines on women's issues and values in the home. I assume we can rely upon the priest's judgment?"

When Rabbi Chaim and Sora Steinmetz first arrived in Sarasota, Florida, they were concerned about the neighbors. Having a regular *minyan* in their living room and programs for children throughout the week made for an active driveway, and cars often had to park in the street near their Chabad House.

But so far, so good.

One Sunday two months after they moved in, Rabbi Steinmetz suggested to his wife that they have a *Tu Beshvat* party.

"Good idea," agreed Sora, "many people don't know much about that holiday, and they may be curious to find out. And if it's a party, they'll bring their kids. I must say, though, I went shopping the other day. With *Tu Beshvat* coming up, I naturally gravitated towards the dried-fruit stands and was surprised to see how expensive they are. Having enough for a crowd will be costly."

Despite this reservation, the couple continued planning.

The morning of the event, their doorbell rang. The caller was a woman carrying a large, gift-wrapped package.

"Hi, and welcome to the neighborhood," she said cheerily. "I live down the block, and noticed that you've recently moved in. You know, greeting a new neighbor is the proper Christian thing to do, but I've been so busy lately, I neglected to do so. I'm so sorry, especially since you seem like nice people. You see, I have a little boy whom I home school, and one day he told me your husband is a rabbi and your children also study at home. It's funny how open and perceptive kids are, isn't it? Anyway, I've brought you this fruit basket as a welcoming gift. Enjoy!"

Sora could hardly contain her surprise at the timely gift.

"Thank you so much for all this dried fruit!" she exclaimed. "Please excuse me, but may I ask what prompted you to think of fruit as a welcoming gift, and why you chose to come over this morning in particular?"

"As I said," the woman replied, "I'd been planning to introduce myself and welcome you for quite a while, but this morning I just had this inner voice compelling me not to put it off any longer. As for the gift, I asked my priest what I should bring to a rabbi's home. He told me that Jewish people eat special food, but I would be safe if I brought a fruit basket. So here you are, and welcome again."

*I*t was the first week in Elul, and Rabbi Menachem Junik of the Jewish Home Network, Chabad's educational program in London, was on his way to Barnard and Levitt Opticians. He had an ongoing learning session with the owner, Mr. Barnard, and they enjoyed a good relationship.

"This business employs a fair number of Jewish people,"

he had thought. "I'm sure Mr. Barnard will be receptive to the idea of having the *shofar* blown on his premises."

Mr. Barnard was indeed agreeable, but with some reservations.

"Rabbi," he said, "there are a number of non-Jewish people here as well, and I wouldn't want them to feel alienated."

"That doesn't necessarily have to be a deterrent," replied Rabbi Junik. "The custom of blowing the *shofar* during Elul is in essence a wake-up call to the awareness of G-d's presence in this world. This is a universal concept, and I can explain the message to Jew and non-Jew alike."

Mr. Barnard consented, and notified his employees that there would be a brief gathering in his office. It was a pensive, introspective moment when the lingering sound of the *shofar* echoed in the hushed room.

As the people headed back to their duties, one of the workers, a British-African gentleman who introduced himself as Albert, approached the rabbi.

"Please excuse me," he said politely, "Can you tell me again what that horn is called? I hope it's not disrespectful of me to inquire. Actually, this is the first time I've ever spoken to a Jewish clergyman, and I apologize if my question is inappropriate."

Rabbi Junik assured him it was quite all right, meanwhile searching for a term that would help the man remember the Hebrew name.

"It's called a *shofar*," he explained, "as in the guy who drives the car for the boss – chauffeur."

"Oh! I get it," chuckled Albert. "Now I'll be able to remember. And thank you for your short sermon and for the ceremony. It was really meaningful."

Rabbi Junik wished him and his colleagues a nice weekend, and the regular hum of activity resumed at the busy office.

The next week, Rabbi Junik returned to Barnard and Levitt to blow the *shofar* again. This time, too, the penetrating sound brought a quiet, reflective moment. And once again, Albert approached the rabbi afterward. This time he had something to relate.

"Last Friday night," he began, "I was out shopping at Tesco in Brent Park with my fiance. As we were standing in line at the checkout counter, I told her about the horn-blowing event in the office. That's a – chauffeur, as in the boss's driver, right?"

Both the rabbi and Albert smiled.

"Anyway, as soon as the customer in front of us left, the checkout clerk looked at me hesitantly and said: 'I don't mean to be intrusive, but I couldn't help overhearing your conversation. Are you Jewish?'

"'Why do you ask?' I responded jokingly, 'do I look Jewish?'

"'Well, not exactly,' she answered awkwardly. 'But I am, and I overheard you speaking about the sound of the *shofar* and explaining its meaning. You know, that was a wake up call for me... I haven't thought about such things for a long time.'"

Albert concluded his story. "So, Rabbi, what do you think about that?"

"Everyone has his mission in this world, Albert," Rabbi Junik replied. "You were G-d's messenger that Friday night, to remind that woman of her Jewish roots."

"Me? G-d's messenger?" Albert asked in surprise. "That sounds more like your occupation, rabbi!"

Rabbi Junik smiled. "I go about all week long spreading G-d's message. But on Saturday I observe the Sabbath, which begins at sundown on Friday. I don't go shopping on Friday nights and could not have met that woman then. So it was you who brought her the message."

*I*t seemed reasonable to Mr. De Vries to call the office of Rabbi Binyamin Jacobs, who is Chief Rabbi of the Netherlands. All Mr. De Vries needed was a signature for his son, George, an idealistic teenager, who had left high school and gone off to Israel to serve in the army. At the end of his service, he had returned home with plans to go back to Israel and join a government-funded educational program, but a letter was required affirming his status as a Jew. Mr. De Vries was certain the rabbi would sign the form, thus enabling a promising young man to continue contributing to the land of Israel.

Rabbi Jacobs would have signed the form gladly; he was only too willing to assist anyone who wished to settle in Israel. There was only one problem. Mr. De Vries was Jewish but his wife was not and so, according to Jewish law, neither was George. The father was enraged. He had been so relieved that his son had found a sense of direction at last after his turbulent teenage years. Here was a young man who demonstrated responsibility and self-sacrifice for the land of Israel. In his eyes, George should be accepted without reservation. But Rabbi Jacobs could not agree to something that transgressed Jewish law. Though he readily acknowledged George's praiseworthy intentions, he would not compromise the Torah's directives.

George was even more offended than his father had been. A tough young man and determined to get his way, he made an appointment with the rabbi. He came with clear intentions to threaten him into signing the form.

Rabbi Jacobs sensed the aggressive approach and, although slightly apprehensive, he tried to diffuse the mounting tension.

"You're a young man with your life ahead of you," he said carefully. "You have many options for your future. Although it looks attractive now, settling in Israel is not your only choice. Your father is anxious for that move. Perhaps his feelings are tied to his own internal conflict, since he married out of his faith. But his faith is not yours. Why rush to settle yourself now? I suggest you return to school in Holland, get an education and pursue a career. You still have plenty of time to decide on your future. As you study and learn more about yourself, you'll be able to make a more thought-out and informed decision about your connection to Israel."

It took a while, but the rabbi succeeded in calming George. He left the office pondering, with a lot to think about. Rabbi Jacobs had one last word with Mr. De Vries. He never heard from him again.

Twenty years later, Rabbi Jacobs was asked to officiate at a funeral in a small town out in the countryside. Shortly after the funeral, one of the participants came up to speak with him.

"Rabbi, you probably don't recognize me. The deceased is a relative of mine and that's why I'm here. My name was George, that hostile young man you counseled so wisely some twenty years ago. I followed your advice and slowly found inner peace and guidance. I have converted properly to Judaism and live with my lovely Jewish wife and children in Israel."

"*R*abbi, you're the only one who can save my son from certain death. Please don't refuse me. You must help!" wailed the distraught woman who appeared one day at the synagogue office in Donesk, Ukraine.

Rabbi Pinchas and his wife Nechama Vishedsky were accustomed to helping others, but this request was clearly out of the ordinary. The rabbi gathered the details from the sobbing woman's tale.

It was 1998. A civil uprising was taking place in Georgia that had been triggered by militants loyal to the followers of the deposed president, the late Zviad Gamsakhurdia, in their attempt to overthrow the government of Prime Minister Shevardnadze. The woman's son, who had served in an elite unit in the Ukrainian army, had been hired by the rebels in Georgia. The woman related that they had promised him a hefty fee for his services, which included terrorist activities targeting the Georgian army. Caught in action, he was now incarcerated in a Georgian prison under sentence of death. The woman insisted that the rabbi could help.

Rabbi Vishedsky found it difficult to agree. He lived in the Ukraine and had no connection to Georgia, much less to its government. He was very much on the outside with regard to the conflict between Gamsakhurdia's supporters and Shevardnadze's government. Nevertheless, he did not approve of terror of any sort. And beyond all that, he had no idea what he could actually do that might help.

But the woman persisted. "I'm sure that if you write a letter to Shevardnadze, he would pardon my son," she implored. "You must write the letter!"

Rabbi Vishedsky was touched by the poor woman's plight. "She is so certain that I can help her, but it's absolutely unrealistic," he thought. "Yet, even though terror is wrong, her son is a Jew, and so I am obliged to respond."

He took the young man's details and promised to write the letter. The woman was overjoyed and thanked the rabbi as wholeheartedly as if he had already facilitated her son's release.

Rabbi Vishedsky was left wondering what to write. Finally, though, he had it on paper. It was a petition on behalf of a naive young man who had become the victim of a band of evil men. He came from a fine, educated home and had served his country loyally, but he had taken the bait offered him by reckless revolutionaries. If he is pardoned," the rabbi wrote, "as a religious clergyman, I will take personal responsibility for rehabilitating him and ensuring his future as a stable, contributing citizen."

At the end of the letter, he included blessings of health and success to the prime minister, in the merit of granting the young man his life.

Rabbi Vishedsky was determined to make good on his promise. He knew that if he merely dropped the letter in a mailbox, it would be just another paper among stacks and reams that might or might not ever reach the prime minister's attention. After making some inquiries, he discovered that the British embassy in Georgia was acting on behalf of local political prisoners. He sent the letter to the British embassy in the Ukraine, requesting that it be forwarded to the British embassy in Georgia, and that they deliver it to Shevardnadze.

"It was a very long shot," recalls Rabbi Vishedsky. "I thought it was highly unlikely that the letter would do any good, and the entire attempt seemed totally futile. But here was a forlorn woman and a Jew whose life was in immediate danger. I felt compelled to do something.

"I didn't hear anything from the woman for two months. Then, one day, a young man knocked on my door and requested to see me urgently. It was the woman's son who had come to thank me for saving his life.

"I investigated the matter and was told by the British embassy that Prime Minister Shevardnadze had been impressed that a rabbi offered to take responsibility for a young man

who had gone astray, and he had signed a pardon. Keeping my
word, I took the youth under my wing. I soon realized that he
was an honest, upright young man. He had never wanted any
part in terror. Gamsakhurdia's supporters threatened him and
compelled him to cooperate. He joined our *yeshivah* and later
advanced his studies further in Israel. Today, he and his family
reside in Jerusalem."

"As the only rabbi in Central Africa, I make periodic
visits to various countries in the region," explains
Rabbi Shlomo Bentolila, who is on shlichus with his
wife Myriam in Kinshasa, the Democratic Republic of the
Congo.

On one of his trips to a certain African country, Rabbi
Bentolila was standing on a street corner trying to hail a cab.
A car slowed and stopped, but it was not a cab. Now, a Jew
traveling in Central Africa must be cautious, in view of third
world security standards, Muslim radicalism and lurking anti-
Semitism. Rabbi Bentolila did not know what to expect.

"Hello there, rabbi, can I give you a lift?"

The driver was a friendly looking gentleman, yet Rabbi
Bentolila knew he must still be careful. Aware of the reason he
was hesitating, the driver smiled reassuringly.

"Don't worry, rabbi, I'm not a fundamentalist in disguise! I
stopped because I'm so happy to meet a Jew in our country. Get
in, I'll be glad to give you a ride. Where do you need to go?"

Rabbi Bentolila was convinced.

"I'm on my way to the Hilton," he told the driver as he
got in. "I appreciate your generosity. I hope I'm not taking you
out of your way."

"Not at all," the driver replied amiably. "Like I said, I'm

pleased to meet a Jew; they're few and far between in our country. My name is Albert, and I'm a diplomat in a European embassy. My father is Jewish, but my mother is not. Even so, my children like their grandfather very much and enjoy his stories and explanations about the religion. As a family, we feel connected to Judaism, and that's why I was so delighted to chance upon you."

As the two men neared their destination, Albert suddenly said: "Rabbi, if you're not in a rush, there's something I think you might be able to help with."

Rabbi Bentolila eyed his new acquaintance with curiosity. "I'd be happy to be of assistance in any way possible."

Albert pondered a moment and began.

"As a diplomat, I often meet people from overseas who are living in Africa. I've encountered a number of young Russian women living here in dire conditions. You may be wondering why Russians would come to Africa. So did I, until I discovered that it's one of the ways to gain exit visas from Russia, in the hope of reaching more promising horizons.

"There's a university called Patrice Lumumba in Moscow where many young Africans go as exchange students. Some of the men befriend Russian women and propose marriage, promising a wonderful new life in Africa. This entitles the women to an exit visa from Russia – their opportunity to enter what they imagine to be an exotic continent. Little do they know what awaits them. Poverty, subjugation in a male-dominated society, and widespread polygamy shock them into reality.

"At that point, though, they're stuck, because their legal husbands are seldom willing to separate. The reason I'm telling you all this is because of a particular young Russian woman I've been trying to help. She is Jewish, has two small children, and her life is miserable. I wonder if you would be willing to visit her. She doesn't live far from here, and your visit would boost her morale."

Rabbi Bentolila consented and accompanied Albert to the woman's home. All that he had been told was affirmed in one quick glance.

"Please help me get out of here," she pleaded tearfully. "I'm bound by the local law, which prevents me from leaving the country without my husband's permission, and he'll never agree to free me. But I am Jewish and you are a rabbi. You must help me."

Rabbi Bentolila was touched by the poor woman's plight. At the same time, he could not be sure her claim to be Jewish was authentic; the situation was complex and potentially perilous, and he wondered if it was wise to get involved.

As if reading his thoughts, the woman implored, "Do you have a cell-phone? Here's my mother's number. She lives in Israel. She will confirm my identity and can get any rabbi in Israel to validate my status."

Rabbi Bentolila made the call and confirmed the woman's statements. He realized that Divine Providence had led him to this desolate woman, and he resolved to help her.

"I don't know how or when, but with G-d's help we will get you to Israel," he said. "Do you have a passport?"

"Yes, my Russian passport, and my children are listed on it as well."

Rabbi Bentolila breathed a sigh of relief. Even if her passport had expired, at least he would not have to accomplish the impossible feat of obtaining an African passport for these foreigners. He took leave of the woman and formed a plan of action.

During numerous trips to the Israeli embassy, he presented the woman's case as the obligation to save Jewish souls. He personally vouched for the woman and took responsibility for her and her children's future in Israel. He then had to deal with the most delicate aspect of the plan. He coached the woman in her role.

"When everything is arranged, tell your husband that your elderly mother hasn't seen you or her grandchildren, and her health is failing. In my experience with Africans, I can tell you that people here are sensitive to family bonds. Take very little with you, so as not to arouse suspicion that this will be a one-way trip."

The ruse worked, and today, she is happily remarried and has established a new Jewish life for her family in Israel.

Rabbi Yehoshua and Chana Goldman knew of the petition to Cesar Maia, mayor of Rio de Janeiro. And what's more, they knew it was justified. Their Chabad House in the Leblon neighborhood had been attracting as many as a hundred people for Shabbos services and other activities. The Goldmans were delighted with the attendance, but this was a residential area and the constant flow of traffic and visitors displeased the neighbors.

But what were the Goldmans to do? This was the largest house in the area, and the only option they had. Trying to maintain peace, the couple apologized frequently, assuring their neighbors that they were continuously searching for a viable alternative. Nonetheless, the uncomfortable state of affairs continued for a few years, until some of the neighbors decided to petition the mayor to take action. The petition had been submitted, and the Goldmans were expecting a summons any day.

About this time, Mayor Maia, on his way to catch a flight,

ran into Mr. Israel Klabin at the airport. Klabin was no mere acquaintance; he was the former mayor of the city and Mayor Maia's previous boss.

"I'm glad to have met you," the mayor told Mr. Klabin as they awaited their flights. "I have a petition that's been sitting on my desk for some time, and I'm not sure how to deal with it. It concerns a complaint against the worship of a Jewish group, and I don't want to offend any Jews living in my city."

He related the details of the petition. "As former mayor," he continued, "you must be familiar with the Leblon neighborhood and can understand that a house of worship there would create a disturbance."

Mr. Klabin smiled knowingly. "Not only am I familiar with the area, I'm part of the problem. I personally attend services at that congregation every week! Yes, there may be some grounds for the complaint, but the situation really isn't as severe as all that, and we both know how hard it is to find a site in that part of the city. But I'll speak to the rabbi and see what I can do."

Shortly thereafter, Rabbi Goldman managed to find a vacant piece of land in a prime location. When he discovered it was city property, he went to see Mayor Maia, accompanied by a strong ally – Mr. Klabin. The response was positive. Today, the beautiful seven-story building that is Chabad headquarters in Rio de Janeiro is much more than the Goldmans had ever imagined when they started.

When the Vizhnitzer Rebbe, Rabbi Chayim Meier Hager, settled in Israel, he guided his community, helping them adapt to their new settings. "One of the things I like in this country," he told his chassidim, "is that when one person meets another

and asks: Ma nishma? (How are things?), the reply is often:
Hakol beseder, (Everything is okay)."They don't realize how
correct they are. The Seder on Pesach night is indeed an ex-
tremely auspicious time. Hakol – everything can be achieved,
beseder – in the merit of the Passover Seder."

Ms. Linda Lingle first encountered Chabad when she was mayor of Maui, Hawaii. Rabbi Yitzchak and Pearl Krasnjansky, shluchim in Honolulu, had sent two *yeshivah* students, Naftali Rotenstreich and Zalman Shmotkin, to the neighboring islands to reach out to Jews. The young men discovered that Mayor Lingle was Jewish and contacted her during their visit. About a decade later, former mayor Lingle moved to Honolulu and became active in the leadership of the local Republican Party. In time, she made a bid for the governorship, but narrowly lost the election. Her efforts to explore her own heritage, in contrast, met with resounding success. Through frequenting Chabad activities and befriending the Krasnjanskys, she was able to advance her knowledge and Jewish experience.

It was the first night of Pesach, one year, when Ms. Lingle appeared at Chabad House shortly after the Seder had begun. Rabbi Krasnjansky publicly acknowledged her arrival.

"Ladies and gentlemen," he announced ceremoniously, "it is my pleasure to introduce to you the future governor of Hawaii! Next year in Jerusalem, but if G-d forbid we are still here, next year's Seder will be held in the governor's mansion!"

"I felt so awkward," Pearl recalls with a smile. "Ms. Lingle had not yet announced her candidacy. Although it was fairly common knowledge that she was planning to run again, it seemed a little audacious to be so outspoken. It must have been the four cups of wine that prompted my husband to make such a statement."

Six months later, Ms. Lingle indeed won the gubernatorial election, becoming the first Jewish governor of Hawaii. As a sign of her Jewish identity, she took her oath of office on a *Tanach*.[14] Shortly after assuming office, she called Rabbi Krasnjansky.

"So when are we going to begin planning the Seder at Washington Place (the governor's residence)?" Governor Lingle inquired.

The Chabad public Seder has now been conducted in the governor's mansion for the past three years. Many share in the joyous celebration. Governor Lingle and her gracious staff are not daunted a bit by the extensive preparations and the total transformation that the gubernatorial kitchen must undergo.

"My only regret," says Governor Lingle, "is that considerations of time must constrain the rabbi in sharing all the inspiring explanations and stories that make the Seder so special."

⤸

"Hi, I'm a university student and saw your ad about the communal Seder. May I join you?"

"Certainly!" replied Rabbi Yosef Shemtov, who operates the Chabad House in Tucson, Arizona, with his wife, Chanie.

"How much does it cost?"

"There's no charge for students," replied Rabbi Shemtov cordially. "Just come; feel free to bring your friends."

Many people participated in the Seder. Rabbi Shemtov addressed his guests with typical chassidic warmth and enthusiasm. Although he did not have a chance to acquaint himself with each of them, the Seder was an uplifting experience for all.

---

14. A Bible.

A few months after Pesach, one of Rabbi Shemtov's congregants, Dr. Wool, approached him.

"Rabbi," he said, "I know you're always on the lookout for
Jewish faces. I've recently met two fellows who work in 'Brake
Masters,' that garage at the corner of my block. It turns out that
they're Jewish. I think you should also get to know them."

Rabbi Shemtov thanked him and soon afterwards visited
the garage. One of the young men looked familiar; he had been
among the guests at the Seder. They introduced themselves as
brothers, Eric and Shalom Laytin.

Shalom, the Seder guest, was now working full-time at
the garage. He was particularly happy to see the rabbi.

"There were so many people at the Seder that I didn't feel
comfortable addressing you personally, but I wanted you to
know I was very impressed," he said. "There was such a variety
of people there, young and old, people with a background in
Judaism and others to whom it was all new. Even people in
wheelchairs joined in the dancing, and there was a real feeling
of being Jewish together. You know, if I ever make it big, that's
the kind of Judaism I'd like to support!"

Today, the Brake Masters chain has over one hundred
branches across the country. It is still owned by the Laytin
brothers, who heartily sponsor a number of Chabad Seders in
Arizona, New Mexico, California, Texas and Nebraska.

"*A*re there any Israelis here?" Rabbi Gavriel Holtzberg
of Bombay called out in the hallway of the primitive
guesthouse frequented by backpackers on shoestring
budgets.

This search for additional guests to the Chabad House
festive table was part of his routine every Friday afternoon and
an hour before any Jewish holiday.

His wife, Rivki, had insisted that he make his rounds this afternoon, despite the assistance she needed at home in preparation for the Pesach Seder.

"Yes," came the answer. A moment later, a dripping-wet young man emerged from the communal shower room at the end of the corridor. He looked at the rabbi in utter disbelief.

"Where in the world did you come from?" he blurted out. "Who sent you here?"

"G-d sent me," the shaliach answered with a smile. "I'd like to invite you to our home for the Seder."

That young man, Ohr Michaeli, became the Holtzberg's guest, and told them the following story.

"I was on my way from a southern village in India to the north, where I had planned to meet a group of backpackers. I was shocked to discover that I had been pickpocketed on the way. I ended up here in Bombay, roaming the streets not knowing what to do, when I came upon some European-looking people I could communicate with. When I told them my plight, they suggested that money could be wired from Israel to a bank in India. I immediately contacted my family and relayed the instructions those kind people had given me.

"The foreigners also directed me to this dingy guest house, which would be a cheap place to stay until the money arrived. Disappointed by my bad luck and exhausted from the ordeal, what I wanted most was to take a shower and go to sleep. But all of a sudden it dawned on me that tonight will mark the beginning of Passover. I'm not an observant Jew, but I've always enjoyed the Seder and had been planning to go to one together with the group I was to meet up north. I was feeling totally dejected, and then suddenly you walked in."

"Nope," replied the head waiter at the Michael On East restaurant, "Mr. Michael's not in. He comes and goes. He may be back soon, though."

It was shortly before Pesach, and for the fourth time Rabbi Chaim Steinmetz of Sarasota, Florida, had tried to meet Mr. Michael Klauber to give him a packet of hand-made matzos for the Seder. Not that he knew Mr. Klauber; someone had mentioned that one of the two partners who owned the eatery was Jewish, and so Rabbi Steinmetz added him to the list he had compiled of Jews in the area to whom he would be giving these Seder gifts.

He continued his morning errands and decided to give it one more try around noon. As he walked toward the entrance, he met two men who were just leaving.

One of them sized up the rabbi and promptly stated: "You must be an emissary of the Rebbe!"

Rabbi Steinmetz was a bit surprised. "Yes, I am, and as Passover is approaching, I'm giving out packages of matzos."

"And I assume that package is for me," the man responded confidently.

"Of course!" Rabbi Steinmetz replied without a question, handing over the box.

"What about me?" the second man inquired indignantly.

"I have a packet for you in my car," the rabbi answered, hurrying off to fetch it.

When he returned, the first man identified himself as Mr. Harvey Rothenberg, from New York. Rabbi Steinmetz listened intently as Mr. Rothenberg filled him in.

"You see, when I was young I had an opportunity to meet the previous Rebbe, the saintly Rabbi Yosef Yitzchak

Schneersohn, and became familiar with Chabad activities. Years later, I became a close friend of Abraham Beame, mayor of New York, and was very active in a number of Jewish circles. It was then that I became acquainted with the Rebbe and his work. Once, at a large *farbrengen*, the Rebbe noted my presence and, in a private encounter, gave me a pair of *tefillin* as a gift. The Rebbe has been sending me matzos each Passover for years. This year, though, I hadn't yet received my packet, and I was really a bit disappointed. But what could I expect? Unpredictably, I had decided to remain in Florida for Passover. How could the Rebbe know where I was? But evidently," he concluded with a smile, "the Rebbe has his ways of tracking me down. So I knew exactly who you were, and I'll accept my matzos with gratitude."

"Yes," Rabbi Steinmetz thought to himself in wonder, "the Rebbe has his ways..."

Rabbi Steinmetz never did meet the restaurant owner that year, but he did pursue his acquaintance with the second gentleman, Dr. Robert Kantor, who became a supporter of Chabad activities in Sarasota.

"Excuse me, Sir," said the flight attendant on American Airlines flight 117 as she glanced at a printout in her hand, "did you order a special meal?" It was her years of experience that had prompted her to address such a question to this Jewish-looking passenger.

"Yes, we did," replied Rabbi Moshe Schapiro, who, together with his wife, Shaindel, and their little daughter, was traveling from their shlichus in Hoboken, New Jersey, to spend Pesach with his sister's family in Palm Springs, California.

"I'm very sorry," the attendant apologized, "but your seat numbers are not on the list."

"That's probably because we were not originally supposed to be on this flight," guessed Rabbi Schapiro.

The Schapiros had been scheduled to fly to Los Angeles the day before, but due to a storm they were now traveling on the morning of the Seder night.

"If we have any extra meals, I'll be glad to give them to you," offered the attendant as she moved down the aisle.

The Schapiros were pleased. Not because they were not concerned with the meal; they had their own provisions. But her words led them to infer that there were other Jews on the flight. This was good news. Chabad distributes special packets of hand-baked matzah worldwide for people to eat at the Seder. Rabbi Schapiro had three packets left that he was hoping to give to Jews on the plane. He would keep an eye on the flight attendant as she made her rounds, in the hope of locating other Jewish passengers.

The first passenger he located was a woman seated not far away.

"Hi, I'm Rabbi Schapiro from Chabad," he introduced himself. "Nice to meet other travelers right before the holiday. Where are you celebrating the Seder tonight?"

"I'm going to be with family in Los Angeles," the woman replied.

"Do you have any hand-baked matzah for the Seder?"

"What's that?"

Rabbi Schapiro explained and handed her a packet. The woman thanked him and wished the rabbi a happy holiday. As he turned to leave, a woman in the next aisle spoke up. "I didn't mean to eavesdrop, but did I hear you say something about home-baked matzah?" she asked.

Rabbi Schapiro was happy to have another potential customer. "That's hand-baked," he corrected and after a pleasant exchange gave her the second packet of matzah.

Meantime, Chanah, Rabbi Schapiro's toddler, decided she had been sitting still long enough. She began to make her way up the aisle, with her father close behind. Chanah apparently considered herself of high status; she waddled innocently through the partially drawn curtain into the first-class section of the plane. Rabbi Shapiro hurried to fetch his wayward child. By the time he reached her, some of the passengers were cooing over her, and soon enough Rabbi Shapiro found himself conversing with a passenger by the name of Rick.

Rick was going to join his wife and children, who had flown earlier, to spend the holiday with his in-laws. Yes, he knew about hand-made matzah for the Seder but unfortunately had not had a chance to get any.

"Not so unfortunate," smiled Rabbi Schapiro, presenting him with a packet. Rick was taken aback and thanked the rabbi profusely. As he turned to leave, little Chanah planted a kiss on another toddler she had met. This renewed the fuss over the sweet little girl, and Rabbi Schapiro found himself the focus of attention.

"So what is this holiday you were talking about?" one gentleman asked.

"Passover – "

"Oh, right, it falls around this time of year."

"You seem to be familiar with the Jewish calendar," remarked Rabbi Shapiro. "Are you Jewish?"

"No, not really."

"What do you mean?"

"Well, my father isn't but my mother's mother is Jewish."

Rabbi Schapiro sensitively explained to the man, whose name was Jonathan, that according to Jewish law he is considered a Jew. This led to further conversation about religion in general, and the upcoming holiday of Passover. Jonathan listened with interest.

Inwardly, Rabbi Schapiro was troubled. "The other three people to whom I gave the matzah are planning to participate at a Seder," he thought. "This man didn't even know he's Jewish! If only I had another packet to offer him, he would have the opportunity to fulfill the mitzvah of eating matzah tonight."

Then he had an idea.

"You know, Passover marks the birth of our nation," he told Jonathan earnestly. "It's springtime, and a season for new beginnings. It would be wonderful for you to have some matzah in honor of the holiday, and to mark your new awareness of your religion. But I don't have any more packets right here. I do have a couple of pounds of matzah in my hand luggage, though, and I'd really like to offer you some. It would be cumbersome to unpack and package it carefully for you now. Won't you please meet me as we deplane? I'll gladly provide you with matzos."

At this point, the captain announced that the plane was beginning its descent, and the conversation ended with a quick farewell.

Rabbi Schapiro returned to his seat, wondering about Jonathan.

"How likely is it for a businessman, who did not even know that he was Jewish and has paid for first-class immediate deplaning rights, to wait around for a stranger whom he has just met? A stranger who has a wife and child to tend to and who is burdened with hand luggage? And for what? For a few pieces of matzah, for a mitzvah and a holiday he knew nothing about."

But Jonathan was there, waiting.

"You know, Rabbi," he said sincerely as he carefully handled the matzah, "I've been thinking about our conversation. It's all very new to me. I was so touched by your concern that I should have this for the holiday. Then I remembered a cousin of mine who is observant. I'll ask to join his family and celebrate Passover for the first time in my life."

The little boys huddling over their papers in the small shtetl *classroom were immersed in writing. Amidst the low tones with which they vocalized the words of their assignment as they filled the page, their teacher overheard a quiet conversation in the back of the room.*

"May I borrow a pencil?" Yossel asked Chayim.

Chayim stared hard at the text on his desk as if oblivious to the request.

"This is not the first time I've noticed Chayim's lack of care for his classmates," the teacher thought to himself. "It's true, he's one of the best students in class. But I'm here to teach more than a text. I must help him work on his character."

Later, as they studied from the Torah, the teacher asked, "Who would like to translate the next verse?"

Chayim's hand shot up immediately.

"Go ahead, Chayim."

Chayim translated the verse word for word: Veharaav— *"And the famine,"* kaveid – *"was severe,"* baaretz – *"in the land."*

"What is the meaning of this verse?" asked the teacher.

Puzzled, Chayim repeated himself.

"Chayim," said the teacher. "You've translated and explained the words, but what is the Torah teaching us?"

Chayim was stumped.

The teacher continued softly: "The verse means give your friend a pencil."

"What does that have to do with this verse?" Chayim blurted out.

"Everything!" explained the teacher.*" The great Sage, Hillel taught us: 'Do not do to others what you wouldn't like done to you. This is the entire Torah. The rest is just explanation.' Every verse in the Torah, even one dealing with a totally different subject, is really teaching us to feel for another person and think about his needs."*

"We have an annual phone-a-thon and need lots of volunteers," says Mrs. Matty Bryski of Agoura Hills, California. "It's a hard job, and no one enjoys sitting all day calling people to ask for money. It can be a humbling experience, and you have to brace yourself for rejection. Some volunteers even believe that the real purpose of the phone-a-thon is to induce them, the volunteers, to make generous contributions, so they can get out of making the calls! 'Any amount' they exclaim, 'I'll give you whatever you want. Just don't ask me to make any more calls!'

"To have enough volunteers, we do what most people would do in such a situation: We ask our children to help out. And, as the letter below indicates, they do in more ways than one...."

Dear Rabbi Bryski,

Please find enclosed my donation to Chabad of the Conejo Valley. The other night I got a call from a pleasant young woman, who identified herself as Chanah Bryski, asking me for a small donation to the Chabad phone-a-thon. I was very tired and maybe a little preoccupied with my current difficulties, and I'm afraid I sounded unpleasant. I told her that I had been laid off a while back, and that my husband had just been discharged from hospital. I said that perhaps some other time I would be more accommodating.

Not only was she polite and warm, but her response was
to ask me if there was anything Chabad could do for us. I
know that Chabad does many acts of kindness, but just then
her gesture brought tears to my eyes, partly because I was so
overwhelmed by our situation and partly because I was touched
by her sincerity. I knew that if I had said yes, any help we needed
would have been forthcoming.

Thank G-d, we're not poor, and in time I hope my husband
will be able to walk and work again. I'm sorry I didn't open my
heart and pocketbook more readily. Chanah must be your wife,
or maybe your daughter. In any case, speaking with her that
night encouraged me and gave me strength. Please tell her how
grateful I am for her sending that moment of heartfelt warmth
into my home and my soul. It was just what I needed.

Sincerely, D.

It was ten o'clock at night when the phone rang in the
home of Rabbi Levy and Chanie Zirkind, of Fresno,
California. The late hour didn't change Mrs. Zirkind's
habitual friendly response.

"Hello, this is Chabad. How can I help you?"

Silence.

"Hello," Mrs. Zirkind repeated, slightly louder. "This is
Chabad, how can I help you?"

This time there was a sound. Not a distinct reply, but she
could hear someone crying softly.

"Hello… hello! I'd like to help you. Won't you please tell
me what's the matter?" Still no explanation, but the sobbing
continued.

"At that point I was considering hanging up," Mrs. Zirkind

recalls. "I thought it might be a prank call." But she stayed on the line a few moments more, hoping to encourage whoever it was to speak. Finally, the caller found some words. She introduced herself as a Jewish woman from the town of Lemoore, California.

"Lemoore," Mrs. Zirkind reflected to herself. "That's a small town about forty-five minutes away. We don't really know of any Jews there, except for those involved with its local Navy base."

The only other connection the Zirkinds had to Lemoore was an annual bill for listing the Chabad House in that town's yellow pages. Several years before, Rabbi Zirkind had come across a directive in the writings of the Lubavitch Rebbe to list the number of Chabad Houses in the yellow pages of nearby small towns. But since then, much time had gone by with no calls from that listing, and Mrs. Zirkind had recently commented to her husband that perhaps that directive wasn't intended for this town. Now, she was no longer wondering.

"Please excuse me for troubling you," the woman was saying. "I'm just feeling so overwhelmed at the moment. Let me explain the reason for my call. I live alone with my treasured cat. For some years now, three women have been part of my life, offering me the wonderful gift of their friendship. They come regularly to visit, bring me food parcels and stay for hours to chat. I honestly considered them my good friends and couldn't be more thankful for their kindness. I really became quite attached to them and looked forward to their visits.

"A few weeks ago, the women came by and, toward the end of a pleasant visit, suddenly announced: 'Well, we've been your good friends for quite some time. You can see that we really care about you and are genuinely concerned with your welfare.

We've given you a lot and would like to continue sharing with you, but we request that you really bond with us by converting to our Mormon religion.'

"I was totally taken by surprise and yes, hurt. I had considered these women to be loyal friends. I hadn't realized that religion had had anything to do with our relationship. I am Jewish. I live alone because my family all perished in the Holocaust, and I came to this country as an orphan. As fate would have it, I never had an opportunity to build my own family. Though I do not practice, I know I'm a Jew. And here are these women telling me to convert to their religion!

"'How can you expect that of me?' I asked them tearfully. 'How could I do such a thing to my family? I could not desecrate their memory; many of them were mercilessly led to their deaths just for being Jews. Nor could I break ties with my heritage.'

"'It's not a problem,' they assured me. 'In the Mormon religion, one can be converted posthumously. We will convert you and your family, and you will all be embraced by our religion.'

"I couldn't think of anything else to say but that I needed time to think. After all, these women were the only friends I had, and they had been very kind to me. They told me they would come back in a few days for my response, clearly implying that I could reciprocate their kindness by complying with their one wish.

"I was at a loss and in turmoil from the moment they left. I truly don't know much about my religion, but I know that it's not right to convert. Yet these women were so charitable, and I didn't want to lose their companionship. I turned to G-d and asked him for a sign that someone out there cared about me.

Perhaps if I could find a compassionate soul in my own religion; it would help me stay firm and face these missionaries.

"I decided to call a synagogue and see if anyone would heed my plight. Though I know it's late, I picked up the Yellow Pages and dialed the number of the first synagogue listed. I was so moved that you answered my call at that hour that I couldn't speak. And then came the very words I desperately needed to hear: '…How can I help you?' said with such compassion and sincerity – that I just broke down and cried."

*T*he screech of tires brought Rabbi Levi and Feige Sudak, shluchim in Edgware, England, racing out of their home. To their horror, their four-year-old son, Mottel, was lying unconscious in the street. He had been hit by a car on his way home from school.

The ambulance arrived within minutes and the crew was swift and efficient. They quickly had Mottel on a special stretcher, with blocks strapped around his head to protect his neck and spine, and the family set off for the hospital. To make sure Mottel would not be shaken if the vehicle drove over a pothole, one of the paramedics stayed in the back and steadied the stretcher. Mrs. Sudak rode in the back as well, while Rabbi Sudak sat in the front.

"As we raced to the hospital," Rabbi Sudak recalls, "I noticed a half-empty bottle of Coca Cola on the floor and thought how dedicated these men must be; they didn't even get a chance to finish their drink. I reached into my pocket and found some change, which I intended to give them so they could get themselves another drink. But as soon as we got to the hospital, the driver and assistant were out of the vehicle, busy lifting Mottel and delivering him to the emergency team that was standing ready. There was no time for thank-you's, so I left the two one-pound coins on the dashboard."

All the doctors who tended to Mottel attested that he was the beneficiary of a miracle. After a thorough examination, he was admitted for overnight observation just as a precaution, and discharged the following day. Thank G-d, he had emerged from the accident with only minor bruises.

A week later, as Rabbi Sudak came into the synagogue on Friday night, one of the members, Aaron, approached him. "Rabbi, we heard about your son's accident and are grateful that all is well. Tell me, though, did you leave any money in the ambulance?"

"Why, yes I did," Rabbi Sudak answered, taken by surprise, "but how would you know?"

Aaron then proceeded to remind him of an episode that had taken place eighteen months earlier. Aaron's niece had married a non-Jew. Her husband was tolerant of his wife's Jewishness and was even thinking about converting. Nevertheless, he was opposed to circumcising their baby son. After seven-and-a-half months of persistent persuasion, the man relented, but refused to attend the ceremony.

The *bris* took place on a Sunday morning, performed by a well-known *mohel*,[15] Dr. H., who often works with Rabbi Sudak. That afternoon, however, something seemed wrong with the baby. The concerned parents called the *mohel*, who in turn asked Rabbi Sudak to join him in attending to the child. The family lived on the other side of London, and they raced over in record time. Thank G-d, everything proved to be in order.

Rabbi Sudak remembered the episode quite clearly.

---

15. One who performs a *bris*, a ritual circumcision.

"But what does this have to do with Mottel's accident?" he wondered.

"My niece's husband was your ambulance driver," Aaron explained. "When he came back to the ambulance, he found the two coins and realized it was a gesture of gratitude. He was touched. He sometimes feels like an invisible participant in the serious and responsible task of administering first aid and then rushing to a hospital. Certainly he understands that those accompanying an injured person are consumed by their own worries, but it's hard to be continuously ignored.

"That's why he was so moved at the gesture; he felt that someone had finally acknowledged his dedication. Later, he told his wife about the incident, wondering if she knew the bearded rabbi in Edgware. A quick investigation confirmed that this was the same rabbi who had hurried across town to attend to their son after his circumcision. As I said, he hadn't been present then, he had never met you."

All this left a profound impression on the driver, and a marked new respect for his wife's religion. Those two coins of acknowledgement were for him a symbol of sensitivity and gratitude. He took them both, had one set as a pendant and the other mounted on a stone, which he displayed in the living room.

Shortly afterward, he decided to begin the conversion process.

Those who turn to Rabbi Shea and Dina Harlig, on shlichus in Las Vegas, know that everyone who encounters Chabad in this gambling capital comes away with a gain. That includes people who are in Vegas on business, for pleasure, or for no apparent reason, as was Arye. An elderly, homeless man, Arye had a weakness for strong drink. The little that the Harligs were able to glean about his background pointed to a bitter, long-ago divorce and desertion. It was evident, though, that this pitiful soul needed a place to sleep.

Arye became a "semi-regular" at Chabad House. "Semi" because he would show up sporadically, stay for a while and disappear again. A small corner in a back room of the center suited his reclusive habits. A couple of years passed in this manner.

One night, Rabbi Harlig's pager went off. "Who needs me so late?" he wondered, as he checked the message. It was a woman who sounded very distraught.

"My name is Peninah. You don't know me. We're originally from Israel and have just moved here from Los Angeles. We know about Chabad. My husband and I got entangled in a messy deal and were arrested. We've been put into the Clark County Detention Center. Our three children have been taken to the Child's Haven Shelter. Please help!"

Rabbi Harlig is a volunteer chaplain at the county jail, so he was able to arrange a meeting with Peninah relatively easily. He learned that the family had no local contacts, and she was desperate to get her children out of the shelter. She begged the rabbi to take custody of the three youngsters, aged four, ten and twelve, and to look after them until their parents' situation could be resolved.

"All in a day's work," sighed Dina, empathizing with the family and mentally calculating where she could set up beds and expand her family on short notice.

The Harligs acted quickly. There was much to be done. Lawyers had to be contacted to arrange for the transfer of custody; the shelter had to be convinced that the Harligs, with five children of their own, were capable of taking charge of three more. Papers had to be signed, and the distressed children had to be eased into a new environment and outfitted with clothing.

"Accommodating the children physically was much easier than settling them emotionally," says Dina. "What else could I do but reassure them over and over again that their parents would come for them soon?"

Rabbi Harlig didn't rest until he had succeeded in raising the $10,000 needed to get Peninah out on bail. "The whole business was far from simple," he recalls, "but the emotional reunion between Peninah and her children after ten difficult days apart was worth all the effort."

Peninah's husband was not eligible for bail, so she and her children became frequent visitors in the Harlig home. In time, Peninah shared some details of the difficulties that had led to their misfortune, as well as bits and pieces of her background. On one occasion, she spoke hesitantly about her own childhood.

"My parents had an unstable relationship; they just never got along. After endless bickering, they divorced. My siblings and I sided with our mother and didn't pursue a relationship with our father. We haven't heard from him in twenty years. At some point we heard he had left Israel and had been seen here in Las Vegas, of all places. If I should ever meet him, I would try for a reconciliation and have a grandfather for my children."

Rabbi Harlig had a hunch and it turned out to be true. Peninah's father was Arye.

"*F*rom the beginning of our shlichus in the university town of Ann Arbor, Michigan," relates Esther, wife of Rabbi Aharon Goldstein, "we involved students in our activities."

"One of my first outreach projects involved visiting people in hospital. The staff would provide us with a list of Jewish patients, and a group of students and I would divide the names among ourselves. We would then spread out on each floor and visit the patients. I must admit, I had a personal interest in this arrangement. I was young and inexperienced. I didn't grow up in a home where shlichus was a regular part of life, and I am shy by nature. So, though we made individual rounds, having the students accompany me was a boost to my confidence."

"On one of our Sunday morning visits during Chanukah, I was feeling apprehensive as usual about dropping in on people I didn't know. Having a *menorah* and candles to distribute gave me an opening.

"Bracing myself, I entered a room where an elderly woman was lying. The multitude of wires and tubes around her bed indicated that she was gravely ill. Gently, I approached her and in a soft tone introduced myself, wishing her a happy holiday.

"Her response was a total blow. 'Don't bother me!' she hissed. 'Get out of here with your Jewish stuff!'

"I was devastated. Yes, I felt sorry that I wasn't able to interest her in Chanukah candles, but I felt much more anguish at having brought discomfort to an ailing woman. The incident haunted me, and I was careful to avoid her room in the following weeks. I prayed for her recovery but hoped I wouldn't encounter her again, since my visit had obviously not contributed to her well-being.

"Yet, week after week, the woman's name appeared on the

patients' list. I felt that I must see her again. I resolved not to say a word; I just wanted to see how she was doing. And so, a few weeks after that initial encounter, I quietly entered the room. She acknowledged my presence right away.

"'Are you the woman who came here a couple of weeks ago with your Chanukah packet?' she asked. I was tempted to deny it, but her inviting tone persuaded me otherwise, so I nodded.

"'I'm so sorry I responded negatively to your kind gesture,' she said earnestly. 'I was having an especially hard day, and the pain just got the better of me. Thank you for coming to see me again.'

"We chatted for a few moments, and then I left her room.

"I was relieved that she was pleased with the visit this time and that we had had a friendly chat. From then on, I continued to visit her. A few weeks later, as I arrived on her ward, a nurse came running toward me.

"'Come quickly,' she called out. 'The patient you've been visiting needs someone at her bedside right now.'

"There was no time to deliberate. The nurse ushered me into the room, and I was confronted with death for the first time in my life. Somehow, I maintained my composure and shared the last moments of life with a woman whom I had almost decided to avoid. She passed away with the *Shema* on her lips."

"*Y*es, I've heard about Chabad here in Baltimore, and I'm pleased to meet you in person," Sigla said with a pleasant smile. "I regret that we haven't met before, though, because we're moving tomorrow to New York."

Sigla was speaking to Rochel, who is on shlichus with her husband, Rabbi Shmuel Kaplan, in Baltimore, Maryland.

The two women had met while picking up their children at preschool. As conversations between mothers often go, the two discussed families and children, comparing notes and sharing personal experiences. Soon the toddlers began lining up at the door and the women wished each other well before parting.

Mrs. Kaplan had the sense she shouldn't overlook this chance meeting, and so, with genuine goodwill, she baked a batch of pastries and brought them to Sigla's house the following day.

"I know about moving," Mrs. Kaplan said sympathetically. "Eating is the last thing on the list, but energy is in high demand. Please enjoy."

Sigla was touched. "You took the trouble to remember my address even though we just met yesterday and are moving today," she exclaimed. "Would you mind staying for a few minutes? The movers know what to do, and I could use a break."

Soon the two women were deep in discussion. Among other things, Sigla shared her fervent wish to have another child. Mrs. Kaplan used the opportunity to broach the matter of Jewish family life and urged her new acquaintance to pursue this vital aspect of Judaism in her new location.

After some time, Mrs. Kaplan bade Sigla farewell and the women went their separate ways.

Months later, Mrs. Kaplan heard from Sigla again. Her family had now settled into their new home and, following Mrs. Kaplan's advice, she had sought guidance in the Jewish lifestyle. She and her husband had begun observing mitzvos and in due time were delighted with the arrival of a new baby.

Mrs. Kaplan was glad to hear the news and happy to know that, with Sigla in a supportive environment, the family would continue its journey of faith.

One winter, Mrs. Kaplan attended the annual Chabad Women's convention in Brooklyn, New York. The weather grew threatening, with a major snowstorm on the way. Mrs. Kaplan decided to leave early Sunday afternoon, foregoing the remainder of the program. With another woman who had asked for a ride, she set out on the four-hour drive back to Baltimore.

The snow was already falling heavily and the roads were treacherous, with bumper-to-bumper traffic. The need to keep the heat on and wipers going full force, combined with the stop-and-go pace was too much for the car's electrical system, and it sputtered to a halt on the Staten Island Expressway. The two women had no luck in flagging someone down to help and had to abandon the stalled vehicle.

Mrs. Kaplan managed to contact the local shaliach, Rabbi Moshe Katzman, and sought assistance. Rabbi Katzman directed them to the closest garage, and the women arranged to have the car towed.

Once in the garage, however, they discovered that the area was not the safest, nor was the mechanic the most upright. The establishment's phone seemed to be set up to block calls to any other garages, putting the two women at the mercy of this particular repair service.

"It'll come to about $500," the repairman was saying, "and considering this weather and your out-of-town plates, I'd like to see it in cash."

Mrs. Kaplan was at a loss. She had to get the car repaired but simply didn't have that much money. She called the Katzmans again.

"Don't panic," Rabbi Katzman calmed her, "we'll figure something out. I'll make a few calls."

"It's all arranged," Rabbi Katzman phoned back a short time later. "There's a very nice fellow in our community who will be glad to help. He'll lend you the money and drive you to our home, where you can stay overnight until your car is ready. He's already on his way."

Mrs. Kaplan and her friend couldn't thank him enough. Their nervous wait in this crime-ridden area was eased by the thought that another Jew was going out of his way to rescue them. When the fellow arrived and introduced himself, Mrs. Kaplan was astonished to learn he was Sigla's husband! Who would have expected that they would reconnect under such desperate conditions?

And that good deed brought an opportunity for yet another. Sigla's mother had passed away a few days earlier, and the chain of events enabled Mrs. Kaplan to pay a visit to the mourners' home in Staten Island.

> In 1972, on the occasion of the Rebbe's 70 th birthday, Rabbi Shlomo Cunin and a group of supporters presented the Rebbe with the key to the new Chabad House opened on the UCLA campus. The Rebbe told them: "If you're giving me the key, it becomes my house. And if it's my house, I want its doors to be open 24 hours a day, 7 days a week, for anyone in need."
>
> And he added: "This is going to start a pattern. It will be like a chain-store. Soon there will be Chabad Houses all over the country."

Those of us who haven't been to Anchorage, Alaska, can trust Rabbi Yossi and Mrs. Esty Greenberg that bundled up Eskimos leading packs of sled dogs are not a common sight. But neither was the individual Rabbi Greenberg spotted one day from his office window. An elderly, slightly stooped chap, with long white hair and a flowing beard to match, wearing faded Bermudas, was walking straight toward the Chabad House door. Clutching a gnarled walking stick, he bore some resemblance to an ancient sage. But his shabby clothing and blank look suggested a very different association; he looked like a homeless person, a rare sight as well in this area.

Rabbi Greenberg wasn't sure what to think, and so, when the bell rang, he opened the door only slightly. The man's toothless mouth and dirt-smudged face seemed to confirm his assessment.

Cautiously, he asked the stranger what he wanted.

"It's about the book of psalms," the man said in a voice that seemed raspy from lack of use. "I wrote you an email. Didn't you get it?"

Rabbi Greenberg did vaguely recall an unsigned email about a psalm book, but the sender's address had been unclear.

"I came to Alaska on a trip and lost my psalm book," the man continued. "Isn't this the place for Jewish things? Well, I need to get a book of psalms."

"How can a homeless person afford a trip to Alaska?" Rabbi Greenberg wondered. "And he doesn't look or sound like a person who recites psalms...."

Though still unsure of the man's intentions, Rabbi Greenberg decided he was harmless and invited him in. Gently, he drew the stranger into conversation.

"I grew up in a large Jewish neighborhood in Chicago," the man related. "I didn't know anything about being Jewish; my family didn't teach me anything. Once, when I was twelve,

I wandered into a bookstore and came across a Bible. I started reading it and couldn't put it down. I got my cousins to read it, too. We were fascinated, but when we asked the adults about the Bible and about being Jewish, they ignored our questions. So I never learned anything about it, but I love reading psalms. I always have my book of psalms with me, and I'm really upset that I lost it. Can you get me a new book?"

Rabbi Greenberg offered the man more than a book of psalms. For the first time in his life, he put on *tefillin* and recited a blessing over food. But when Rabbi Greenberg invited him to join the Chabad House programs, he became timid.

"I guess I had to lose my psalm book so that I would end up here and have a private bar mitzvah," the man said earnestly. "But I don't like to be among people much. It makes me nervous."

And so, stick in one hand, his new book of psalms in the other, he turned and walked out of the Chabad House. His back did seem a little straighter than it had been when he hobbled in.

It was a few days after Rosh HaShanah, and Rabbi Yosef Groner, who is on shlichus with his wife Mariasha in Charlotte, North Carolina, was talking with a couple of members of his synagogue after the morning service. Other synagogue members were also on their way out, when in walked Mr. Walter Shechter.

"Fellows," he announced, "I have a story to share that I think you will appreciate. I play racquetball every week with my friend, Larry. He has a daughter, Debra, who lives in Los Angeles. She has a successful career and is comfortably settled on the West Coast. She has her own personal views on Judaism, which are not in accord with her father's. He called her before the High Holy Days to wish her a good year and urged her to attend services.

"'Debra,' he reminded her, 'Rosh HaShanah is a very significant day, a day when a Jew should be connected to G-d. Going to the synagogue adds meaning to the day.'"

"'Dad, I'm not going to the synagogue,' she replies. 'It just isn't very meaningful to me. Besides, I have loads of work at the office and it will only pile up.'

"Larry doesn't argue; he loves his daughter too much to spend time debating. He wishes her well and hopes that in the future she will be more receptive.

"After the holiday, Larry receives a call from his daughter. She tells him of an experience that moved her to the core.

"On Rosh HaShanah, about the same time her father was at services here in Charlotte, she was walking down Wilshire Boulevard toward her office. She stops at a red light and sees a young bearded man in chassidic garb walking over to a homeless man sitting beneath the awning of a Persian rug store. She overhears the following exchange.

"'Good morning, Sir!'

"The homeless man looks around uncertainly, as if to say: 'Nobody says good morning to *me*....'

"'Good day, Sir!' the chassid says again, louder this time. Now the homeless man was sure the greeting was intended for him. His face lights up.

"'I hope you don't mind me asking, but are you Jewish?'

"'Yes – my name's David.'

"'David, today is the beginning of the Jewish New Year. It's Rosh HaShanah, and we blow a special horn, a *shofar*, whose sound arouses us to be aware of the presence of G-d. Have you heard the *shofar* yet today, David?'

"'Nope.'

"The chassid takes out a *shofar* from the bag he is carrying. He removes the *kipah* from under his hat and places it on David's unruly, matted hair. He then recites the blessing and blows the *shofar*.

"'Dad,' Debra said, as she concluded her account, 'Watching that religious man's gesture toward a homeless person, whom most people try to steer clear of, was a profound spiritual experience for me. That was my synagogue this Rosh HaShanah.'"

"*I* welcomed the couple that strolled into our Chabad House," relates Shachar, who is on shlichus in Venice with her husband, Rabbi Rami Banin. "Venice is a tourist haven, and thousands of people walk about this beautiful city.

"I chatted with them and at some point suggested that perhaps the husband would like to put on *tefillin*. The man shook his head adamantly. 'I did that many years ago, but it did nothing for me,' he declared. 'I'm not interested in that sort of thing.'

"We spoke a little more, and although it was only the beginning of the week, I invited them to join us for the coming Shabbos. They thanked me politely and departed, leaving me wondering if I would ever see them again.

"We were expecting our first child, and the next day I had an appointment with my obstetrician. My husband accompanied me to the hospital, which was in a residential part of town, far from the tourist attractions. Yet whom did we meet as we made our way to the hospital there but the couple from the day before! They were equally surprised as I greeted them and introduced my husband. We asked if they were lost, as this was an unlikely place to run into tourists.

"'Oh, no,' the wife answered. 'We just like to wander about a city we are visiting and catch a glimpse of the local life. What a coincidence that we should meet again!'

"Our conversation continued for a few more minutes, and once again I invited them for Shabbos. Their response was a look that said, 'We've already planned our itinerary…'

"On Wednesday, as I was hurrying down the main street – a crowded area that runs parallel to the famous Grand Canal in the heart of 'tourist country' – lo and behold, there they were again! At that point it no longer surprised either of us. We exchanged a few words, and I repeated my invitation to join us for Shabbos.

"The woman looked at me with what appeared to be sympathy for my repeated invitations, and quipped good-naturedly: 'So where are we going to meet tomorrow?'

"I imagine she thought me to be a one-track Jew, obsessed with Shabbos. She didn't know that Shabbos is indeed the focus of much of our outreach. In the summer we often have over five hundred people join us for Shabbos. Winters are much quieter, but even then we usually host fifty to sixty visitors. The atmosphere is exhilarating, and the meal on Friday night inevitably leads to joyous dancing that spills into the street along the canal.

"We didn't meet or hear from the couple the next day, and assumed that they had left Venice, but somehow I couldn't get them out of my mind. On Friday night, shortly after we recited the *kiddush*, in they walked, and we joyfully greeted one another like long-lost friends. They were happy to join us, and blended right in.

"As usual, the meal was followed by outdoor dancing; the cold weather couldn't compete with the warm atmosphere, and all the men danced while many of the women went out as well, clapping along. Suddenly I realized I was alone at the table with the woman I had run into so many times before. This is no accident, I realized. I got up and sat down next to her.

"Evidently, our conversation was meant to be, because despite the chilly night, the dancing went on for over half an hour. As we talked, she told me that life was good. She had been married for eighteen years and had three lovely children.

"'Good can always be better,' I remarked wholeheartedly and shared with her the basic guidelines for Jewish family life. She listened with marked interest. Soon, the dancing was over, and our private conversation with it."

The couple left Venice, but took their newfound awareness with them. In time, the woman contacted the Banins and related that she had seriously thought about their conversation that Friday night. The couple pursued the topic and eventually committed themselves to the laws governing Jewish family life.

Whoever would have caught sight of Rabbi Nosson Gurary that day in the cafeteria at the State University of Buffalo, New York, would have looked twice. Not that Rabbi Gurary, who is there on shlichus with his wife, Miriam, was never seen in the cafeteria. On the contrary, it was a great place to meet students, and that was his whole objective.

Just then, though, it might have raised an eyebrow or two. It was late in the afternoon of Yom Kippur, and there he was, garbed in the traditional white *kittel*[16] and wrapped in a *tallis* on this holy fast day, sitting in a cafeteria!

But, indeed, he was doing what he usually does, seeking

16. Yom Kippur robe.

out Jewish students. At that particular moment he was waiting for a fellow he had just met.

It hadn't been an easy day. The Gurarys had begun their shlichus only recently, and even though a member of a Jewish fraternity had volunteered to help organize an evening *minyan* for the *Kol Nidrei* service, which marks the beginning of Yom Kippur, pulling it together had proven to be quite a feat. Then, serving as cantor, the rabbi was stunned to find that his "congregation" had slipped out on him in the midst of the prayers, opting to relax in the dorm instead. He had managed to regroup the *minyan* for the morning services but was short one person for the vital afternoon and *Neilah*[17] prayers.

The sun was nearly setting as he made his way to the cafeteria, his last resort. There he came across Joe, a Jewish student, holding a dinner tray. Joe had never even heard of Yom Kippur, let alone concepts like *minyan* or *Neilah*. Rabbi Gurary tried to convey the urgency of his request, but Joe replied that this particular dish was one of his favorites. He had already paid for the food and was looking forward to enjoying it. The Rabbi's description of the sumptuous repast Chabad had prepared to break the fast didn't change Joe's mind, but he agreed to join the prayers after he had finished eating.

That's how Rabbi Gurary found himself sitting in a cafeteria waiting for a Jew to finish dinner on the holiest day of the year. But never mind; the rabbi had his *minyan*, and that was worth waiting for, even in a cafeteria on Yom Kippur.

Following this unlikely first encounter, Joe began exploring his Jewish identity, and eventually went on to study at a *yeshivah*.

---

17. The final service of Yom Kippur.

*G*uests at the table of Rabbi Moshe and Leah Shemtov of Stamford, Connecticut, were enjoying the festive atmosphere, the good company, and the special foods they were eating on Rosh HaShanah. Their hosts suggested that they take on a resolution for the New Year and commit themselves to it for at least a month. Among the guests were Mrs. Dena Graber, her husband, Howard, and their five-year-old daughter, Rachel, who was attending the Chabad preschool.

Mrs. Graber volunteered her resolution.

"Years ago, when I attended Hebrew day school, I remember learning about a short prayer called the *kriyas shema* that's to be recited before going to bed. I think that's something I could put into my routine."

After the holiday, Leah gave Dena a copy of *kriyas shema* in Hebrew and English.

The year went by, and as registration for the following school year approached, Dena contacted Leah about a dilemma.

"I would really like my daughter to attend Hebrew day school like I did, but my husband is opposed to the idea. He's a strong supporter of the public school system and maintains that we have excellent schools in our area. What's more, we have two children and the cost of private schooling is quite high. He sees no reason for such an expense. As he's the sole breadwinner, I feel it would be wrong to pressure him to pay for something he considers unnecessary."

Leah echoed Dena's conviction that Hebrew day school was the right choice and sympathized with her situation. She voiced her hope that things would work out.

Leah and other shluchim worldwide are only too familiar with this problem. To address it, the head shluchim of Stamford, Rabbi Yisrael and Vivi Deren, invest a good deal of their time in encouraging Jewish families to enroll children in Hebrew day schools. Mrs. Vivi Deren's weekly schedule includes house calls to meet with parents and discuss the issue, so vital to their children's education. She paid a visit to Rachel's home and spoke to Howard, but he only reiterated his staunch opposition.

The matter weighed heavily on Dena. She was convinced that her children should be given a formal Jewish education but could not see how it would be possible.

Some time later, the phone rang in the Shemtov's home. It was Dena.

"I must share something with you," she said excitedly. "I had been losing sleep over the school issue. Tossing and turning last night, I suddenly remembered the commitment I had made to recite the *kriyas shema* before retiring. I got up and took the prayer sheet. As I was reciting the words, they jumped out at me with a compelling force. "…and you shall teach your children diligently… and I will give you rain in the right time…"

"'That's it!' I said to myself. 'If we enroll our child in Hebrew school, financial blessings will shower down from above. I must convey my deep concern for the need of a Jewish education for our children. I know that, for my husband, the issue is mainly financial. Things will work out somehow.'

"The next morning I spoke to him before he went off to work at his law firm. Later that day, he called home. 'The most unexpected thing happened today at the office,' he told me. 'Do you remember that hefty insurance case I was working on, the one that was going on and on, with the insurance company only too happy to prolong it indefinitely? It could easily have taken years before my client saw a penny. Well, out of the blue, the company's representative called, and they're ready to settle! This means an immediate payment to my client and unexpected

income for us. I think I have an idea as to how you would like
to spend the money. What was the name of the school where
you wanted to enroll Rachel?'"

> *Once, a youth from an observant home strayed from Jewish
> practice. His family tried, without success to influence him to
> find his way back to observance.*
>
> *After several years, this youth encountered a Lubavitch
> mitzvah mobile[18] and was invited to put on tefillin. At first
> he declined, but the polite persistence of the rabbinical student
> manning the mitzvah mobile convinced him to perform the
> mitzvah. And that changed everything. After having been
> away from Jewish observance for so long, fulfilling this one
> mitzvah whetted his appetite for more. He underwent a quiet
> transformation, and with the help of the Lubavitchers, returned
> to his Jewish roots.*
>
> *His father, overjoyed at this sequence of events, went
> to the Rebbe to thank him for the efforts of his chassidim. He
> explained that previously he had not understood the Lubavitch
> outreach campaign, but now he appreciated the validity of
> that approach.*
>
> *The Rebbe accepted his thanks graciously, telling him:
> "You have suffered the pain a father feels when his son departs
> from the Torah's ways, and the joy he experiences when he
> returns. I feel such pangs for every Jew estranged from his
> Torah heritage and derive similar happiness whenever one
> returns."*

---

18. The mobile units manned by Chabad students which have enabled
    Jewish outreach activities to be taken to the streets of many major
    cities.

"ello? My name is Shmuel. Umm, you don't know me, but before I go on, could you tell me if your Chabad House in Carlsbad also covers the La Costa area? It's very important. There's a woman in La Costa who really needs help. I don't know her so well. Actually, I do, or rather I did, about sixteen years ago. She just called me out of the blue. She didn't give me her phone number but told me her address. She's really troubled. Can you help her?"

Rabbi Yeruchem and Nechama Eilfort of Carlsbad, California, are not the type to be daunted by a slightly disjointed phone call. Nechama calmly replied that La Costa is indeed close to Carlsbad, and that she would be glad to be of assistance. Her composed response prompted the man to take a deep breath and start again from the beginning.

"Sixteen years ago, when I was at college in New York, I became acquainted with a girl who was probably the only other Jew in my class. We kept in touch throughout school, but after we graduated we lost contact. Just a couple of minutes ago, I got a phone call from her. She sounded very low and dispirited. She told me that she had drifted away from Judaism, married a non-Jew and has just had a baby. She feels that their relationship is on the rocks and that she's losing control of her life. I really feel sorry for her, but you know it's been a long time since we've spoken. I'm here in New York and don't really see what I can do. But I know that Chabad helps people all over the world. I wonder… would you be willing to contact her?"

Nechama took the address and discovered the woman lived only two miles away. The phone number was unlisted, so she drove over and knocked on the door. A Mexican housekeeper answered the bell and excused herself, as she was in the middle of caring for the baby. Left alone for a few moments, Nechama had a chance to glance around. She was surprised to

see that the living room, dining room table and bookshelves
were laden with Jewish books.

"How strange, for the home of a Jewish woman who has
married out of the faith!" she mused to herself.

Meanwhile, the housekeeper returned and told her the
couple was out and that she didn't know when they would be
back. Nechama gave the woman her Chabad House business
card and asked her to tell her employer she was welcome to
call. Shortly afterward the woman indeed phoned.

"Please come over," she pleaded, "I really need to talk to
someone knowledgeable." Nechama came and spent quite a
while with the woman, who introduced herself as Masha. It
turned out that the numerous Jewish books had been acquired
by Masha's husband, who had undergone a Reform and then
a Conservative conversion and was genuinely interested in
Judaism. The couple's difficulty was with their relationship.
It had continuous ups and downs, and she felt that marriage
should be steadier, giving each one strength and security.

Nechama was unsure of how to deal with the situation.
"Should I encourage this woman to invest in a relationship
with a man whose conversion is questionable according to
Jewish law? And there is a Jewish child here, too," she mused
silently. After she decided that she didn't know enough about
the couple at this point to give sound advice, a thought crossed
her mind.

"I suggest that, as a start, you learn about the concept of
marriage from a Jewish perspective," she told the woman. "Try
reading the book, *Doesn't Anyone Blush Anymore?* by Rabbi
Manis Friedman. We'll talk again after you've read it."

Some time later the woman's husband called Rabbi Eilfort. Both he and his wife had read the book, and they wanted
to learn more about the Jewish lifestyle. They had come to

realize that the disharmony in their marriage was linked to their mutual lack of direction and purpose. Rabbi Eilfort set up classes, and the couple became involved in Chabad House activities.

"Bill was very serious about his learning," relates Rabbi Eilfort. "Soon enough, he realized that he was not considered *halachically* Jewish; it was forbidden for him to live with a Jewish woman. He promptly moved out of his home – and moved in with us. Directly after his proper conversion, we held a joyful wedding for the couple. It was a very moving occasion, as Masha's family (who had not participated in the first, out-of-faith ceremony) were now present."

"This is truly an auspicious day," the groom-husband-father (now known as Yakov) announced after the ceremony. "Today happens to be my daughter's birthday; it is also my own birthday in a sense, for it is my first day as a Jew, and it will be our wedding anniversary – the beginning of a proper Jewish relationship."

～

"No change for a $100 bill!" snapped the teller at the Kingston Avenue subway station in Crown Heights, Brooklyn.

Rabbi Sholom and Chana Lew of Glendale, Arizona, groaned. It had been an uplifting trip but not an easy one in the sweltering summer heat, with two small children, suitcases and baby carriages. And it wasn't over. After a weekend in Crown Heights, they were taking a train to Hartford, Connecticut, to visit Mrs. Lew's family. This side trip had seemed simple enough in the planning stages, but now the need to search for change presented an unexpected difficulty.

As they began moving their luggage out of the way so, Mrs.

Lew could wait with the children while her husband set out on the search, they heard a pleasant voice from behind them.

"May I be of assistance?"

A friendly stranger was rummaging through her pocketbook. She soon had the required change and handed it to Rabbi Lew.

"Thank you ever so much," he said appreciatively. "We're from out of town and aren't familiar with the fare regulations here."

After the Lews boarded the train and settled down, they noticed that the kind woman had taken a seat nearby. Rabbi Lew approached her and thanked her once again.

"Oh, don't mention it!" the woman exclaimed. "I'm glad I could help. Traveling with young children isn't easy, I know. Where are you headed?"

Rabbi Lew described the details of their trip.

"I'm not from the area myself," the woman commented. "I'm doing some research on Jewish communities and have come here to meet people and take photographs."

They had been conversing for a while, when Rabbi Lew realized the train was approaching his stop. Before getting off, he asked her if she was familiar with the practice of lighting Shabbos candles.

The woman shook her head. "That's not for me," she stated flatly, "I'm not observant."

Rabbi Lew explained the virtue of lighting candles regardless of the level of one's religious commitment.

"I'm not sure it would be relevant to me," she insisted. "Besides, what's the point of keeping this one commandment if it's followed by the violation of others?"

The woman's position brought to mind an exchange that Rabbi Lew's grandfather, Mr. Zalman Jaffe, had had with the

Rebbe. It was around the time the Rebbe had first decided to publicly encourage the mitzvah of lighting Shabbos candles. Mr. Jaffe had mentioned an attempt he had made to influence a neighbor. The neighbor had voiced the same arguments as the woman on the train. Mr. Jaffe related to the Rebbe that he had stressed the inherent value and personal gain derived from each mitzvah, regardless of previous or subsequent actions. The Rebbe had replied that this was the correct approach.

With that in mind, as they prepared to leave the train, Rabbi Lew again urged the woman to just light candles, independent of her other activities. The train's closing doors brought an end to the conversation.

Three years later, Rabbi Lew received the following email:

Rabbi Lew,

I met you and your family in Crown Heights in July 2001 and looked up your email address on chabad.org. My name is Melissa, but I don't imagine you remember me. I gave you change for $100 so you could get a subway ticket. On the train you urged me to just light candles. Well, I did 'just light.' A few years have passed, and I'm now married to a wonderful Jewish man, Marty. We observe most of the Shabbos laws, eat kosher meat, and don't eat other non-kosher foods. We have an incredible Jewish home and observe the laws of family purity, believe it or not! I've thought about your advice to 'just light' many times over these past few years, and wanted you to know that you helped me become the Jewish person I am today. Thank you so much for your kindness, and thank you for caring and helping me on my spiritual journey. Keep in touch if you can,

Melissa

A while later, Rabbi Lew called his father in England, Rabbi Shmuel Lew, and related the story.

"What perfect timing!" exclaimed the elder Lew. "I've just returned from the engagement party of the granddaughter of Mr. Jaffe's neighbor. His grandchildren are fully observant and lead exemplary Jewish lives. Who can measure the effect of fulfilling a mitzvah, and the Divine Providence that suffuses every one of life's encounters?"

While still a high school student in London, England, Mrs. Leah Namdar and her classmates devoted Thursday afternoons to visiting Jewish women in the hospital and distributing candles.

"One of my friends, Channah Negin, was remarkably talented," she recalls. "She had the legendary Jewish nose! I don't mean in shape, but in her ability to 'sniff out' the Jewish women from the rest of the patients. More often than not, she was right."

One week, as the girls were making their rounds, they came upon a young woman who the nurses affirmed was Jewish. She was lying in her bed, her long black hair strewn over the white hospital pillow, her cheeks streaked with mascara-stained tears.

Softly, the girls approached.

"Hi, we're from Lubavitch and...."

The girls had barely uttered these words when the young woman pulled herself up with a start and flung open her arms.

"Lubavitch!" she cried. "I knew you would come! Come closer and let me hug you. I want to make sure you are real."

The girls were completely taken aback. Then the young woman told her story.

"My family immigrated to England from Israel when I was a little girl. I went to a Jewish school in Stamford Hill, but I learned very little about Judaism there. There was one time, though, that I actually did have an authentic Jewish experience. One weekend, Lubavitch organized a Shabbaton for a group of girls. My parents are not observant at all, but they agreed to send me.

"We were hosted by different families and had a program that included lectures, games and discussions. It was a long time ago, and I don't remember everything, but there was one thing that stuck in my mind. It was the Vogel family, on Darenth Road, that hosted me. Funny I should remember their name. We were sitting around the table on Shabbos, and their children started to sing. It was so beautiful, all those voices together. Then each one talked about the Jewish things they had learned in school. All of a sudden, I felt something I had never felt before. I thought to myself: 'I still don't know if there really is a G-d, but maybe, just maybe, if there is, He must be right here in this room with this Lubavitch family.'

"Since then, I haven't thought much about G-d. Until now, that is. A couple of days ago I was in a terrible motorcycle accident. My legs were crushed and the doctors say they can't save them. They're scheduling a double amputation. And I'm only twenty-four!"

Her tears began anew.

"So I started thinking about G-d. I prayed: Dear G-d, I still don't know if You are really there, but I remember thinking You were there with that Lubavitch family. If it's true that You exist, and that You can help me, please, please, give me a sign.

I just lay here crying, and praying for the first time in my life. That's when you walked in saying: 'We're from Lubavitch.'

"Now I know He really is there."

The girls sent a letter to the Rebbe asking for a blessing. Shortly afterwards, the doctors discovered that they would not need to amputate her legs, and the young woman left the hospital much sooner than expected.

"When we first arrived 'down under,' relates Rabbi Yisrael Rosenfeld of Australia, "we lived in a small apartment building that had only four flats, two upstairs, and two downstairs. We lived downstairs. Our upstairs neighbors were an Israeli brother and sister, Sharona and Yigal, who had come to Australia after their army service. My wife, Sarah, and I tried to get to know them, and invited them with their friends for Shabbos and holidays. But though we had a cordial relationship, we didn't feel we were affecting them in any apparent way."

The Rosenfelds later opened a Chabad House in Glen Waverley, a suburb thirty minutes away, and lost contact with their former neighbors. Their new location required more commuting, and the cost-conscious shluchim decided to switch to a more efficient type of fuel, sold at the Solo Gas chain. One such station was owned by Israelis and operated by a series of Israeli backpackers keen on gathering funds for their treks in the Australian outback. Rabbi Rosenfeld began to use this gas station chain, thus combining good economics with shlichus, as he knew he would meet Jews there.

"After filling up my van," says Rabbi Rosenfeld, "I would go into the station to pay. I would greet the attendants with a cheery 'Shalom!' hoping for a response. Some Israelis abroad are not eager to be identified as Israeli or Jewish. My greeting would often go unanswered; at most, I might get a slight nod of acknowledgement. But there was one fellow called Kobi who always returned my greeting. We became acquainted, and I used my brief encounters with him to share messages of Jewish content before the next customer came in to pay."

Those short meetings apparently made an impression. One evening when Rabbi Rosenfeld came to fill up, Kobi told him that he was engaged to be married and wanted to learn how to set up a Jewish home. Rabbi Rosenfeld congratulated him and gladly scheduled an appointment for a learning session.

The next week when he came to fill up on gas, Rabbi Rosenfeld noticed a young woman sitting on a car in the parking lot.

"She looks familiar," he mused. "Where could I know her from?"

Then it hit him. "The upstairs neighbor in our old house!" Was she Kobi's future bride?

It was indeed Sharona.

"You're not going to believe this, Rabbi," Kobi told him after the initial re-acquaintance was made. "When I suggested to Sharona that we both take some classes in Jewish studies in preparation for our marriage, she agreed, but felt it had to be with the right kind of people. She said she had just the right people in mind – old neighbors of hers who were very friendly. She had liked their way of sharing their Judaism with others. But they had moved, and she didn't have their new address.

"I insisted," Kobi continued, "that the friendly rabbi I had met was the person to learn with. Can you imagine how happy we were when we realized we were both talking about the same rabbi?"

Kobi and Sharona married according to Jewish law and

eventually moved back to Israel. Kobi became a scribe, and he and Sharona now have an open home where they too spread the message of Judaism in a friendly manner to their Shabbos guests.

*R*on is a regular at the evening classes at Chabad House in Copenhagen, Denmark, operated by Rabbi Yitzchak and Rochel Loewenthal. One Tuesday night after class, Ron approached the rabbi with a query.

"Rabbi, under your guidance I've learned to recite parts of *shacharis*, the morning service, and I'd like to learn how to pray the afternoon *minchah* service as well. I recall you telling us in class that *minchah* has a special importance, since it is recited right in the middle of our business day. Would you please instruct me in how one prays *minchah*?"

Rabbi Loewenthal was more than happy to fulfill this request and duly guided him. Ron thanked him for his assistance, and the two men parted.

Rabbi Loewenthal's day was not yet over. For some time now, he had been weighed down by financial worries. A substantial payment for the Chabad winter camp had to be made on Thursday. He had made numerous efforts to raise the funds, but with little result. He pondered the matter well into the night.

Beginning early Wednesday morning, he had made many calls. By mid-afternoon, he still lacked the majority of the funds.

That evening, Rabbi Loewenthal had a strong feeling that he should address Ron. He had not wanted to speak with him about it, as Ron was already a Chabad supporter and had committed himself to a fixed contribution every couple of months. However, for a reason he couldn't explain, Rabbi Loewenthal just had the sense Ron was the person to talk to. He resolved to speak with him later that evening, after the Wednesday night class.

Ron attended, but left early; Rabbi Loewenthal had no alternative but to phone him afterward. It was now ten o'clock at night.

"I apologize for calling so late," he began, "but there's something urgent I had planned to discuss with you after the class."

"I'm sorry I had to leave early," Ron answered. "Would you like to come over now and talk?"

"If it wouldn't inconvenience you too much, I would be grateful," replied Rabbi Loewenthal, "but the drive might take me longer because of the snow. Are you sure it won't be too late?"

"No trouble, just drive safely."

Rabbi Loewenthal arrived at Ron's home close to eleven o'clock and explained his predicament.

There was a moment of silence as Ron absorbed the rabbi's words. He was clearly moved, with a look of amazement on his face.

Then he slowly responded, first reminding the rabbi of his earlier request to learn about the *minchah* prayers.

"For some time now, I've been having problems with one of my overseas suppliers. This difficulty was going to cost me a large, unforeseen expense. I tried to negotiate, but with no apparent success. I resolved to intensify my connection to G-d and take on an additional commitment to prayer, including *minchah* in my daily schedule. This afternoon, I had a telephone appointment with that supplier. I recited the *minchah* services and prayed for G-d's help in solving the problem. I prayed that, instead of losing money, I would be able to use my finances to further His work. My prayers were evidently answered, for the business meeting went very well. G-d indeed desires that I direct my money to His business. Now, how much did you say you needed?"

The hospital in S. Germain-en-Laye, a town outside Paris where Rabbi Mendel and Chanah Sabag live on shlichus, doesn't usually have many Jewish patients. Nevertheless, Rabbi Sabag makes a point of visiting before the holy days so that, should a Jew be there, he can offer assistance.

One year, he made his usual round before Rosh HaShanah but didn't find any co-religionists. On his way home from synagogue the next day, his thoughts drifted back to the hospital. He felt drawn there. "But I checked yesterday and there were no Jewish patients," he argued with the force that was prodding him. Before he had finished this internal debate, he found himself at the hospital entrance.

He made his way to the nurse's station on the first floor.

"Are there any Jews here?" he asked.

"I don't know," came the curt reply.

"I'm a Jewish clergyman," explained Rabbi Sabag. "Today is one of our holy days, and I have always been given permission to check the list of patients to identify anyone Jewish, so I may visit them."

The nurse shrugged indifferently and handed him a list. Rabbi Sabag couldn't see any names that struck him as Jewish, but decided that, having come this far, he might as well check the next floor – just in case.

This time, a name on the list caught his eye. "Memouni,"

he mused. "It could be either Arab or Jewish." He decided to give it a try.

"I'm here to see Mrs. Memouni," he declared.

The nurse eyed him doubtfully.

"She's in the maternity ward," the nurse said. "She gave birth last night and may not be feeling up to visitors. Are you sure she would want to see you?"

"Today is a Jewish holy day, and I'm convinced she will be happy to see me," Rabbi Sabag said.

"I'll ask her," offered the nurse. She returned shortly, nodding in the direction of the woman's room.

When Rabbi Sabag entered and introduced himself, Mrs. Memouni looked shocked yet somehow elated. The nurse had only told her that she had a visitor; she was totally surprised at the rabbi's visit, and began to cry as he offered to blow the *shofar* for her.

"Rabbi, you have no idea how thankful I am that you came. I'm not observant, but I do know about some of our holidays and practices. I always go to the synagogue on Rosh HaShanah to hear the *shofar* blowing. It's been bothering me that I wasn't able to fulfill the commitment this year. Then suddenly you appear with a *shofar* in hand…"

Esther stood at the door of the Chabad House in Brighton Beach, Brooklyn, New York, where she is on shlichus with her husband, Rabbi Zushe Winner. It was her birthday, and she was graciously ushering in the guests who had come to celebrate with her. She was grateful for the large turnout – over one hundred women – all of whom she and her husband had met during the course of their shlichus work.

"I am indebted to the Rebbe for encouraging us to celebrate birthdays in a meaningful way," Esther thought to herself. "Everyone likes parties, and this is such an opportunity to share lessons in Judaism."

As she glanced at all the familiar faces, she noticed Betty Malakoff, a woman in her nineties whom the Winners had met during Sukkos. They had been sitting in their sukkah (which they had built in the alley, easily accessible to passersby) when Mrs. Malakoff, intrigued by the strange shed, knocked on the door.

"I hope I'm not disturbing you, but can you explain why you're having a picnic in this outlandish-looking hut?" she had asked.

That question led to others and to a friendly bond. Since she lived alone, Betty appreciated the weekly gifts of homemade goodies that Mrs. Winner delivered to her door and had recently shown a pronounced interest in eating kosher food.

Another woman's face caught Esther's eye. This was Miriam Eberman, and Esther smiled inwardly as she recalled how they had met. The Chabad House operated a model matzah factory which attracted many school children. Parents often came along, helping the teachers with the chaperoning, and Mrs. Eberman had been one of those parents. As she did with many visitors, Esther had used the opportunity to brief her visitor about the upcoming holiday.

"I know all about it," Mrs. Eberman responded with a hint of indifference. "I went to a religious school."

"Really?" inquired Esther, "which one?"

"Beth Rivka, in Crown Heights."

"So did I!" Esther said. "What year did you graduate?"

Mrs. Eberman's response caused Esther to exclaim, "Why, that's the same year I graduated! I don't recognize you, but if we weren't in the same class, we must have been in the same grade."

The woman looked from Esther to her teenage daughter, Yehudis, who was guiding a group of children through the factory.

"You must be Esther Sperlin! That girl – she must be your daughter – looks just as I remember you!"

Esther was delighted to reconnect with an old schoolmate and added her to the Chabad House mailing list. As a result of that unexpected meeting, Miriam had resolved to be more meticulous in lighting Shabbos candles. Esther had previously been in contact with Miriam's sister, Elaine Wineberg, who often attended Chabad House functions, and invited her to come with Miriam to the party.

As she continued welcoming guests, Esther noticed that Laura Zukin had arrived. Esther had been speaking with Laura about the laws of family purity for some time. Laura was interested, but reluctant to make a commitment. Just recently, though, she had called Esther and announced that she was ready to study this vital aspect of Jewish family life more seriously.

Esther pressed Laura's hand, acknowledging Laura's presence and continued to greet newcomers. As the women entered, they marveled at a striking display of three beautifully wrapped gifts placed atop handsome pillars. The packaging was transparent and the contents were clearly visible. One was a stunning set of silver candlesticks, the second was a unique cookbook and novel kitchen utensils, and the third was an attractive collection of health and beauty items.

"Oh, how lovely, that's exactly what I've been looking for!"

"That gift is just right for my daughter-in-law."

"Who is selling the raffle tickets?"

The excitement continued a few minutes more, until Esther began the program.

"Today is the eve of the seventh day of *Tishrei*, the day of the passing of the Rebbe's mother, Rebbetzin Chanah, of blessed memory. I would like to dedicate this birthday program to her."

The evening included many stories and insights into the life of this exceptional woman. Esther also explained the Rebbe's directive to celebrate birthdays in a meaningful way.

"One's birthday is a time for introspection, and for making resolutions for the coming year," she said. "Inviting others to a party in celebration and sharing one's resolutions in public reinforces personal commitment. It's also an opportunity to encourage others to take positive steps in Torah observance.

"Rebbetzin Chanah's Hebrew name is an acronym for the mitzvos that pertain to women – keeping kosher, family purity and lighting Shabbos candles. Accordingly, I would like to propose that we raffle these three beautiful gifts, each of which represents one of those mitzvos."

The women nodded and began rummaging in their purses, but Esther waved her hand to dissuade them.

"The raffle I'd like to hold is somewhat different. In place of tickets, all you need to do is resolve to make a further commitment to one of these mitzvos."

Her proposal created quite a stir. The women had been thoroughly enjoying the evening, and many were inspired to make resolutions. Those who hesitated were encouraged: "If you're concerned about committing yourself to lighting Shabbos candles every week, resolve to light at least this week. If you already keep kosher, resolve to try to teach a friend about it."

Soon all the women had 'earned' their raffle tickets.

Mrs. Malakoff won the kosher cookbook and kitchen gift, and Laura Zukin won the beauty assortment. Elaine Wineberg won the candlesticks and decided to give them to her sister, Miriam. Now Miriam had two beautiful new candlesticks in addition to the two she had committed herself to light, and decided to begin to light for her children as well.

> *It began soon after Egypt's closure of the Straits of Tiran and two days before the outbreak of the Six Day War in 1967. At a farbrengen, the Lubavitcher Rebbe cited the Biblical promise[19] that, "all the nations of the world will see that the Name of G-d is proclaimed upon you and will fear you" and our Sages' interpretation[20] that this verse refers to tefillin. He highlighted how the observance of this mitzvah endows the Jewish people with added strength and emphasized the contemporary relevance of this message – that in the current moment of crisis, too, observing this mitzvah would bring the Jews awe-inspiring victory.*
>
> *Throughout the world and particularly in Israel, chassidim eagerly responded to the Rebbe's call, using every possible means to reach out to their fellow Jews, soldiers and civilians alike, and to offer them the opportunity to perform this mitzvah. And just a few short days later, many jubilant soldiers acknowledged the miraculous nature of the victory in which they had participated by putting on tefillin at the Western Wall, reestablishing the Jews' connection to that holy site.*

---

19. *Devarim* 28:10.
20. *Berachos* 6a, *et al.*

*R*abbi Sholom Ber Gordon, who served on shlichus with his wife Miriam in Maplewood, New Jersey, was a man of sterling character. His exemplary guidance and many good deeds are well remembered by all who knew him. In his later years, although his health was deteriorating, his efforts to reach out to others did not wane. He seemed driven by a desire to fulfill his shlichus as long as he could. He was especially active in helping men and boys put on *tefillin* and jokingly described himself as addicted to the *tefillin* campaign.

In the summer of his last year, despite his illness, he was determined to visit the Rebbe's burial site at the beginning of the month of Tammuz. The decision was made to go the day before the third of Tammuz,[21] as navigating the crowds and enduring the long wait on the date itself would be too taxing. That decision proved to be a wise one, but there was still a sizeable crowd, as well as a traffic jam on the drive back to New Jersey. It was close to five o'clock in the afternoon before he got home.

Throughout the period of his illness, his children, including those who are on shlichus themselves, took turns attending him.

"I was driving my father home that day," relates Rabbi Yossi Gordon, "and I could tell he was agitated. I was sure it was due to his illness. But after a short rest at home, and even though he was still exhausted, he directed me to drive him to the hospital where he was chaplain."

"'It's already six in the afternoon, and I still haven't put on *tefillin* with a single Jew today,' he insisted.

---

21. The date of the Rebbe's passing when chassidim are accustomed to visit his gravesite.

"My father's illness and extreme fatigue from the treatments were insignificant to him when weighed against his determination to help another Jew put on *tefillin*. Especially during the months in which he was struggling with his final illness, he was resolute not to miss a day in helping other Jews with this mitzvah.

"I drove to the hospital parking lot, heading for the area designated for staff. I knew he had a special permit to park there, and at this point it was most necessary. It was visiting hour, and the closest parking was very far away. Imagine my distress when we discovered that the permit was not in the car; it had probably been taken accidentally by one of my siblings who had attended our father earlier.

"Having no other choice, I navigated the maze of parked vehicles, ending up quite far from the hospital entrance. Undeterred, with labored movements, my father braced himself to get out of the car. Suddenly, out of nowhere, a man appeared at the car door where I had been standing, ready to assist.

"'How good to see you, Rabbi Gordon!' he said. 'I haven't seen you for a while, but I'd like you to know that ever since you helped me put on *tefillin*, I've been doing it every day.'

"A full dose of pain killer could not have made my father feel better! But that was not all. The man quickly assessed my father's condition and, knowing his determination, he insisted that my father stay put. 'I have a few friends nearby who would be happy to put on *tefillin*,' he declared.

"True to his word, he soon came back with five people to put on *tefillin*. He then gently helped my father out of the car and led him to the hospital to find two more 'customers.'"

After putting on *tefillin* with seven people in less than thirty minutes, the rabbi agreed to go home.

"Excuse me, would you like to put on *tefillin*?"

"NO!"

Having regularly manned one of the mitzvah mobiles in New York, Rabbi Nissan Dubov was well versed in the many and varied responses he might receive to that question. But this person's furious refusal and hasty departure caught him off guard.

"Of course, it wasn't the first time I had been refused, but I had never encountered such a hostile reaction," says Rabbi Dubov. "I really took it to heart. Perhaps I hadn't seemed friendly enough? Maybe I had unwittingly offended him? It took me a while to regain my composure."

Rabbi Dubov kept up his weekly excursions on the mitzvah mobiles from Brooklyn to Manhattan. He did not have a steady route and often jumped on the first mobile that was ready to leave. One Friday, three months later, he found himself with the same "crew" and in the same "work station" where the unpleasant experience had occurred.

Many thousands of people walk down Fifth Avenue, but there was no mistaking the fellow Rabbi Dubov spotted out of the corner of his eye. He had almost forgotten the incident, although the sour taste still lingered. Instinctively, his legs took him across the street to avoid any more unease. But the fellow had seen him and was making a beeline in his direction, obviously intent on confronting him.

Rabbi Dubov braced himself.

"I've been looking for you," the fellow began. "I wanted to thank you." Rabbi Dubov could only stare at him, stupefied.

"I was brought up in a modern Orthodox home," he continued. "I had a bar mitzvah and continued putting on *tefillin* for quite a while afterward. But then, when I went away to college, I became lax in my commitment. When you approached me, I knew exactly who you were and what you wanted. Even though you spoke in a friendly tone, your question echoed loudly in my ears. I became acutely aware of how I had lapsed, and at that moment all I could do was shout back in self-justification. Afterwards, I made a firm resolution to start putting on *tefillin* every day and have done so ever since. I owe you both an apology for my outburst and my sincere gratitude for reminding me of my religious obligations."

"I was very moved," recalls Rabbi Dubov, "and also thankful to G-d for allowing me a peek into the ways of His Providence. Had I not met the fellow again, I would still be troubled by the thought of having offended a fellow Jew."

The town of Cocoa Beach, on the "space coast" in Florida, was buzzing with excitement. Congressman and space pioneer John Glenn was back on earth after a return from orbit, and the city was getting ready for a ticker-tape parade. Rabbi Zvi Konikov knew the procession would be passing near the Chabad Center and decided to join the festivities. The years he and his wife Shulamis have spent on the space coast have taught them that, given the opportunity, Jews tend to gravitate toward Judaism. What better place to be available than among the crowd?

He parked himself right in the center of town, securing a good place to set up a *tefillin* booth. This also happened to be a great spot from which to greet the returning astronaut. People were milling all over, the media were stationed on every corner, and helicopters were hovering overhead, their rattle drowned out by the din of the crowds.

Looking around, Rabbi Konikov noticed a group of young skinheads gliding by on rollerblades. Suddenly, his eyes locked with those of one of the boys.

"Eli, is that you?" Rabbi Konikov called out on impulse.

"Heeey, Rabbi Konikov!" came the response from the boy, who turned towards him.

Eli, now a teenager, had studied with the rabbi in Chabad's Hebrew School until he was eleven. His grandfather had brought him every Sunday to learn about his heritage, hoping he'd live long enough to see the boy celebrate his bar mitzvah. Unfortunately, this was not to be. Shortly before the grandfather's passing Rabbi Konikov visited him, and the elderly man reiterated his wish. But Eli stopped coming to Hebrew School, and the bar mitzvah never happened.

All this flashed through his mind as Rabbi Konikov took Eli's hand and shook it warmly.

Impulsively, he said, "Eli, your grandfather wanted so much that you should have a bar mitvah – we can do it right here and now!"

Eli's skinhead friends, the throngs of people and the clicking media watched in amazement as Rabbi Konikov assisted Eli in putting on *tefillin*. To onlookers, it may have seemed like a scene from outer space. For Eli, it was an inward-bound journey.

No sooner had they finished than the open cars came rolling down the street. Congressman Glenn came within hand's reach and saluted Rabbi Konikov.

*H*oward Butcher, a member of the Palo Alto Chabad House Advisory Board, talked and walked frequently with the director, Rabbi Yosef Levin. Three times a week, Howard and the rabbi would exercise together, improving their health and solidifying their relationship.

Once, when discussing the effort of persuading other Jews to put on *tefillin*, Rabbi Levin mentioned that he was at a disadvantage because he is left-handed.

"It's awkward, adjusting *tefillin* made for a lefty on a person who is right-handed," he commented, "because the straps and knots must be positioned differently."

"Why don't you just get a separate right-handed pair for your outreach purposes?" asked Howard.

"*Tefillin* are expensive," the rabbi replied candidly.

"What does a pair cost?" Howard wanted to know.

"Costs vary, but you can purchase a quality pair for about $450."

A few weeks later, Howard presented the rabbi with a stack of checks made out to Chabad House. The memo line stated: "toward the purchase of *tefillin* for outreach," and the total added up to $450. "People were happy to have a share in your *tefillin* outreach efforts, Rabbi," explained Howard.

Rabbi Levin was very touched by the gesture and immediately placed an order with a scribe in Israel. Three months later, the *tefillin* arrived. Rabbi Levin put them in his car, along with a packet of brochures explaining the mitzvah of *tefillin*.

A few days later, Howard's daughter called Rabbi Levin urgently.

"My father is in the emergency room at the hospital," she said. "We rushed him in with severe chest pains."

Rabbi Levin knew it was a serious situation; Howard Butcher was in his eighties and had a heart condition. He quickly drove to the hospital.

"As we speak I am having a heart attack," Howard said with a wry smile. "They gave me medication for the pain, but not for the heart because they want to do a second EKG during the attack."

"How soon will the test be done?" inquired the rabbi.

"Right now."

Rabbi Levin asked Howard if he had put on *tefillin* that morning.

Howard shook his head.

"Well," the rabbi said encouragingly, "you will be the first one to put on the *tefillin* that you sponsored!"

He quickly approached one of the doctors. "Can I please have a minute with the patient before you proceed with the EKG?"

The doctor was busy setting up equipment and told the rabbi that he really needed to do the test immediately.

"Just two minutes?" Rabbi Levin implored.

"All right, but only two minutes."

The doctors and nurses left the cubicle and closed the curtains. Rabbi Levin had the new pair of *tefillin* with him. He quickly put them on Howard's head and outstretched arm.

As soon as the rabbi left, the doctors and nurses swarmed back and the second EKG was administered.

The hospital cardiology team reviewed the scroll of results. The note on the doctor's printout stated: "Attack arrested without any intervention."

One of the cardiologists had been a *yeshivah* student in his youth. He modified the note to read: "Attack arrested without any medical intervention."

*R*abbi Mendel and Chanah Sabag devote their energies to a shlichus that spans numerous towns outside Paris. "Paris itself has many shluchim, but we decided to serve those Jews living in the outlying areas," explains Rabbi Sabag. "They are few and far between, but they too need Jewish contact. Even if it is a community of only twenty families, we feel honored to reach out to them."

He takes care to visit each of these outlying locations at least once a month, but since there are many of them, it means he's on the road two or three times a week. Or should we say, on the rails? He often boards the T.G.V. express train, which speeds along at three hundred kilometers an hour, enabling him to reduce travel time.

"Once, after visiting the city of Laval, I was waiting on the platform for the next train with a crowd of other travelers. As the train pulled in, I could see that its ten passenger cars were already packed. I knew that an additional car would probably be latched onto the first to accommodate the overflow. Although I had an assigned seat in the front car, I thought the second would be more spacious, so, on the spur of the moment, I decided to forgo my assured place in the overcrowded first car and board the attached one. I waited patiently until everyone was seated and then took an empty seat."

It proved to be a wise move, as this less-crowded car was more comfortable, and Rabbi Sabag settled in. But no sooner had he stretched his legs than he felt a tap on his shoulder.

"May I sit next to you?" asked a fellow passenger.

Rabbi Sabag quickly sized the man up. He nodded cordially, but inwardly he groaned. "He's probably a Muslim," he was thinking. It wasn't the first time a Muslim had chosen to engage him, visibly Jewish, in prolonged and futile arguments about the state of affairs in Israel.

Indeed, no sooner had the man taken his seat than he expressed a wish to speak. Much to Rabbi Sabag's surprise, though, he introduced himself as a Jew.

"My name is Frank. I live in a small town that has only a few Jewish families. I'm already in my thirties but have only recently begun contemplating my religion. There's no one around to ask, though, so I've been ignoring this inner calling. Then I noticed you as you were standing in the isle waiting to take a seat. I felt that chancing upon you was a G-dsend, and I want to take the opportunity to ask some questions."

Rabbi Sabag realized that his choice of train cars had involved more than his own comfort. He and Frank conversed for some time. Then Rabbi Sabag said, "Talking things over and learning about Judaism helps a person connect to G-d, yet our religion teaches that deeds surpass everything else. Through performing one of G-d's commandments, a Jew binds himself directly with the Creator. Have you ever heard of *tefillin*?"

"I've heard the term, but I don't know exactly what it refers to."

"Here, let me show you."

Rabbi Sabag opened his briefcase and took out his *tefillin*. As he explained, Frank seemed interested.

"How about putting them on right now?" Rabbi Sabag offered.

"What?!" Frank recoiled. "Here on a train? In public?"

"Why not?" Rabbi Sabag urged him gently. "In Paris it's not an uncommon scene. Besides, look at all the people around us. They're munching away at their snacks, drinking in public and talking loudly. Don't worry, it won't offend anyone."

Frank was hesitant but eventually allowed himself to be persuaded to put on *tefillin*, albeit not at his seat, but in the passageway between the train cars.

This 'chance' meeting marked the beginning of Frank's Jewish education and led him to pursue his journey towards Judaism.

"*I*'m sorry, Levi. No one called to report finding a pair of *tefillin*."

Levi Abayev hung up the phone, disappointed. Not that he had expected this call to Rabbi Danny and Bat Sheva Cohen, the shluchim in Chevron, Israel, to solve his problem.

Every Friday, Levi joined a group of *yeshivah* students who, under Rabbi Cohen's direction, visit soldiers at the numerous army bases in the Chevron area. It was late Friday afternoon, on the boys' ride back to Jerusalem, when Levi discovered that his expensive *tefillin* were missing. He reckoned that he had left them at one of the bases, but it was too close to Shabbos to turn back.

The following Friday, when Levi and his group returned to Chevron, Levi inquired about his loss at the various stops the boys had made, but to no avail. Their final destination was a large base, which included a variety of units. They visited the officers, commandos, mechanics, reservists, *nachal* brigade and others. Their last stop was a platoon located at a caravan site at the far end of the base. As the boys neared the site, a soldier came forward and called out, "Is one of you Levi Abayev?"

The boys were a bit surprised; in the course of putting on *tefillin* with soldiers, there is often an exchange of heartfelt wishes, but not necessarily names, and certainly not family names.

"I am Levi."

Visibly moved, the soldier embraced Levi. Then he ran into the caravan and returned with a bag of *tefillin*. "This must be yours," he said, still emotional.

Levi was very grateful but wondered why the soldier had been so affected by the find. He didn't have long to wait before the soldier explained.

"I'm not really an observant Jew," he began, "but since my

bar mitzvah, I have been putting on *tefillin* every single day. I am not quite sure why, maybe I feel it's a good omen, especially for a soldier in combat. Anyway, that's what I do.

"Last Friday, I was on the way back to the base from the northern part of the country. Halfway through my journey, I discovered that I had forgotten my *tefillin*. I was devastated. I had to be at the base on time, and I knew it would be very close to Shabbos by the time I got there. I know you don't put on *tefillin* on Shabbos. No one else in my unit has a pair, and there would be no time to search elsewhere for a pair. I had never missed a day, and was really upset.

"I thought to myself, 'It's really not so serious; after all, I don't observe other mitzvos.' But still it bothered me, because I'm meticulous about this one mitzvah. I concluded that if G-d really cares about my fulfilling this mitzvah, He would work it out for me.

"Imagine my amazement when I arrived at my caravan and found a pair of *tefillin* lying on my bed!"

> In the summer of 1974, in response to a call by the Rebbe to intensify the *tefillin* campaign, several *yeshivah* students rented a step van, parked it along a major thoroughfare in Manhattan, and invited passersby to come in and put on *tefillin*.
>
> When the Rebbe heard about their initiative, he was very pleased. At the next *farbrengen*, he named the vans, "*mitzvah tanks*" and explained: "Our Sages teach that gold was created solely for the Temple, implying that everything in the world was brought into being to be used for G-d's purpose. A tank has the ability to enter terrain otherwise inaccessible by soldiers. Similarly, a *mitzvah tank* can bring Jewish practice to places that would otherwise be difficult to reach."
>
> Similarly, the Rebbe welcomed all the new developments

in technology and communications, seeing them as means to spread the Torah and its mitzvos.

When Yossi, Zalman and Mendel, *yeshivah* students from New York, drove into Highland Park, Illinois, in a large mitzvah mobile, the shluchim there, Rabbi Yosef and Michla Schanowitz, were pleased to greet them. Their "mitzvah tank" was one of five similar vehicles that their colleague Shmuel Strasberg had organized. The tanks had been sent on a cross-country trip in an attempt to arouse more Jewish awareness. The colorful messages on the exteriors prompted curiosity, and an effort was made to reach out to Jews in as many places as possible.

"Where would be a good place to park the tank and meet people?" the young men asked Rabbi Schanowitz.

"Teenagers may get a kick out of it," he replied. "There's a large high school in Highland Park that many Jews attend. The fields and park adjoining the school are full of students during breaks. I suggest you try there."

The boys drove to the school and parked close by. As they got out, the school guard glanced at their vehicle and the boys saw him placing a call. It looked as if he were informing someone of their presence. Soon enough, he waved them in. Encouraged that the school administration had apparently allowed them to enter, they turned toward the throngs of students who filled the area. It was perfect timing; lunch break had just begun. In a short while, their hands were busy putting *tefillin* on boys, who were amused as well as intrigued by the tank and the *yeshivah* students.

About half an hour later, the guard came running, waving his hands in disapproval.

"You have to leave," he said in an authoritative manner.

"Why?" asked the *yeshivah* students.

"Principal's orders," the guard retorted.

"May I speak with the principal?" Yossi asked the guard politely.

"She's right in there," the guard replied, pointing to a glass-enclosed office in the school building which faced the yard.

Yossi approached the office and introduced himself, explaining the boys' mission.

The principal shook her head. "Sorry, that's against school policy."

"Of course we don't want to violate any policy," Yossi assured her. "But the guard saw us drive up and let us in. We thought he had informed the school of our arrival."

"It was a mistake," admitted the principal. "Our school is scheduled to be interviewed today by a team from the Good Morning America news program. Broadcasting teams often travel in vehicles like yours. When the guard saw the signs, he thought it was the television crew."

What was it that had confused the guard? Could it have been the message in bold letters spelling out "Good News, America"?

The message continued below – "Mashiach is on the way."

∽

"We just have to put up a billboard!" insisted Avrohom Rapoport. His parents, shluchim Rabbi Shmuel David and Tova, sensed their son was right. They had been discussing the issue for quite a while already. A billboard seemed to be one of the most appropriate ways to promote Jewish awareness in Atlantic City, New Jersey. After all, every road into this gambling mecca is lined with flashy billboards advertising casinos. It was shortly before Chanukah, and an attractive billboard reminding Jews to light a menorah would be in the spirit of our Sages' directive to publicize the miracle commemorated on this holiday.

There were some hurdles, though. First, an available billboard had to be found; high demand compelled would-be advertisers to book far in advance.

"We need one only for a short time," Mrs. Rapoport explained to one agency after another. "Perhaps you have an opening between bookings?"

Nothing was available.

But Avrohom persisted. He wrote a letter to be read at the Rebbe's gravesite requesting success in their efforts. Shortly afterwards, Mr. Manny Levine, owner of one of the agencies, called back.

"You're in luck!" he informed the Rapoports, "I just got an unexpected opening. In my business it's called the 'Rolls Royce' – the largest size and most desirable location. I've thought about it, and want to donate it to your cause. By the way, who's doing your sign?"

Rabbi and Mrs. Rapoport rapidly learned that preparing a sign for a billboard requires special skills and can be quite expensive. This was the second hurdle. Mr. Levine put them in touch with a Mr. Terry Steer, whose son-in-law had recently returned from an inspiring trip to Israel. His son-in-law's enthusiasm persuaded Mr. Steer to create the sign at no cost.

The third hurdle was mounting the sign. This, too, would have been a pricey job, but once again Mr. Levine directed the Rapoports to a fellow who volunteered to do it for free.

The wording on a billboard has to be minimal yet punchy, so that drivers could get the message. That Chanukah, an eye-catching sign on Atlantic City's main highway proclaimed: "Light up the world, light up your soul."

The Rapoports had miraculously gotten their billboard for a fraction of the usual cost, but all in all, a great deal of effort had been invested in pulling it together. Avrohom echoed his parents' thoughts when he mused: "After all that, I wonder if anybody was really affected by it."

The winter months passed and Mrs. Rapoport's niece, Chana, from Brooklyn, came to visit during Passover. She shared the following story.

"My friend Rachel Leah told me that her family had a Shabbos guest who had recently committed herself to becoming more observant. One of the family members asked what had prompted her to begin this spiritual journey.

"Funny you should refer to it as a journey," the woman replied. "It actually began in a fleeting moment while on the road through Atlantic City. There was this huge billboard...."

The completion of a Torah scroll and the celebration of its arrival at a synagogue is always good news. And so, Rabbi Sholom and Aliza Leverton of East Windsor, New Jersey, decided to spread the word. They informed the local papers of the event, which was to take place a week before Rosh HaShanah.

One of the local publications, the *Jewish State Newspaper*, responded with enthusiasm. "We would be happy to do a full article on this festive event," said the editor.

Rabbi Leverton was gratified and began to offer the relevant information regarding the date and location of the ceremony. The newspaper staff, however, had other ideas. "We're interested in publishing an article about the event now," they said.

"It's mid-August," Rabbi Leverton thought to himself. "Most people are away, and there's probably little other Jewish news worth printing. Of course, publicity would be most effective as close to the date as possible, but a full article as opposed to a small notice is nothing to sneeze at."

The Levertons contacted the family that had largely subsidized the writing of the scroll, and asked their permission for an interview.

"We appreciate the offer," they replied, "but we must decline. We prefer to remain behind the scenes and don't really want the publicity."

Meanwhile, someone from the paper contacted the Levertons once again, requesting other related items of interest and some photos and created the impression that the article might be put on the front-page.

"I went through my files and dug up some information and publicity from the Torah Launch ceremony we had held over a year earlier, when we began the writing of the scroll," says Rabbi Leverton. "Without putting too much thought into my choices, I also pulled out a bunch of photos of that occasion and delivered it all to the newspaper."

True to its word, the paper published a full article, with a color photo on the front page. The picture chosen featured a member of Rabbi Leverton's synagogue, Mr. Tzvi Pomper, a man honored at the ceremony.

"Mr. Pomper is an elderly man," recalls Rabbi Leverton, "one of the sweetest *yidden* you could ever meet. He's a Holocaust survivor whose family perished in the war, but despite his hardships, he radiates joy and a love for Judaism. All in all, I was thankful for the publicity, although it was really last year's story."

The day after the article was published the Levertons received a call from a Jewish lawyer who lived about half an hour's drive away.

"Rabbi," he said with audible excitement in his voice, "I read the front-page story in the paper. I'm calling about the elderly man in the picture, one of your congregants. His name appears in the caption beneath the photo. I have the same last name, and I believe we may be related!"

"I'm sorry to disappoint you, Mr. Pomper," replied Rabbi Leverton sympathetically, "but Tzvi Pomper is a survivor of the Warsaw ghetto. He never married; he told us that his entire family perished in the war, and that he has no living relations."

"But we know that my grandfather, who emigrated from Warsaw in 1935, left family members behind. For all these years, there's been a lingering hope that someone may have survived," insisted the caller. "We've made many inquiries, but to no avail. And here is this photo of an elderly man bearing our family name who's a survivor of the Warsaw ghetto!"

Rabbi Leverton promised to pursue the matter and contacted the elderly Mr. Pomper at the first opportunity. Gently, he asked for more details about his painful past, inquiring specifically about any family members who might have left Warsaw before the war.

"Oh…yes. I remember when I was a little boy there was a farewell party for some relatives who were leaving for America," he said slowly. "When I arrived in the States, I searched for them a long time. Finally I gave up and decided to get on with my life. Why do you ask?"

The story came full circle when the two Mr. Pompers, indeed related, had an emotional reunion at the joyous dedication of the Torah scroll at Chabad the week before Rosh HaShanah.

"And I thought it was last year's story," recalls Rabbi Leverton.

The writing of this scroll led to other fortuitous events as well, although these were not mentioned in the article. It had begun with a $15,000 donation by a member of the community toward the writing of the scroll. Rabbi Leverton was grateful for the generous donation, but it lay dormant for a year.

"Why has the Torah scroll not been written?" the donor finally asked.

Rabbi Leverton tactfully explained that the sum donated was enough to buy a fine second-hand scroll, but not enough to commission a new one.

"I would really like our community to acquire a new Torah scroll, and I've been working to raise the additional funds, but haven't yet succeeded," he said.

"Give me a week, rabbi," the donor requested.

A week later the man returned with a pledge for an additional $15,000.

"It's from my sister and brother-in-law, who live in Florida," he explained. "They are happy to participate in such a worthy cause."

Rabbi Leverton was moved, both by his community member's efforts and by the generosity of his relatives to a cause and a community to which they didn't even belong. As the completion of the scroll drew near, Rabbi Leverton insisted that the couple from Florida participate in the ceremony. They were being honored, and the community wanted an opportunity to thank them in person. The couple's modesty dissuaded them from such a place in the limelight, and it took some convincing to get them to come. Little did they know how fortuitous their visit would be.

This couple had lived in New York before moving to Florida. Prior to their move, the wife had been diagnosed and treated for cancer. Now, back up north for the ceremony, they

arranged to visit old friends, among them the doctor who had
treated the woman in New York. The woman's next check-up
was scheduled for two months later, but since she was right
there, the doctor suggested an examination. The woman agreed.
To their dismay, they found that the disease had returned in
an aggressive form. It was decided to send her for immediate
surgery. The doctors who treated her informed the couple that,
had her condition not been detected at that time, it might have
been too late.

When the vacationers at the French Riviera first
looked in the direction of the rhythmic hum above
their heads, they were stumped. Amidst the colorful
gliders soaring above the pristine beaches was a small aircraft
towing a banner. The Jewish tourists were the first to figure
it out. As the aircraft neared, they were able to make out the
banner's message – "Chabad Lubavitch wishes you Shabbat
Shalom."

The banner noted the time for candle lighting as well.

Rabbi Yehuda and Tsherna Matusof of Cannes, France,
coordinated this appealing demonstration of Jewish awareness
each Friday throughout that summer. It was a quick run for
pilot Phillip, and he evidently enjoyed watching the beach-go-
ers craning their necks.

One Friday in August, however, the gusts were too strong
for his small aircraft, and he was forced to abandon his "cargo"
in a nearby field, as the banner would have caused dangerous
control problems. He flew to a nearby airport and waited for
further instructions.

Mr. Ayache, owner of the aviation company, informed

Rabbi Matusof's son Mendel, who was overseeing the banner project, of the difficulty.

"We would still like the banner flight to take place if possible," Mendel answered. "Could you please make another attempt later, weather permitting?"

Mr. Ayache promised he would. He added, "You're lucky that the pilot dropped the banner where he did. These small planes often take off quite a distance from here, and the banner could have been dropped too far away for me to retrieve it and try to fly it on another plane."

Mendel felt this was a good sign, and indeed things eventually worked out. Later that Friday the banner flew as usual.

In the meantime, Mendel busied himself with ground activity at the Chabad Houses in the area, one of which is in S. Tropez, an exclusive resort. With the assistance of *yeshivah* students, one of his objectives was to gather Shabbos *minyans* in as many small towns as possible. The boys sought out Jews and invited them to attend prayers while they were vacationing. Numerous Torah scrolls were brought from Cannes and Nice and sent out weekly to each *minyan* that the boys had managed to organize.

An hour and a half before Shabbos that windy Friday, one of the boys, Daniel Belaich, told Mendel that he had arranged a minyan in the town of Ramatuelle. He was calling for a Torah scroll.

Mendel marveled at the turn of events. At the beginning of the summer, a scroll had been found unfit for use. A scribe was contacted immediately to repair it, but his arrival had been repeatedly postponed. Two days earlier, the scribe had finally arrived and the scroll was corrected. Just in time, as it turned out, since every other scroll had already been reserved.

But the town of Ramatuelle was a two-hour drive away. How was Mendel going to get the scroll there in time?

Suddenly, it dawned on him. He dialed Mr. Ayache's number.

"Hello, this is Mendel. Is that plane that was grounded this morning still parked in the nearby airport?"

It was. The Torah scroll made it to Ramatuelle in time for Shabbos.

Walk-ins are welcome in the study hall at the Melbourne Lubavitch *kollel*.[22] So when Robert Hanner, a young medical student on a break from the University of Tasmania, requested a learning session with Rabbi Yossi Gordon, the latter readily agreed. Rabbi Gordon and his wife Mina had recently arrived in Australia, and he was then a *kollel* student. Little did Rabbi Gordon know that this would lead to his intensive connection with the island of Tasmania, a one-hour flight from the Australian mainland, but light years away from Torah practice.

After they had studied together for a while, Robert asked Rabbi Gordon to help organize prayers in Tasmania for the upcoming High Holidays. With much effort, they succeeded in organizing a *minyan* for Yom Kippur in Hobart Hebrew Congregation, the oldest existing synagogue in Australia (established 1845).

"There weren't more than a handful of Jews on the entire island who had Jewish spouses," recalls Rabbi Gordon. "I discovered that the woman responsible for Jewish education was a Christian. In short, there was a lot to be done, and so I set

---

22. An institute of higher Jewish education.

to work, encouraged and aided by Rabbi Aharon Serebryanski and an extremely dedicated Tasmanian couple, David and Peninah Clark."

One of the first people to respond to Rabbi Gordon's programs, a woman who was later to become part of the shlichus herself, was Mrs. Bonnie Seigal. She lived in the suburb of Launceston and participated regularly at Chabad activities in Hobart.

At some point, Rabbi Gordon proposed that a program be organized in the long-unused synagogue in Launceston. The program was planned for Sunday, November 25, the first day of the Hebrew month of Kislev. A handful of Jews from Hobart promised to attend, but no one knew how to contact other local Jews. Yet suddenly, on November 21, the phone began ringing off the hook!

On November 15, the Willesee Show, a nationally broadcast TV program that highlights human-interest stories, had featured ninety-one-year-old storekeeper Harry Joseph. Mr. Joseph was the proud owner of a quaint store that preserved the charm of a 1920's haberdashery. His store stood out as a rare sight on a busy modern boulevard. The cameramen were keen on using the unique mannequins hanging in the window display as the perfect backdrop for the interview, but Mr. Joseph would hear nothing of it.

"Those mannequins are silent remnants of times gone by," he had said. "I want to focus on life today. I'm a member of the Jewish community, and I insist that the background for the interview be the second-oldest synagogue in all of Australia, right here in Launceston, which, unfortunately, has been closed for the past twenty years."

The cameramen knew better than to argue with a ninety-one-year-old, and so the interview was filmed as Mr. Joseph wished, including his sad memories of coming to an empty synagogue each Shabbos until he finally gave up. On the show, he expressed his heartfelt wish to attend a *minyan* in his precious synagogue one more time before his passing.

Many people in Melbourne who saw the show and knew of Rabbi Gordon's work in Tasmania were touched by the man's request.

"People called and urged me to help fulfill Mr. Joseph's wish," Rabbi Gordon recalls. "They were eager to donate funds, if only to bring an hour of gratification to an elderly Jew. The timing was perfect. We placed an ad in the local paper inviting people to join us for a *minyan* and the program at the Launceston synagogue. That was when the phone started ringing, and a large crowd showed up on November 25.

After the official reopening of the synagogue, Rabbi Gordon planned another Sunday morning *minyan*. Seven local Jews, one tourist from Sydney and the rabbi were committed to attend. Only a tenth person was missing. Several days before that Sunday, Rabbi Gordon had gone to visit Mr. Joseph, who resided in a nursing home. This proud Jew, who felt so strongly about his Judaism, said he had never heard about *tefillin*, but would be glad to start putting them on at the age of ninety-one.

Although his health did not permit him to attend the *minyan* himself, he had an idea. "I remember another Jew by the name of Harry Lewis," Mr. Joseph said. "I don't know his number or where he lives, but I'm sure he's still around and would attend."

In a city of 65,000 people, finding an individual named Lewis is no small feat, even for a determined rabbi. On Friday, still one man short, Rabbi Gordon was walking down the street to buy some fruit and vegetables.

"Excuse me, Rabbi," a man on the sidewalk addressed him. "I heard you were looking for Mr. Harry Lewis. Well, he's standing right over there across the street."

The man indicated the person he meant and walked off, leaving the dumbfounded rabbi wide-eyed. Later, he discovered that this non-Jewish man managed the store for Mr. Joseph, and had been in the hallway of the nursing home to discuss something with his boss at the time of Rabbi Gordon's visit. Harry Lewis was delighted to be the tenth man.

Surfing the net brought "Ado422" to an "Ask the rabbi" web page. "Ado422" liked the web rabbi's style and became a regular visitor to the site. Among the issues raised there were Jewish history, questions of faith, Torah study and observance.

At some point, "Ado422" came across a link regarding the Birthright program, which enables young people to visit Israel and acquaint themselves with their Jewish heritage. "Ado422" applied and was accepted as a participant. His experience in Israel was very inspiring, and he resolved to encourage other young people to benefit from the program. As an active recruiter, "Ado422"s enthusiasm subsequently earned him a number of trips to Israel as chaperone of the groups he had organized and contributed to his involvement in Judaism.

One year, Rabbi Eliezer Sneiderman, on shlichus with his wife Roni at the University of Delaware, served as accompanying rabbi of a Birthright group of students sponsored by the Chabad Mayanot *Yeshivah* in Jerusalem.

Once in Israel, his group was combined with others. This enables the participants from various places to share programs and trips. A chaperon from one of the other groups, a serious young man called Alex Dekterman, met Rabbi Sneiderman. Alex's family had emigrated from Russia. Over a period of time, he had learned more about Judaism, leading to a commitment to a Torah lifestyle. With Rabbi Sneiderman's guidance, he now introduced the added dimension of Chassidism to his life.

When the program was over, Alex promised to stay in touch.

Some time later, he sent Rabbi Sneiderman an email. The address caught Rabbi Sneiderman's attention; he was sure he had seen it before. Suddenly, it clicked. "Ado422."

> When Reb Pinchas Horowitz first became a disciple of the Maggid of Mezritch,[23] the Maggid advised him to study with Reb Zushe of Hanapoli.
>
> Reb Pinchas went to Reb Zushe and told him of the Maggid's advice. Reb Zushe humbly replied that he could not understand why the Maggid would send anyone to study with him, but that he would be happy to join as great a sage as Reb Pinchas in his intellectual endeavors.
>
> "What should we study?" Reb Pinchas asked.
>
> "Whatever you are studying," Reb Zushe replied.
>
> Reb Pinchas took out a volume of Talmud and began explaining the following passage. "When there are only nine people in the synagogue, there is an opinion that the ark of the synagogue can be counted to complete the quorum of ten necessary for congregational prayer. The Talmud then asks: 'Is the ark a person?!' For no matter how holy the ark is, it is people that are required to make up a minyan."
>
> As Reb Pinchas stated this, Reb Zushe interrupted:

---

23. The successor to the Baal Shem Tov as leader of the Chassidic movement.

"What does the *Talmud* mean: 'Is the ark a person?!' Everyone knows the ark is only an object."

Reb Pinchas was puzzled; the question was obviously rhetorical. Didn't his partner appreciate that?

Reb Zushe continued: "Maybe the intent is that a person can be like an ark in which the Torah is contained, a veritable repository of knowledge, but unless he is a person, unless that knowledge is integrated with his humanity, there is a question if he can be counted."

Reb Pinchas understood that this was the lesson the *Maggid* had wanted him to learn from Reb Zushe: not how to augment his knowledge, but how to use his knowledge to refine himself and transform his character. Such a person attracts attention; others look up to him as an example of a person who lives by the Torah.

For over four decades, Rabbi Nissan and Rochel Pinson have been on shlichus in Tunis, the capital of Tunisia. It has never been easy for Jews in this nation, living among millions of fundamentalist Muslims, but one particular Sukkos season was especially perilous. The arch-terrorist Yasser Arafat, who had been out of the country for some time, was back, and his presence had made tensions rise. Having stones thrown at them was an everyday occurrence for Tunisia's Jews, but now the stones were accompanied by gestures that depicted throat slicing and worse. People were justifiably afraid.

That year, the Pinsons had wanted to travel to New York and personally receive a set of the four species, which the Rebbe sent them annually. They reported the state of affairs to the Rebbe, wondering if a temporary leave of absence might be wise. The Rebbe instructed them to stay, commenting that if he had anyone else to send to Tunis at that time, he would do so.

The Pinsons understood. It seemed clear that the Rebbe would not compel someone to travel into danger but wanted those who were already there to stay and continue their work. After all, were they to leave, what would the other Jews think?

"The Rebbe said 'if I had someone to send...'" the Pinsons pondered. "That implies that it would be the right thing to do. If someone were to arrive here at this time, it would certainly boost the people's morale. But who would come to Tunis now?"

There was only one possibility in the minds of this dedicated couple – their children. They contacted their daughter and son-in-law in Nancy, France, and invited them to come, although doing so would be no simple feat.

"Of course!" Rabbi Yehuda and Tsherna Matusof responded. "If we can help the community in any way, we'll be there."

"And the children?" asked the concerned grandparents, referring to Levi and Mendy Matusof, aged one and three.

"They are children and grandchildren of shluchim," replied the Matusofs. "The Rebbe said 'if I had...'. Who could be more appropriate for this mission? We'll all be honored."

The Matusofs caught the last flight out and landed Friday afternoon, just before Sukkos began. News of their arrival at that tense time spread quickly and generated a wave of encouragement to the local Jews.

The ability to provide support and spread calm is part of the very fiber of the Pinsons' personalities. The gentle warmth of this extraordinary couple affects everyone they meet. With characteristic humility, Mrs. Pinson claims this quality is not their personal achievement.

"Living a constantly tension-filled life due to our surroundings," she relates, "has always made me keenly aware of the need for inner peace. Once, on the occasion of a private encounter with the Rebbe, I expressed appreciation of the tranquility I sensed upon entering his study. I asked for a blessing to have unending reservoirs of inner peace to enable us to continue our shlichus.

"The Rebbe gave me the blessing I requested and added: '… and to spread that calm to others as well.'"

"We had heard about the South American's reputation for warmth and friendliness," relate Rabbi Eliezer and Rochi Shemtov. "But the greeting we were given when we arrived in Montevideo, Uruguay, seemed a bit much."

Rabbi Eliezer recalled, "As I walked into shul the first Shabbos morning, an elderly gentleman, who was soon to be identified as Mr. Leibel Zyman, came over and surprised me with a hug and kiss. I was quite taken aback by such an effusive welcome and asked him why he was so moved to see me."

"I know that the Lubavitch Rebbe has sent shluchim to many places around the world, even to communities much smaller than ours," Mr. Zyman explained. "I always wondered why there was no shaliach here. I was concerned that perhaps the Rebbe saw something negative in this community and for that reason had sent no shaliach. These thoughts made me feel somewhat uncomfortable continuing to live here.

"When I found out that a shaliach was coming to Montevideo, I was elated. In my eyes, it's as if a *mezuzah* has been put up on our city. All of a sudden, I felt safer and more protected.

"So, now that I see the Rebbe's *mezuzah*, is it not proper to kiss it?"

"**W**e live on the bottom floor of a town house," says Chanah, who is on shlichus with her husband, Rabbi Yirachmiel Kittner, in Milwaukee, Wisconsin. "Our activities focus mainly on the many Russian Jews who live in the area. We go out of our way to make contact with these families, and they know they can turn to us for all their needs. So it bothered me that we hadn't been successful in creating a relationship with a Russian couple who were our immediate neighbors.

"Mr. and Mrs. Pyatetsky are a lovely elderly couple with whom we had tried to connect, but they seemed very private and introverted. Try as we would, our interactions didn't get much beyond the occasional polite greeting.

"Then one Friday morning, Mrs. Pyatetsky appeared at our door. I was delighted at her unexpected appearance. In a shy but resolute manner, she told me that she had a request.

"'I'll be happy to help if I can,' I assured her.

"She handed me a pen and paper. 'Would you be kind enough to write down in Russian the blessing one recites when lighting Shabbos candles?'

"I was taken aback by this request. It was the first time we had exchanged more than a brief 'hello,' and I was happy that she was opening up and had taken the initiative to turn to us for advice on Jewish matters.

"'I can certainly do that for you,' I replied, 'but if you would excuse me for a moment, I'll go get you a calendar. It's an attractive piece displaying Jewish art and has much useful information on it, all in Russian. It has the blessing you want written out and, most important, it states the proper times for candle lighting.'

"My neighbor shook her head. 'Please don't trouble yourself. All I really wanted was the blessing.'

"Gently, I stressed the importance of lighting at the correct time, explaining the transgression involved in striking a match once Shabbos has come in. I repeated my desire to give her the calendar.

"'It's unnecessary,' she insisted with a hint of discomfort.

"'But how will you know the correct time to light?'" I persisted.

"My neighbor seemed a bit intimidated, but confided nevertheless. 'I hope you will not consider it rude of me but, you see, my dining room window on the second floor overlooks your apartment. I admit that for a long time now I have noticed you lighting candles every Friday. I resolved that I, too, should light candles in honor of Shabbos. But I am not familiar with the proper blessing, so I decided to ask you to write it out for me. I don't need a calendar; I'll just look out my window and light when you do.'"

Rabbi Shneur Zalman and Chanie Trebnik prefaced their shlichus in Stuttgart, Germany, with a two-week preliminary visit to find out more about the location. They introduced themselves to the community leaders and met some local residents. During their visit, a community celebration was held in honor of Jerusalem Day (the day Jerusalem was reunited by Israeli forces in 1967). The Trebniks were invited to participate in the event, which was to be held in the afternoon. In the morning, the couple decided to walk about the city to start becoming acquainted with its neighborhoods.

That afternoon, they arrived at the ceremony and seated themselves at random. The elderly gentleman sitting next to

Rabbi Trebnik introduced himself as an entrepreneur from Cholon, Israel, who had business ties in Germany.

The Trebniks are also Israeli, and the two men quickly entered into conversation. But much to Rabbi Trebnik's consternation, the subject soon turned to the strife between observant and non-observant Jews in Israel.

Rabbi Trebnik tried to steer away from that highly charged subject.

"We've just met," he proposed in an agreeable tone, "We hardly know each other. Instead of discussing Israeli politics, let's talk about our lives."

"I'm totally unaffiliated," the man offered. "I know when Yom Kippur is, because everything is closed. And I can figure out when Pesach falls because there's no bread in the stores. But that's about as far as my connection to Judaism goes. If I didn't live in Israel, I would probably know even less."

The two men continued to converse a few minutes more. Shortly before the program began, the elder man took Rabbi Trebnik's hand and said, "My personal lifestyle is my own business. Please don't regard me as antagonistic. I'd actually like to share something else with you.

"You're probably assuming that we've just met, but I saw you this morning in town. I was walking slightly behind you and your wife. Not that I knew who you were, but your appearance is obviously that of observant Jews. I noticed two German men standing on the street. One of them pointed at you and said mockingly to the other, 'Look, the Jews of yesteryear are back in town....'

"At that moment, my heart swelled with pride. To me, your appearance here in Stuttgart symbolizes the Jewish response to the Holocaust, and the promise of Jewish survival fulfilled. It's uplifting that observant Jews proudly walk the streets of

Stuttgart today. I was so moved that had I had the nerve, I would have gone over and embraced you!"

*T*he two mothers sat on the park bench chatting as their brood played together. Leah Namdar, shluchah in Gothenburg Sweden, was spending an afternoon with Mrs. K., a visitor from Antwerp.

"Belgium isn't exactly a haven for Jews these days," Mrs. K. was saying, "but we live in a Jewish neighborhood and I'm not overly alarmed by the mounting anti-Semitism in Europe. Still, here in Sweden, in this very non-Jewish environment, I feel uneasy. As you see, I insist that my sons wear caps and tuck in their side curls so they don't look obviously Jewish. This lets me feel more relaxed. But your children are wearing *kipos*, and very noticeable ones too! Aren't you worried?"

"We're proud of our Jewish heritage, and this pride is something my husband, Alexander, and I want to transmit to our children," Leah explained. "Even small children who walk around as proud Jews strengthen Judaism here in Sweden, and that, after all, is our whole purpose of living here on shlichus. Let me share an incident with you.

"Every summer, hundreds of Chabad *yeshivah* students are sent to remote towns and villages worldwide, seeking out Jews and promoting Jewish awareness. At the end of one summer, two boys returned discouraged and downcast. They felt that, although they had traveled extensively and met many Jews, they had not had the kind of impact they were hoping for. They felt they had been ineffective and sent an account of their trip to the Rebbe in which they expressed their frustration.

"In a public address the following summer, the Rebbe referred to that note and reported that some time earlier a letter had arrived from a woman who lived in one of the places those boys had visited. The two had not made personal contact with her, but she had seen them from afar, and the mere sight of them had struck a deep chord within her. Their appearance had reminded her of her own identity. She felt a need to express this spiritual stirring and uttered the only Hebrew words she knew – the *Shema* prayer. Later on, she inquired who the boys were, obtained the address of the organization that sent them, and wrote a letter of gratitude."

The two women continued talking for a while and then called their children. "We're moving on to the petting zoo," they announced. Seven excited little boys and girls came running. As the bouncy group made their way up the path together, a young woman suddenly approached Leah, who was holding one of her boys' hands, and began speaking.

"You must be Leah Namdar!" she said.

The two women were speechless as the stranger continued.

"My name is Lisa. I'm originally from South Africa and I'm Jewish. While I was growing up, my family was not religious, but my parents have recently become observant. I visit Sweden regularly; my friend is Swedish and I might settle here one day. My mother knows Mrs. Yona Lazarus of Chabad in Capetown, and she got your number from her. She sent it to me and has been nagging me to contact you.

"I basically told her that it wasn't going to happen; no way was I was going to call up a rabbi's wife, introduce myself, and say I wanted to meet her. I just don't do that kind of thing. But I told her I wouldn't mind making contact if I happened to bump into you sometime. The likelihood of such a thing happening in this big city was so slim that I assumed it would never happen. But then I find myself in this park, and here you are!"

Leah smiled warmly. "Pleased to meet you, Lisa," she said cheerfully. "But tell me, how did you know who I am?"

Lisa pointed to the *kipos* on the boys' heads. "Who else would have children wearing these here in Gothenburg?!"

Rabbi Mendy and Chaya Harlig were walking home with their children from Chabad House in Henderson, Nevada, after services on Pesach morning. As they were crossing a street, they greeted a fellow crossing in the other direction, wished him good morning, and asked if he were Jewish.

"Well, yes," he replied, "but many years ago I married a devout Christian and have been following her religion. Unfortunately, she has passed away."

After a few more minutes of conversation, Mrs. Harlig invited the man, Bernie Lester, to drop into Chabad House in honor of the holiday.

"Me? Go into a synagogue?" Mr. Lester objected. "I haven't stepped foot in a synagogue for the past forty years! I wouldn't even know what to do in there."

Mrs. Harlig assured him that there was no need for extensive knowledge or intense preparation; he was welcome to come to Chabad House any time.

Mr. Lester did not respond to the invitation, but their street meeting did mark the beginning of an acquaintance. The Harligs began sending him Shabbos packages and holiday greetings. He accepted the gestures, such as the tasty *shalach manos* for Purim, with gratitude but did not come to the synagogue.

The following year, as the High Holy days approached, the Harligs again encouraged Mr. Lester to attend services.

"Forty years is a long time," they insisted.

Eventually, he agreed. "But don't expect me to do anything, because I just don't have a clue."

Bernie spent that Rosh Hashanah wrapped in a *tallis* immersed in prayer. The longer he stayed, the more the tunes and prayers came back to him.

Later, he asked Mrs. Harlig what had compelled her to stop him in the street at their initial meeting.

"It was my four-year-old daughter, Chanah Sarah," admitted Mrs. Harlig. "When she spotted you, she tugged my arm and said 'Mommy, there's a Jewish man. Let's wish him a happy holiday.' I wasn't sure, but you know how little children are…"

"*I* wasn't the religious type," Carol Posner relates. "I had nothing to do with synagogue or religious practices of any sort. Except of course on Yom Kippur. Once a year, I would hear the cantor recite the *Kol Nidrei* prayer. I enjoyed the singing and all, but that was it. I would leave, feeling satisfied that I had fulfilled my obligations.

"One Yom Kippur, after the evening services at the Seabreeze Jewish Center in Brighton Beach, I got ready to leave. As I walked out, little eight-year-old Chanah Winner said sweetly to me, 'Have an easy fast!'

"I smiled at the innocent child. Inside, though, something stirred. I usually fast on Yom Kippur, but I was feeling a bit queasy and hadn't planned to complete the fast that year. But the child's gentle words replayed in my mind, and the more I thought about it, the more certain I became that it was only right that I fast. And so I did. The next morning, feeling rather spiritual, I came to the synagogue early, stayed the entire day, and fasted until the end. I was gratified and felt that child's friendly wish had empowered me to make the commitment."

hether or not the multitudes that tour Surfers' Paradise in Queensland, Australia find the nirvana they are looking for is a matter of opinion. But many can vouch that they found genuine warmth and calm in a place they were not necessarily looking – the home of Rabbi Moshe and Bluma Serebryanski.

"It's common for us to host forty to fifty tourists on Friday night," says Rabbi Serebryanski. "During the meal I often raise a cup of wine, say a hearty '*l'chayim*' and wish my guests blessings of goodness and success. One Friday night, I raised my cup in the direction of a young woman from Brazil who had been coming by, on and off, for a while."

"I hadn't singled her out in particular, but my eyes happened to turn to her. '*L'chayim!*' I wished her enthusiastically, 'You should have a beautiful future!' My blessing wasn't deliberately chosen; the words just came of themselves."

Some time later, the young woman, Natasha, confided in him.

"Rabbi, you don't know what an effect your blessing has had on me," she said. "I had been having a really terrible time for weeks now. Everything was going wrong in my life. Your blessing gave me such a positive lift. I felt I could pull myself together again. But how could you have known what was going on inside me?"

e must have been quite a curiosity to the locals as we walked the streets of Madrid," admits Shifra, who is on shlichus in Spain with her husband

Rabbi Yitzchak Goldstein. "But then again, that's precisely why we were there, trying to encourage Jews in Spain to be openly comfortable with their Judaism. Our message is evidently not lost on the non-Jewish population as well.

"Once, as we were strolling down the avenue with our children, an elderly Spanish gentleman stopped us. He pointed to the *kipah* on the toddler in the carriage. 'Just look at you Jews! In our religion, we have to devote years of study to earn the honor of wearing a head covering. But you Jews? Even a baby in a carriage wears one.'

"Of course, it is the Jewish population that we are striving to attract, but the sad history of Spanish Jewry, with the forced conversion of the Marranos, has created a situation in which Jews are not always identifiable.

"I was cycling down the street one day and stopped at a red light," relates Rabbi Goldstein. "A man who looked like a typical Spanish *senor* turned to me from the curb and said, "If you are what I think you are, then – Shalom, *hermano* (brother)! Before I had a chance to respond, he had walked away."

"This almost mystical notion about Jewish origins has led many a guest in our home to explore his or her roots. Miriam (Maria) is a local Spanish girl who was on the road to conversion. Scheduled to stay with us on Pesach, she arrived some time before the onset of the holiday, when all our household members were busy preparing for the *Seder*. Some of our other guests, American students, watched, a bit puzzled, as we inspected the lettuce, holding it up against the light.

"What are you looking for?" they asked.

Maria looked at them in surprise. "For bugs, of course!" she announced. "We always check our lettuce for bugs. Everyone does."

The students were not convinced. "Never heard of such a thing," they retorted.

Maria insisted that this was normal practice at her home. Soon enough, she discovered that some of her family's practices were not as normative as she had thought. It was this simple kitchen procedure at Chabad House that led her to uncover the Jewish roots in her family – a family that had always presented itself as staunch Christians, while retaining many vestiges of Jewish customs.

"We have hosted many foreign students who have shared experiences with us similar to Maria's. One of those students was Steve, who told us about a visit to acquaintances in Valencia. On a Friday afternoon, they were chatting in the living room when suddenly all the family members rose. Some walked toward the paintings on the walls that depicted religious themes. Turning the hangings around, they then headed toward the basement. Steve looked on, bewildered. He was invited to join them.

At the bottom of the staircase, they entered a large, clean room, which was empty but for a table bedecked with a white cloth and candles. The mother lit the candles and everyone marched back up the stairs, turned the wall hangings back around, and resumed the conversation.

Curious, Steve inquired about this strange procedure.

"Oh, that's just an old family custom we have on Fridays at sunset," was the indifferent reply. They could not explain the origin of the custom.

But Steve could not remain indifferent, because he knew the reason for that family's actions. He had just witnessed a telling remnant of Jewish life in Spain. He contrasted that experience with the openly joyous Shabbos he was used to at Chabad House and appreciated the opportunity to express his own Jewishness by experiencing a real Shabbos in modern Madrid.

"We often don't realize how far-reaching simple gestures, or just being there, can be," says Rabbi Benyamin Karniel, who is on shlichus with his wife, Chani, in Gedera, Israel. "Time and time again, I am moved by people for whom practical Judaism is a foreign concept, yet who are somehow affected by the way we live.

"One of our upstairs neighbors is a fellow who had a pronounced animosity to religious practice. He was so biased that when I asked for his signature on a form that had to be signed by all the building's residents, he grumbled, 'Why do you compel me to sign a piece of paper that has the words "with G-d's help" in the top corner?'

"But then, one day, he came knocking on our door and asked for a *mezuzah*. 'You're probably wondering why a non-believer like me would want to get a *mezuzah*,' he said wryly, but grew serious as he related the following incident.

"'I was on the highway, and to my horror I saw an eighteen-wheeler in my rear-view mirror roaring up behind me. It seemed oblivious to my presence on the road.

"'In the split second before my car was squashed, I called out to G-d and pleaded for my life. I knew I had no business turning to Him, because I habitually go out of my way to ignore His existence. So I prayed for salvation in the merit of my righteous neighbors, yourselves. As you can see, my prayers were answered. I firmly believe that it was your good deeds that enabled me to crawl out of the wreck without a scratch.'

"On another occasion, a neighbor who lives downstairs

from us remarked: 'You wouldn't know it, but thanks to you we make *kiddush* every Friday night.'

"'What do you mean?' asked my wife.

"'Well, you sent us a very nice Purim basket, remember?' the neighbor replied. 'One of the things in it was an attractive wine flask. It was so striking that we decided to keep it on the dining room table. One Friday evening, our younger daughter suddenly said, "Let's make *kiddush* like grandpa does. Here, there's already wine on the table." Well, we did, and we've continued to do so every week.'

"I was most moved by the initiative taken by Ben Shochat and his friends. Ben was about sixteen when he and a few friends started dropping by the Chabad House. They may have come for the joy, the food, the classes, the warmth, the authenticity, or all of the above. But come they did, especially on Simchas Torah.

"It's customary to hold a chassidic gathering before dancing with the Torah, and this was done in true holiday spirit. I turned to the participants and announced: 'Since this is a day of celebrating with the Torah, each of you is encouraged to take upon yourselves a resolution promoting more Torah observance.'

"One after the other, the participants shared their resolutions.

"'And what will you take on?' I asked when it was Ben's turn. Ben was ready.

"'Starting this Friday, I will man a *tefillin* booth at the market place in the center of town,' he announced.

"I was taken aback. It was only a short time ago that Ben had been called up to the Torah for the first time in his life. He had no notion what a serious commitment he was proposing to take on. From the sidelines it may seem like a 'cool' thing to do, but few people know how difficult and frustrating it can be. Maybe Ben should have been encouraged to think of something more realistic, but I didn't want to burst his bubble. I nodded and moved on to Ben's friend, Shachar Reitzer.

"'I'll join Ben at the *tefillin* booth,' Shachar announced promptly.

"On Friday, I passed through the center of town on my way home, and there they were! Ben and Shachar, in T-shirts and jeans, were helping two Jews put on *tefillin*. And they kept at it, week after week.

"But it didn't end there. Shachar's older brother, Eyal, wasn't pleased with Shachar's growing involvement with Judaism. He would come to Chabad House every so often to challenge what he considered my 'brainwashing' attempts.

"In time, Shachar decided to pursue Torah study in an out-of-town *yeshivah*, but he felt guilty about abandoning his post at the *tefillin* booth.

"'Eyal, brother, do me a favor,' he pleaded. 'I made a commitment, and it's not right to leave Ben there by himself. You don't have to do anything if you don't want to; just stand there with him at the booth.'

"'I have my own views, but I'll do you the favor,' Eyal returned. 'I'm not prepared to be a hypocrite, though. Before I start, I guess I should put *tefillin* on myself.'

"Today, Ben, Shachar and Eyal all lead a Torah lifestyle."

> *The Rebbe Maharash, the fourth Lubavitcher Rebbe, once said:"People usually say that when encountering an obstacle, at first try to squeeze under. If one can't squeeze under, attempt to climb over. And I say: The first option should be to climb over."*

Our Rebbe translated this statement into a charge for action, urging his followers never to hesitate in their mission. For the recognition of difficulty is a self-fulfilling prophecy. When, by contrast, a person unflinchingly dedicates himself to a purpose, motivated by the knowledge that he is based on a rock-bed of truth, he will often be amazed at the serendipity that enables that goal to be achieved.

"What did you say you wanted?" the pet shop owner asked, his eyebrows rising. "Two goldfish?! Male and female?!"

On a regular day, he would have taken it all in stride and proceeded with the sale. But this was no regular day. Hurricane Jeanne had suddenly changed course and was heading toward southern and central Florida. The wind was already strong and the sky was darkening. There was talk of evacuation. People were hurrying about purchasing water, batteries, provisions and gas. The pet shop owner was trying to devise a plan in case his store stood in the hurricane's path. And this customer was looking for goldfish?!

The customer, though, was no ordinary pet lover. He was Rabbi Zvi Konikov, who is on shlichus with his wife Shulamit in Satellite Beach, Florida. And the day was far from ordinary for other reasons as well. Perhaps Hurricane Jeanne should have consulted the Jewish calendar before making her arrival. It was the day before Yom Kippur and, Jeanne or no Jeanne, a Jew must do *kaporos*.[24]

This custom is usually performed with a chicken, but with no chickens readily available, Rabbi Konikov decided to follow the halachic opinion that, in a pressing situation, any kosher living creature can be used. Well, goldfish are kosher, and they were the creatures most readily available. Hence his trip to the pet store.

After carrying out the custom, Rabbi Konikov then made his way to a river to put the fish back into water. People were scurrying all around, securing their boats and yachts, but Rabbi Konikov was concerned about securing something else: a *minyan* for the holiest day of the year. It looked as if much of the island's population was being evacuated, and he just hoped things would work out somehow.

They did...sort of. Although many people had left, over one hundred gathered to attend the Chabad House services. Given the circumstances, *Kol Nidrei* (the prayers that usher in Yom Kippur in the evening) and the morning prayers were moving and heartfelt. But that afternoon the police announced they were closing the causeway connecting the island of Satellite Beach to the mainland.

Only nine men remained in the synagogue for the afternoon *minchah* services. The congregants were distressed. They all clearly recognized that the situation was beyond their control. Still, it was hard to accept that for the first time in fifteen years it looked as if there would not be a *minyan* for the highlight of the Yom Kippur prayers, the *Neilah* service.

When the Temple was standing in Jerusalem, the High Priest would enter the Holy of Holies on Yom Kippur. There he would stand alone, facing the Divine Presence. This experience is recreated in microcosm during the *Neilah* service, for *Neilah* means "locking." At that time, the gates of Heaven close, and every Jew is "locked in" with G-d. For this special prayer, everyone wanted a *minyan*.

---

24. See *Shulchan Aruch, Orach Chayim*, sec. 605, where this custom is described.

But who would come? Rabbi Konikov refused to give up. He knew there were people who would not evacuate, choosing instead to stay home and ride out the storm. But who were they, and were they within walking distance? He suddenly thought of Arthur. Arthur lived about a mile and a half away and did not frequent the synagogue. But the congregants were desperate. Trying not to deliberate too long, lest the raging wind and rain might change his mind, Rabbi Konikov set out.

"I was literally blown that mile and a half," he recalls. "Though the hurricane was still six hours away, storm winds were raging. Many roofs had already blown off and fallen electric lines snaked dangerously up and down the roads. Police cars, their sirens wailing, kept stopping to give me a lift, but I howled above the winds that I was fine. I must have been quite a sopping, pathetic sight when I arrived at Arthur's place."

Arthur's wife, beside herself with astonishment, ushered Rabbi Konikov into the house. In the background, the television blared with warnings of impending danger. Hurriedly, Rabbi Konikov explained the situation.

Arthur's response vacillated between shock and annoyance. "Have you lost your senses, Rabbi? No one should go out in that storm! Come on, G-d will surely understand."

While Arthur adamantly refused, his wife looked on thoughtfully.

"Arthur," she said softly, "this is the holiest day of the year. You've been presented with a unique opportunity to do something that is beyond all reason. Your father would have been very pleased to know that you enabled services to be held on Yom Kippur."

Arthur sighed. "It's hypocritical," he said quietly, "I've just eaten dinner."

"Every moment and deed has its own worth," Rabbi Konikov encouraged him.

After a long moment of silence, Arthur consented, "Okay. Count me in, I'll be there."

The outpouring of prayer inside the only synagogue with a *minyan* was a match to the downpour outside. And the vitality of the joyous singing at the close of the day contrasted sharply with the powerless city.

At eleven o'clock that night Hurricane Jeanne hit with full force.

Of all the people who had attended the *minyan*, only Arthur's house had its roof blown off. No one was hurt.

The rabbi expressed his empathy wholeheartedly. In an attempt to take the sting out of the situation he added with a smile, "You're the first Jew in Florida to have his sukkah up already!"

Arthur grinned.

Everyone loves Teddy, a big man with a big heart, whose outgoing personality and generosity endear him to others. So when Teddy first encountered Rabbi Chaim and Charna Mentz, of Bel Air, California, they naturally struck up a friendship. Teddy enjoyed the lively spirit at Chabad House, and he and his wife Michelle became frequent attendees at Chabad functions.

One Thursday, on a trip with his three young daughters to the East Coast, Teddy phoned Rabbi Mentz from his limousine.

"Hey, Rabbi, you're not going to believe where I'm coming from. I just visited the Rebbe's gravesite in Long Island. You're always talking about him, so I decided that, as long as I was in the area I would take my kids and say a prayer at his grave."

Teddy was right. True, he frequented the Chabad House and readily supported its activities, but his own involvement in Jewish practice was minimal, and Rabbi Mentz could hardly believe that a visit to the Rebbe's gravesite had been on his agenda.

"I asked for a blessing for health and prosperity," Teddy continued, "so that I may continue to support all the good work you and the others are doing. It was really an uplifting experience."

Rabbi Mentz was not going to let this opportunity go by without linking it to a positive step toward spiritual growth.

"Good move, Teddy!" Rabbi Mentz responded. "You know, we've often spoken about the need to transform an inspiring moment into tangible practice. How about connecting the feeling to a *mitzvah*?"

"You're right, Rabbi, I guess it's time. So why don't you order a pair of those black boxes for me? You'll teach me how to put them on when I get back home."

The *tefillin* were ordered immediately.

That Saturday night, Teddy's wife Michelle called, frantic.

"Rabbi, Teddy's in the hospital."

"Hospital?! I just spoke with him the other day. He sounded so vigorous. What happened?"

"The doctors don't know. He's really sick. Please pray for him."

On Sunday morning, Rabbi Mentz went to the hospital. Teddy's room was full of family members and friends. Rabbi Mentz went straight to the bed where Teddy was lying, looking pale and weak.

"It's my leg, Rabbi," he mumbled. "Here, take a look."

Teddy's leg was covered with a large red blotch that looked as if it were consuming the skin. Someone in the room said, "It's a staph infection; it came from a small cut that got infected."

Rabbi Mentz did not intend to continue discussing the ailment. He pulled a velvet bag out of the case he was carrying and said gently: "Come, Teddy, let's put on *tefillin.*"

"My new pair?" Teddy's eyes lit up.

"No, yours should arrive tomorrow. Meanwhile, you can use mine."

Teddy put the *tefillin* on, and after him, all the men present in the hospital room did so as well.

On his way out after the visit, Michelle introduced Rabbi Mentz to the chief physician in residence, one of Teddy's childhood friends, Dr. Michael Chaiken.

"Not good news," the doctor said grimly. "It's a fairly rare condition, and the last few people who had this disease in the States didn't make it."

On Monday, Teddy's condition worsened. The infection had spread, and he was given strong medication, which caused him to drift in and out of consciousness.

When Rabbi Mentz came to visit on Tuesday, Teddy had been sleeping the entire day. He stayed at the bedside anyway, hoping for a conscious moment so that he could put on the new pair of *tefillin*. But nothing had changed by evening, and Rabbi Mentz had to leave to give a class.

In the middle of the class, Michelle called, emotionally spent.

"Rabbi, this is it. You really have to pray now. All of the top doctors from S. Joseph, Kaiser and Sinai Hospitals are here to study Teddy's case. They may learn something about treating others, but they say it's too late for Teddy."

When Rabbi Mentz came to the hospital Wednesday morning, Teddy was no longer in his room.

"He's been transferred to the intensive care unit," a nurse informed him. "Nobody but his wife can go in."

Michelle, who was at the entrance to the i.c.u., looked desperate.

"You must have faith," Rabbi Mentz said to her earnestly. "Your husband has always been a robust, healthy man. It's uncanny. A perfectly healthy man goes to the Rebbe's gravesite, asks for a blessing for health, commits himself to put on *tefillin*, and gets sick?! Stay positive and have trust. G-d will not forsake a man who has just taken a major step in His direction."

On Thursday sixty people, including family, friends, the rabbi, and members of the Reform Temple with which the family was associated were assembled in a room adjoining the i.c.u. The atmosphere was somber when Rabbi Mentz arrived. Dr. Chaiken hastily approached him.

"Go on in and see him," he said, instructing the attendant to let Rabbi Mentz in. 'You're the only positive person around here."

Dr. Chaiken accompanied the rabbi into the isolation room. He lifted the bed sheet slightly, exposing a terrible sight. The infection had spread mercilessly. "It will enter his lungs in ten to twelve hours," he said sadly. "We've done all we can."

"But Dr. Michael," Rabbi Mentz said softly, "there is something else you can do. You can put on *tefillin*." The doctor had been the only one who had adamantly refused to do so throughout the ordeal.

"Rabbi, I'm a non-believer."

"Perhaps you will do it for the sake of Teddy's recovery?"

"Look, Rabbi. I do my thing for him and you do yours. If you want to stay here and pray, I'll make sure the attendant doesn't interfere."

Rabbi Mentz stayed in the room and recited Psalms. When he came out into the lobby where the others were assembled, he heard the Reform rabbi consoling the teary-eyed crowd, explaining that death is an inevitable part of life. Rabbi Mentz felt a need to distance himself from all the gloom and anxiety, and told Michelle that he would be back soon.

Once out of the hospital, Rabbi Mentz struggled for some clarity. "What is this?" he thought. "I can't allow all this negativity to continue! We have heard numerous times from the Rebbe that doctors are given permission to heal, not to depress. That positive thinking is powerful and can bring about positive results, that a person who makes a commitment to take a step toward Jewish practice will have great merit, that joy breaks through all barriers. This is it. I am a chassid and I have options. I will make a conscious decision to break through this barrier with positivity and joy. I'd better get to it right away, before I lose my nerve."

A short while later, Rabbi Mentz and eighteen boys from the *Yeshivah* Ohr Elchonon Chabad packed themselves into a van. As they filed into the dread-filled room, the depression was tangible.

Rabbi Mentz pulled out a *tzedakah* box and passed it around.

"My dear friends, I would like to propose an alternative to this negative atmosphere. No more helplessness. We must do something. Let's give charity, which our sages say can avert calamity. Let's muster up inner strength and generate positive energy in Teddy's direction, and focus on recuperation and health. Let's heal ourselves of our own negativity, and we may have an impact upon Teddy's condition as well. Let's think good thoughts of miraculous outcomes and joyful thanksgiving. I will go into Teddy's room with these *yeshivah* boys and pray, and you do your part in positive thinking."

Somehow, the boys managed to bypass the hospital staff and squeeze into the tiny room. Rabbi Mentz fervently led them in prayer and Psalms. Then he spoke to the boys in earnest. "We are chassidim. We have values and axioms that govern our lives. We are taught never to give up hope, and to use positive energy and joy to overcome hurdles. Well, this man needs life, and we'll use all our strength to do what we've been taught, to generate life force and direct it toward him. Not in theory, but for real. Joy penetrates barriers, and we want to break through those barriers. So join me in song and joy. Right here, right now."

The boys sang – hesitantly at first, and then strongly enough to bring a nurse running.

"What in heaven's name is going on here?!" she bellowed.

"It's o.k.," came the reply. "It is indeed in heaven's name."

Rabbi Mentz gestured to the boys to follow him down the hospital corridor, still singing. The astonished staff looked on in amazement as the strange procession returned to the room with the assembled crowd.

Rabbi Mentz addressed the people. "Do you believe in miracles?"

Many nodded.

"Then why must we wait until we see them? Let's celebrate Teddy's recovery now!"

The rabbi's words fell upon ready ears. The men joined hands and danced as the women clapped. Then Rabbi Mentz led them in prayers and Psalms and shared a Torah thought.

"We have adhered to the directives of our sages," he concluded. "Certainly our efforts will bear fruit. May I suggest that we all go home with hopeful hearts and uplifted spirits, and may we meet again tomorrow to share good news."

He bid everyone a good night and dropped off the boys. Then Rabbi Mentz voiced a silent prayer. "Please G-d, Torah teaches us to live with simple faith and have trust and joy. I have tried to do all I can. I have put Your Name and the Rebbe's teachings on the line. Please answer our prayers."

When he came home, Mrs. Mentz was busy in the kitchen, cooking up a storm. In response to her husband's quizzical look, she said matter-of-factly: "Tomorrow is Friday. All those people at the hospital keeping vigil have to eat on Shabbos."

At 11:00 Friday morning, Rabbi Mentz and his daughter drove to the hospital, laden with trays of food. They went straight to the familiar room next to the i.c.u. It was empty. They weren't sure what to think. Then Rabbi Mentz spotted Dr. Michael down the corridor and hastened toward him.

"How's Teddy?" he asked anxiously.

"Before you ask me, I have a question for you," snapped Dr. Michael. "I know that rabbis make use of all kinds of kabbalistic formulas. What did you do here last night?"

Rabbi Mentz shook his head. "Nothing of the sort. I just tried to generate positive energy to affect a morbid situation."

"Don't play games with me," the doctor retorted. "Teddy's condition took an unexpected turn and his body is fighting the infection. It looks like he's going to make it!"

"Is this a miracle?" inquired Rabbi Mentz.

"Yes! For the moment, at least, I must admit there is a supernatural force up there and it's not modern medicine. A sheer miracle."

Rabbi Mentz smiled. "Miraculous enough for you to put on *tefillin*?"

The doctor paused before nodding. The change of roles was poignant. Now it was the doctor that rolled up his sleeve, and it wasn't for an injection.

Teddy remained in the hospital for two more weeks and was finally able to don his own pair of *tefillin*. What's more, five of the friends and relatives who had been together throughout the ordeal purchased *tefillin* and committed themselves to putting them on daily.

Time: The day after Yom Kippur, in the first year of the Kantor family's shlichus

Place: Bangkok, Thailand

Problem: The four species required for Sukkos, which could not be shipped directly to Bangkok due to customs regulations, had been sent to Hong Kong instead. The package arrived there only that day, and the Kantors know of no one planning to travel from Hong Kong to Bangkok who could bring them the package.

Solution: One of the community members returning from a trip to Israel would bring a few sets of the four species with him.

Time: The day before Sukkos

Problem: The community member informs Rabbi Kantor that he did not bring *aravos*, the willow branches, as they would have wilted on the way.

Solution: Find a way to get the set from Hong Kong after all.

Problem: Who would know how?

Solution: Mr. Abi Kashani, a friend of Chabad, is a gem dealer with business connections in Hong Kong. He would find a Chinese acquaintance to bring the packet.

Problem: How do you describe to a Chinese gentile what he's being asked to carry on the plane?

Solution: Plant needed urgently for herbal health treatment.

Time: 10:00 a.m. morning before onset of holiday. The Chinese gentleman arrives.

Problem: Rabbi Kantor is informed that the delivery of *aravos* to the airport in Hong Kong had not gone as planned; they were not brought.

Solution: Mr. Kashani promises to find an Indian in Hong Kong with a valid visa to enter Thailand. That individual will be paid to make the trip, scheduled to arrive in the early afternoon.

Time: Noon before onset of holiday.

Problem: The hired man from Hong Kong has a car accident on the way to the airport and misses his flight.

Solution: The man is instructed to get on the next flight – scheduled to arrive an hour before the holiday begins – at all costs.

Time: Always!!!

Problem: Heavy traffic on all Bangkok roads

Solution: The man is instructed to take a motorcycle taxi in order to bypass traffic.

Time: Afternoon, *minchah* services at onset of holiday

Problem: Rabbi Kantor has to leave for the synagogue to lead the prayers.
Solution: Mr. Kashani agrees to stay in the office and wait for the *aravos*.

Time: Evening of the festival of Sukkos, time for *maariv* services
Problem: Mr. Kashani arrives at shul without the *aravos*. The congregants were not aware that the royal procession of the king of Thailand was holding up all traffic in the city.
Solution: Abide by the directive "…and you shall be joyous on your festivals."

> The package finally arrives later that night.

Time: Sukkos morning
Problem: The *aravos* appeared all dried out.
Solution: Close inspection and intense examination of the details of the law lead to the conclusion that two of the ten wilted branches could be considered acceptable. All the members of the synagogue fulfill the mitzvah of the four species on this one set.

> Those *aravos* alone had cost $1,800 and much worry. The blessing of *shehechiyanu*, which expresses our thanks to G-d for enabling us to perform His commandments, is said with immense gratitude indeed.

Time: After the prayers – Rabbi's sermon
Problem: What can be learned from the entire adventure?
Solution: The four species symbolize the various levels of Jewish observance and Torah study. The *aravos*, plants with no smell or taste, symbolize the Jew who has not yet

had an opportunity to learn and practice. Every Jew, in particular those who are likened to the *aravos*, is valued and cherished. Regardless of the effot necessary, we must reach out to all.

*E*verything was ready and Rabbi Shabsi and Esther Alpern, shluchim in Sao Paulo, Brazil, anticipated the next step of the project with zeal. It was shortly after the Rebbe had requested that the *Tanya*, the basic book of Chabad chassidic philosophy, be printed in as many locations around the world as possible. The newly published editions of the *Tanya* were to be studied with local Jews straight from the pages that rolled out of the press. This would exemplify the concept of spreading the wellsprings of chassidic teachings worldwide.

Rabbi Alpern immediately got to work. He would see to it that the Jews in far flung towns across Brazil would be given the opportunity to be part of this unique endeavor. To that end, he equipped two vans with a mobile printing press, an accompanying technician, a group of *yeshivah* students and cases of kosher food. The vans would travel cross-country, seeking small towns and cities whose Jewish inhabitants are seldom contacted.

One hundred locations were on the itinerary. Why 100? As soon as Rabbi Alpern had heard of the Rebbe's request to print the *Tanya* worldwide, he traveled to New York to tell the Rebbe of his plans to fulfill that directive.

That Shabbos, the Rebbe held an unexpected *farbrengen*. The Rebbe announced that one of the reasons for the gathering was the pleasure he had derived from Rabbi Alpern's resolution.

During the break of singing between talks, the Rebbe inquired about the number of places in which he was planning to print.

"Eighty-three," Rabbi Alpern replied, as the number corresponded with the Rebbe's age.

"No one will object if you add more locations," the Rebbe said smiling.

Rabbi Alpern upped the number to one hundred. After Shabbos, the Rebbe's secretary handed Rabbi Alpern two thousand dollars from a special fund set up by the previous Rebbe to supplement the printing expenses.

Now, Rabbi Alpern watched with satisfaction as the vans embarked on their long journey.

Thirty-three days later, after successful logistic organization and much dedication, the *Tanya* was printed in one hundred locations in Brazil. At each stop, the van became a central attraction for the local Jews, and they were invited to a study session culminating with a joyous *l'chayim*. The printed material was sent to Sao Paulo to be bound, and in time Rabbi Alpern took a special case of one hundred *Tanyas*, with the location in which each had been published imprinted on the cover, to the Rebbe.

Soon thereafter, Rabbi Alpern was traveling back to Brazil from a trip overseas. As the plane neared its destination, he contemplated with gratitude the pleasure the Rebbe had derived from his efforts.

Suddenly an announcement was made that the plane would be landing in a different airport, a two-hour drive from Sao Paulo.

"It was strange," Rabbi Alpern relates. "I had been living in Brazil for over twenty years, traveled extensively, and have never landed at this airport. As all is Divine Providence, I sensed there must be some reason for this unexpected extended journey. But what was it?"

After he collected his luggage, he set his mind to seeking a means of transportation home. Suddenly, he spotted a familiar face. It was George Fisher, a congregant at the Chabad synagogue in Sao Paulo.

"Hello, Rabbi," George called out, "can I offer you a ride?"

"Thank you, yes!" Rabbi Alpern responded most gratefully.

The long drive afforded the two men a pleasant chat.

"You'd probably appreciate hearing this, Rabbi," George commented at one point. "You're always eager to hear about Jewish people. Well, recently I met a very interesting fellow. His name is Roy. He's originally from Israel but he lives in Sao Paulo and is one of the engineers who built the Brazilian Scientific Base in Antarctica."

George was going on about his new acquaintance, but Rabbi Alpern's mind had shifted gears. "Antarctica?" he mused to himself. "A Jew who has connections to Antarctica? And just now, on this unexpected leg of my journey, I've learned of his existence. There must be a reason."

Recalling his earlier thoughts, he concluded that it must be about the *Tanya*. "Why has this information been presented to me right now? I'm going to try to have a *Tanya* printed in Antarctica! After all, I've just been told about a Jew who works there and I've been given his name and number."

Rabbi Alpern called Roy, and they arranged to meet the following day. At first, Roy had no idea what Rabbi Alpern wanted. Patiently, Rabbi Alpern explained about Chabad, the Rebbe, his shluchim and the book of *Tanya*. Soon Roy had a clearer picture of the rabbi's intention and said that, in principle, he was willing to help. Practically speaking, though, it wouldn't be so simple.

"Nothing about printing *Tanyas* worldwide is simple," smiled Rabbi Alpern. "Tell me what it entails."

"Well," replied Roy, "first of all, I don't exactly live in Antarctica. I travel there periodically to work at the base. Every two to three months a ship laden with supplies sets out southward."

"Good," said the rabbi. "Just tell me what port it leaves from and I'll deliver the original films and printing paper. I am also giving you this *kipah*. When the printing is done, call me and we'll study a portion of the book from the freshly printed pages. On the next ship back, send the box of prints and we'll bind them here."

"Rabbi, you may not realize this, but equipment at the base in Antarctica is very minimal. A printing press is just not on the lists of provisions!"

Rabbi Alpern was not deterred. "No problem! I have two mobile printing presses. I'll pack one to be delivered to the ship."

Roy shook his head.

"Every inch on the ship is taken up with necessary equipment: food, clothing, scientific apparatus, tools and machinery. I can't see any of the officials making allowance for a printing press!"

Rabbi Alpern decided to try a different approach. "Look, everyone knows that Antarctica is not the most stimulating of environments, even for scientists! Why don't you suggest to your supervisors that a mobile press would enable the employees to produce their own publications; I'll donate this press to the base. That could serve to enhance their extended stay at the base and reduce boredom."

It all sounded a little far-fetched, but Roy came around to agreeing with the rabbi, especially on the boredom issue. Surprisingly, his supervisors also acknowledged the possible benefits and proved to be quite enthusiastic about the initiative. And so a government-approved mobile printing press and films of *Tanya* made their way to Antarctica.

One night, at 3 a.m. Brazilian time, the telephone rang in the Alpern home.

"*Shalom*, Rabbi, it's Roy. I've got the *kipah* on my head and I'm ready. Which chapter are we going to be reading from?"

A few weeks later, shortly before Purim, an official government vehicle delivered a case of printed papers to Rabbi Alpern's office. The Antarctica *Tanyas* were bound and one was sent straight away to the Rebbe.

"It's *shalach manos* for the Rebbe," Rabbi Alpern told Rabbi Groner, the Rebbe's secretary.

Directly after the *Megilah* reading, Rabbi Groner called Rabbi Alpern and conveyed the abundant blessings that the Rebbe had bestowed on him. "But the Rebbe commented on the inscription," Rabbi Groner added. "You wrote that the *Tanya* was printed in Antarctica, but to date there are fourteen bases there. You printed at only one base."

Rabbi Alpern had new stickers made up, stating the exact base, and covered the original inscription on all the books. He sent a revised copy to the Rebbe's office.

A few weeks later, the Alpern family arrived in New York where they would be spending Pesach. On the afternoon before the Seder night, Rabbi Alpern was called to the Rebbe's office.

The Rebbe greeted him with a broad smile. Among other things, he said, "It's very cold in Antarctica; you've warmed it up."

*T*he group that assembled that morning at the Alabama Jewish Federation offices included many lay members of the community. All were concerned about the importance of Jewish life and pride in Jewish identity. Many were anxiously seeking ways to infuse local youth with stronger connections to their roots.

"Last year's statistics describing synagogue membership, participation in Jewish Community Center programs, and turnout at holiday events showed a decline. And in spite of all our efforts, this year's statistics aren't much better," the chairman reported. "What are we going to do?" he asked emphatically.

There was silence as this troubling question lingered in the air. Then one of the participants, Frank Siegal, stood up. "We are discussing Jewish continuity. Let me tell you about Jewish continuity! Two years ago, Rabbi Yossi Friedman, from Chabad of Birmingham, phoned me. Some of you may know Rabbi Yossi and his wife Miriam, who work at Chabad. Well, he asked me if I would like to set up a 'lunch-and-learn' session with him at the office. You fellows know me. I enjoy a good lecture, and I was genuinely interested, but I'm a busy man and didn't want to make a commitment. Still, I'm a well-mannered guy, so I asked him to call me back in two weeks. It was a gentle way of letting him know how busy I am and giving him the brush off, you know....

"Two weeks later, Rabbi Friedman called again. Politely, he asked again about the 'lunch-and-learn' class. I thought he hadn't gotten the message the first time, so I again excused myself, pleading deadlines, and asking him to call in yet another two weeks. Sure enough, he called back again two weeks later. I guess some people just don't take no for an answer. I reckoned it would be easier to say 'yes' and see what it's all about than to continue shrugging him off without giving it a chance.

"Now, two years later, what started as a two-member class consists of twenty 'lunch-and-learners,' who continue to meet regularly. You tell me – if Rabbi Friedman's persistence is not a practical demonstration of Jewish continuity, what is?!"

> *No encounter happens by mere chance. Rabbi Yosef Yitzchak Schneerson once related:*[25] *"G-d's providence governs every minute creation. . . a fallen leaf that has been rolling around in someone's yard. . . or a bit of straw that someone used when thatching a roof some years ago. To move them from one place to another. . . a stormwind breaks out, shaking heaven and earth in the middle of a warm sunny day, thereby bringing to fulfillment the Divine Providence that governs this small stray leaf and old wisp of straw."*
>
> *If this is true with regard to the creation as a whole, it certainly applies with regard to mankind.*

*M*ost people who set out to open a new venture pack their bags with concrete assets: substantial seed money, a list of key contact people, potential team members, and the like. Such things would also be of great assistance to any shluchim opening a Chabad House, but Rabbi Yossi and Nechama Harlig of Kendall, Florida, maintain that the most valuable asset is a dose of Divine Providence.

"We made a trip down to Kendall to 'scout the land,'" Rabbi Harlig relates. "We drove around, getting a feel for the city and investigating its neighborhoods. At some point, we visited a realty business at random to get information about

---

25. *Likkutei Dibburim* (English Translation, Kehot), Vol. 1, p. 177–179.

housing. A helpful agent seated my wife (who was holding our six-month-old) and me at the desk, and we began discussing options.

"A man soon walked by us and, noticing our infant, commented, 'What a cute baby! I remember when my little boy was that age. I can see him in my mind's eye now when he was only eight days old and had his circumcision.'

"The man gave a soft pat to our baby and walked away. I immediately asked the agent who the man was. 'He's the owner of this business,' the agent replied.

"'I'd like to speak with him,' I requested.

"Soon we were seated in the owner's office. We introduced ourselves and explained that we were seeking to bring more Jewish awareness to Kendall.

"'Chabad?' the man, whose name was Carl, queried. 'I've never heard of Chabad Jews. Are you the ones who throw rocks at people who aren't observant? Or are you connected to those far-right racist Jews?'

"We assured Carl that Chabad was nothing of the sort, but he persisted with his questions.

"'I've never heard of it, but I have a son up in Delaware who mentioned that he's been studying with some rabbi. Maybe he knows.'

"He picked up the phone and called his son, asking him if he had heard of Chabad. 'Sure, Dad, I've been learning with a Rabbi Vogel, whom I met here, for a year now. He's Chabad and he's a great guy. They are good people, these Chabad fellows.'

"That was enough to make us legitimate in Carl's eyes. We now had a contact in the realty business, as well as a friend who was instrumental in helping us learn the ropes in Kendall.

"Three months later, I returned to Kendall to sign a lease on a house. We were offered three choices, all of which were in a neighborhood with many Jews. Each of the homes had its advantages, and none of them had clear superiority over the others. But I had to make a quick decision, sign papers and close the deal. So I just chose one without any definite rationale.

"The owner turned out to be David, an unaffiliated Jew, who told me he was delighted to have a rabbi renting his home. David couldn't understand why we were choosing to live here and not in Miami Beach, for example, which boasts a large Jewish community. I explained why we had come to Kendall. David was intrigued and offered to show me around town and be helpful in other ways. Later, I asked him to introduce us to his friends.

"Now we had a contact and access to a group of potential participants in our programs. Rosh HaShanah was approaching; we made a *minyan* in our home and twenty-five people who did not habitually attend services joined us. At some point I asked David if he had had a bar mitzvah. He shook his head. We organized and held the ceremony. At the event, David became very emotional and admitted to everyone present, 'A mere two months ago, if any of you would have told me that I would be celebrating my bar mitzvah in my own home with a rabbi, I would have scoffed at the notion.'

"David became one of Chabad's biggest supporters, and his wife, Tziporah, was instrumental in helping start the Chabad Hebrew School in Kendall."

*   *   *

"With G-d's help it was soon necessary to move our home-based synagogue to a larger place. There was only one shopping center within walking distance. It appeared to be an ideal location, and a storefront seemed to be available. I took down the number and called to inquire about the rent. I phoned a number of times but no one answered. At last I reached the owner.

"'I'm interested in renting your store,' I said. 'What are you asking?'

"'Very high,' was the curt reply. 'What kind of business do you have?'

"'Well, it's not exactly a business. I'm looking for a place to hold some gatherings and classes.'

"'What kind of gatherings?'

"'For Jewish people.'

"'Are you a rabbi? What group do you belong to?'

"'Chabad.'

"'Really? I'm associated with the Chabad community in North Miami. You know Rabbi Lipskar of Miami? He was the one who started me on my journey back to Judaism. Why don't you come by and we'll meet?'"

The owner, Ronny Emmano, proved to be very supportive and enabled the Harligs to operate Chabad out of that storefront under extremely generous terms.

"We once brought a leading American rabbi out to speak at one of our functions in The Jewish House," relates Rabbi Pinchos Woolstone, who is on shlichus in Sydney, Australia, with his wife, Aviva. "Afterwards, I kept in touch with him. We met again some time later, when I was on a trip to New York, and he invited me to participate in a *melaveh malkah*[26] at the home of a chassidic Rebbe who was a relative of his. I was introduced to the Rebbe and enjoyed an uplifting evening. It was a small gathering, and I was honored

---

26. A Saturday night festive gathering.

to be one of the guests but didn't expect anything more than this one-time experience. So it was a surprise to be informed that the Rebbe had asked to see me privately."

"I would appreciate your assistance," the Rebbe said, "in a pressing matter. A certain family has been struck with misfortune. Their daughter experienced great difficulty in her marriage, and after six months she disappeared. We have word that she is now in Australia, and I implore you to look for her."

"I'll do all I can to help, of course," replied Rabbi Woolstone, "but with all due respect, Australia is a huge continent. I don't imagine that a woman in hiding would be frequenting the local Jewish shops and social gatherings."

The Rebbe nodded. "You're right. I realize it's not a simple matter. But we will pray, you will search, and G-d will help."

Rabbi Woolstone was given details concerning the young woman and a photograph of her. He stuck the picture in his pocket diary, as it was Saturday night and he didn't have his briefcase with him.

Later, back in Australia and busy as usual, Rabbi Woolstone pondered how to begin the search. At some point, he was flying from Sydney to Melbourne for a family wedding. With the intent of using the one-hour flight to set up the schedule for his stay, he pulled out his diary. As he leafed through it, the picture fluttered out. He retrieved it and placed it in the crevice of the drink tray so it would be secure while he worked. He was immersed in his planning when the woman sitting next to him suddenly spoke up.

"Is this woman your relative?" she asked, pointing to the picture.

Rabbi Woolstone made a gesture that could have been interpreted as a 'yes.'

"But I haven't seen her for a while," he added quickly. "Why do you ask? Do you know her?"

"I own a small chain of clothing stores. This woman works in my store in Cairns, Queensland."

"Cairns!" Rabbi Woolstone thought to himself in disbelief. "That's a three-and-a-half-hour flight from Sydney. I would never have thought to search there." Not wanting to alert the woman that anything was amiss, Rabbi Woolstone casually asked for the store's business card.

"My wife may want to drop by if we're in the area," he said with a smile.

That was the truth. The Woolstones indeed visited the store, though it wasn't exactly for shopping purposes.

The meeting led to the young lady's return to New York, where a divorce was arranged. She has since remarried and has a wonderful family.

⁐

"*I* regularly make rounds in the jewelry district of Chicago," relates Rabbi Aron Wolf. "I meet many Jews there, both local and visiting businessmen. We often arrange a *minyan* for *minchah*, which many people attend.

"One Thursday afternoon, while speaking with people after the service, I met two Israeli salesmen. We conversed for a while and then went our separate ways. Some hours later, these two men and I met again in an elevator. We greeted one another and chatted briefly before they bade me farewell. They were scheduled to travel back to Israel the same evening.

"I handed them my card, half thinking that it was pointless, as they were about to leave the country."

That evening, the two Israelis made their way to the airport, but a storm was raging. Fierce gusts had toppled trees and the heavy rains had caused flooding. Many passengers decided to stay put, knowing that most of the flights had been cancelled, but some continued to arrive at the airport nonetheless in the hope of flying, the two Israelis among them.

Chaos reigned at the terminal. It was the end of a business week, and scores of travelers wanted to get home. All the harried clerks could suggest was to try again Friday morning. The two Israelis were scheduled to spend the weekend in New York and then take a connecting flight to Israel. "It's not so bad," they reckoned. It was a long Friday, and they would arrive in New York well before Shabbos. So they went outside to catch a taxi back to their hotel until their flight the next morning.

For other passengers, however, the delay created a more serious problem. One such stranded traveler was Dr. Patric David from Paris. He had come to Chicago to attend a medical convention in his area of expertise. Because of the delay, he would have to make arrangements to spend Shabbos in Chicago. Not knowing a soul in the city, he had been striding up and down the airport lobby searching for a Jewish face, without success.

Unsure of how to proceed, he ventured outside to continue looking. It was then that he caught sight of the two men with *kipos* waiting for a cab. He rushed over and explained his predicament.

"We're not local either. We don't really know people here," one of the businessmen told him regretfully.

"Wait a minute!" the other exclaimed, rummaging through his pockets. "We ran into this friendly rabbi here. He gave me his card. I think I may still have it."

A thorough search for the business card, originally thought to be of no use, finally produced results. The Frenchman was extremely thankful. Then he glanced at the name on the card and gaped.

"I can't believe it," he exclaimed. "Before I left home, a congregant in my synagogue who heard I was traveling to Chicago mentioned that he knew a certain Rabbi Aron Wolf. Half jokingly, he asked me to send his regards if I should bump into him among the millions of people in the city!"

The Wolfs were delighted to host Dr. David for Shabbos. Indeed, it proved to be a mutually beneficial and enjoyable encounter. Mrs. Bracha Wolf is originally from France, and staying with a fellow countryman put the doctor at ease. Moreover, the doctor's expertise was in an area in which the Wolfs had urgently been seeking advice on behalf of an acquaintance. The physician's timely arrival proved to be of great assistance.

"Just part of the job," sighed Rabbi Yehoshua Rosenblum, who is on shlichus in Caracas, Venezuela, with his wife, Chanie. He put down the receiver and added the task to his "to do" list. Finding time to visit a community member's son was not a problem, but there was the added heartache of having to make the visit in a prison. Jaime was a young man who had fallen in with the wrong crowd, and had been arrested for illegal activity.

The call from his family had come on Friday, and Rabbi Rosenblum intended to go and see him the following week. That Shabbos, the Rosenblums hosted a young man by the name of David Goldberg. David knew Jaime and asked about the rabbi's plans to visit him. Although prisoners' visitation rights are closely monitored, supervisors are often more lenient when the visitor is a clergyman.

"When you go to see him, I'd like to come along," said

David. "If I accompany you, I'll probably have a better chance of getting in."

David showed up at Chabad House on Sunday morning. "Let's go today," he suggested.

"I'd like to," replied Rabbi Rosenblum, "but I have a number of pressing matters that I have to take care of, and I don't know how long it will take. Why don't you go about your plans for the day, and I'll call you as soon as I have some time."

"My schedule's not so full today," said David, "so I'll settle myself in the Chabad House library and wait for you. I have some reading to catch up on."

The morning hours passed quickly, too quickly for Rabbi Rosenblum. He really didn't see how he could fit in the prison visit. But knowing that David had been waiting all this time, he felt increasingly uncomfortables and by midday decided to put other things on hold.

When Rabbi Rosenblum and David arrived at the prison, they were disappointed to find out that the supervisor, whose authorization was necessary to gain entry, was not in.

The guard on duty would not let them pass.

"May I at least leave the prisoner a package of food and a note?" Rabbi Rosenblum inquired. The guard nodded, indifferent.

"Please mention that I came to visit him, too, and send him my regards," David reminded Rabbi Rosenblum as he wrote the note. They left the parcel and the note. The unsuccessful visit was over.

A few days later, Rabbi Rosenblum made another attempt to visit the young prisoner. This time the supervisor was there, and the visit was more productive. Jaime appreciated the rabbi's efforts, put on *tefillin*, and they spoke for some time.

"There's another Jewish inmate here," he told the rabbi. "He's from South Africa. Maybe you could visit him, too."

"What's his name?" Rabbi Rosenblum asked. He would need it when requesting visiting rights.

"Ian Clark," responded Jaime.

Rabbi Rosenblum raised an eyebrow. The name didn't sound Jewish; it wouldn't be the first time a non-Jewish inmate claimed to be Jewish in order to merit visiting rights from a rabbi and, in addition, an accompanying food parcel.

Jaime understood the rabbi's hesitation.

"Rabbi, he must be Jewish. He knows all kinds of Jewish stuff."

Rabbi Rosenblum decided to take Jaime's word for it. After taking his leave, he approached the supervisor once again, asking to visit Ian Clark.

Permission granted, Rabbi Rosenblum found himself facing a gentle-looking young man who gave the impression of being well-educated and cultured. What's more, when the rabbi invited him to put on *tefillin*, it did not take much convincing for Ian to consent. He even put them on himself with the ease of an old-timer.

The inmate saw the rabbi's puzzled look.

"I know you're wondering about me," he began. "I don't blame you! What could a Jewish boy who calls himself Ian Clark know about *tefillin*, and what is a South African, as you probably detected from my accent, doing in a prison in Venezuela?

"Well, I grew up in a traditional Jewish home and received a typical Jewish education in my hometown. At some point, I ventured into other circles and eventually dropped all my Jewish practice. My new acquaintences were involved in shady financial activity. For me, the need to feel accepted and the lure of the quick buck was too great. Still, I wanted to spare my family's reputation, so I took on a new identity, used false papers, and dropped out of sight.

"Though I succeeded in dodging the law for a long time, it finally caught up with me.

"I'm thankful that I had my false passport and identification when I was arrested, because I don't want my family to suffer any further on my account. So here I am, with plenty of time to contemplate things.

"And that's just what I've been doing. I've been thinking about the meaning and purpose of life, and about my identity as a Jew. I've drifted so far away, though, that I have many conflicting thoughts. When I was arrested, I hadn't imagined there were Jews in Venezuela, and I certainly didn't think that I would meet one in prison. So when I chanced on Jaime and he told me he was getting kosher food and had Jewish books to read, I was stirred.

"I began struggling to find my real identity. Then something uncanny happened, and I knew it was time. You know, I haven't used my Jewish name for many years. Then, last week, Jaime showed me the note you left. My real name is David Goldberg. Someone up there was sending His regards...."

*P*eninah, the secretary at Chabad House, transferred the call to Rabbi Yisrael Hershkowitz, who heads the shlichus in the city of Ofakim, Israel, with his wife, Sarah.

"It's Rabbi D.," Peninah informed him.

Although he was very busy, Rabbi Yisrael took the call. Rabbi D., a dedicated activist, is not chassidic but recognizes the success of Chabad in this southern Israeli city and has great respect for the shluchim. He appreciates their commitment and enthusiasm and, on occasion, seeks advice regarding his own projects.

"So tell me, Rabbi Hershkowitz," he was saying, "how does one go about building a school for teenage immigrant girls here in Ofakim?"

Rabbi Hershkowitz realized his colleague wasn't seeking a one-minute plan. He knew Rabbi D. as a serious person, one who would have scheduled a proper meeting if in-depth advice was being sought. No, this call was an appeal for encouragement and inspiration.

So he responded straight from the heart. "How does one open a school? With unwavering determination and self sacrifice."

"Look," insisted Rabbi D., "that approach and the inner strength to follow it are gifts the Rebbe bestowed on his shluchim. I'm looking for some down-to-earth, rational advice."

"Believe me," Rabbi Hershkowitz replied, "when one does all one can, it draws a blessing from above, all the way down to earth. Know, my friend, that commitment to your worthy goal, untiring effort, trust and prayer – those are the materials that enable one to succeed in any endeavor."

Rabbi Hershkowitz would have given similar advice in any number of situations. In fact, though, he himself had been trying for some time now to raise funds for equipment urgently needed by the Chabad educational facility in Ofakim. After pursuing numerous unsuccessful leads, he resolved to make an appeal to a certain individual from the center of the country, a man who had supported Chabad in the past.

He called at the beginning of the week, but was told the man was busy and to try again in a few days. Two days later, he was given the same response. Rabbi Hershkowitz was a bit discouraged, wondering if he was being given the brush-off. But he decided to call again today, and reached the fellow at last.

"You've called on an auspicious day," the man said good-naturedly. "Never mind the details; I'm happy to assist you. I would, however, like to make the donation precisely today, and so I would request that someone be sent to pick up the check right away. I know that you habitually send letters regarding your activities to be read at the Rebbe's gravesite. Please mention me for a blessing in your next letter."

Rabbi Hershkowitz thanked him wholeheartedly, and arranged right away for one of his drivers to travel north to the donor's office. That evening he set aside time to write the letter. As he was sitting down to write, though, a call came in.

"Rabbi Hershkowitz, this is Rabbi D. I'm sorry to bother you again, and at this late hour, but an urgent matter has come up that only Chabad can help me with."

Rabbi Hershkowitz wondered what it was all about.

"One of our community members, a Russian immigrant, went to Belarus for a visit," Rabbi D. continued. "While there, he collapsed in the city of Homel and was rushed to hospital in critical condition. When I heard the news, I made contact right away and learned that the local hospital is not very well equipped.

"The closest metropolis is the city of Minsk. As I know of the worldwide Chabad presence, I called the shluchim in Minsk and spoke to Mrs. Tamar Gruzman. She's well acquainted with a fine doctor who will take the case and see to it that the man receives the best treatment. Transferring the patient, hospital fees and related costs will be expensive, though. I am committed to raising the funds, but it will take some time. Meanwhile, I am anxious to send a first payment of $3,000, so that the hospital in Minsk won't stint on the necessary treatment.

"In what I see as Divine Providence, Mrs. Gruzman told me that her husband, Rabbi Yosef Gruzman, is presently in Israel, in Kfar Chabad, and is due to fly back to Minsk tomorrow morning. I must get the money to him tonight somehow. It's 10 p.m. now. I don't have a car available, and I don't even know how to get to Kfar Chabad. I was hoping you might have a suggestion."

Rabbi Hershkowitz was silent for a moment, stunned by the turn of events.

"Rabbi D.," he replied, "the matter is solved, thanks to a man whose donation to Chabad will now fulfill two *mitzvos*. I have a fellow from Ofakim who's on the road a short distance from Kfar Chabad with a check for me. I'll instruct him to deliver it to Rabbi Gruzman instead, and you can pay me directly. The check is made out for $3,000."

"*A*ny person I meet is invited to drop in at Yeshivah College," says Rabbi Baruch Lesches, on shlichus with his wife, Shterna, in Sydney, Australia. "One day, as I was taking a train across town, a man came up to me and introduced himself. During our short ride I didn't learn much about him, other than his name and that he was from Israel. I don't know what prompted him to come over, perhaps a desire to communicate with a fellow Jew while far from home. As is my custom, I gave him the address of the *yeshivah*, and we parted ways."

The next day, the phone rang in Rabbi Lesches's office. The caller was a rabbi from a prominent *Beis Din* (Jewish court) in Israel. "Shalom," he began. "Perhaps you can help us. There's a woman in our city whose husband has disappeared, leaving her in a desperate situation. After thorough investigation, we have reason to think he may be in Sydney. We know that people are attracted to Lubavitch all around the world. True, it's like trying to find a needle in a haystack, but perhaps you're willing to take his name? Who knows? You may run into him one day and be able to help a distraught woman 12,000 miles away."

Rabbi Lesches said that, of course, he would be glad to help and took pen and paper to write down the name.

It was the name of the man he had met on the train only the day before.

"What a shame you didn't call yesterday!" he exclaimed to the stunned rabbi. He told him of their chance meeting the day before and added, "I regret that we met too briefly for me to find out any more details, but I promise to keep my eyes and ears open."

Rabbi Lesches's habit of inviting people to Yeshivah College paid off for the abandoned woman in Israel. The man indeed showed up one day at the *yeshivah* "just to see what it's all about." Rabbi Lesches tactfully confronted him and helped solve a difficult situation on the other side of the globe.

"*I* was one of the first twelve students at the Chabad *yeshivah* in Budapest," relates Rabbi Shmuel Raskin, who is now on shlichus there with his wife, Devorah Leah. "The *yeshivah* was established by Rabbi Baruch and Batsheva Oberlander, and, in addition to our studies, we assisted them in their activities. Today, we serve not only the vibrant Hungarian Chabad community, but an Israeli community as well, composed of several hundred families and over a thousand Israeli students. In the Central Chabad Center we have our own 'Israeli' shul. The center is called Keren Ohr.

"It all started with an exceptional man named Yossi Prial. He first arrived at Chabad in response to an ad announcing High Holiday services for Israelis in Budapest. Because of the overflow attendance at the main Chabad shul, we had started to hold services for Israelis in rented premises. Shortly afterward, Yossi called me.

"'The services were o.k.,' he stated bluntly, 'but you need to improve.'

"I explained that we were just beginning to establish services for a distinct Israeli community and were happy to get feedback and suggestions. I asked how he thought we could improve.

"'Oh, everything was fine, Rabbi,' he said. 'I just think you need a better venue.'

"Yossi had hit a soft spot. I agreed, but explained gently that we needed help to obtain a more appropriate place.

"'Let's meet and talk things over,' suggested Yossi.

"At the meeting, Yossi pledged to help fund a building, and to get others involved as well. We decided to begin searching for a site immediately.

"Now, as we became more acquainted, Yossi asked me if I could prepare his son for his upcoming bar mitzvah.

"'With pleasure,' I replied. 'We can conduct the ceremony at the main Chabad shul in Budapest.'

"He thanked me for the offer but explained that he'd been planning to hold the ceremony in Israel.

"I began instructing Yossi's son, Itamar, and all went well until a week before the bar mitzvah, when a terrible car accident left Yossi's seven-year-old daughter Keren in a coma. Attending to his daughter round the clock, Yossi called us from her hospital room. He was adamant that his son's ceremony be held as planned, but obviously with some changes. He asked if he could impose on me to make the necessary arrangements and hold the celebration at the Chabad shul. Of course, I agreed.

"The bar mitzvah was charged with energy and joy, mingled with concern for Yossi's daughter. Itamar performed beautifully, and Rabbi Oberlander led everyone in heartfelt prayers for his sister's full recovery.

"Only a few weeks later, the little girl herself was a happy guest at Chabad for the bar mitzvah of a family friend. At the *kiddush*, tears flowed from everybody's eyes as she stood on a chair and in a sweet voice thanked Rabbi Oberlander and the whole community for praying on her behalf.

"It was at about this time that Rabbi Oberlander and his assistant, Rabbi Shlomo Koves, received a call from Mr. Paul Steiner, mayor of Budapest's Fifth District.

"'Rabbis, you've contacted me in the past regarding a site for your center,' began the mayor. 'My father was Jewish, and I have decided to assist you. I'd like to propose a site in the center of the city, at 20 Károly Körút.

"We could hardly believe our ears. The location was indeed central and easily accessible; we couldn't have hoped for better. Renovations were soon under way and, true to his word, Yossi Prial undertook the funding. The complex would serve as Chabad's central offices as well as a synagogue for Israelis.

"So the Chabad Center in Budapest was named 'Keren Ohr,' which means 'ray of light,' in commemoration of little Keren's miraculous recovery."

*　*　*

"When I first arrived here, the Israeli community we now serve didn't yet exist as a distinct group," relates Rabbi Raskin. "My friend, Yosef Solomon (who is now on shlichus in Bulgaria), and I were Israeli, so it was natural for us to work with other Israelis. Rabbi Oberlander directed us to businesses and offices, in order to connect with Israelis living here and interest them in Judaism. That's not an easy job, as you can imagine, and we didn't always meet with success.

"One of our duties was to visit Jewish prison inmates. Once, we were instructed to visit a prison outside the city. We followed directions, but got lost and ended up in a small village near Budapest. Looking for directions, we came across a young woman.

"'Do you speak English?' we asked.

"'No,' she replied in Hungarian, but we understood from her gestures that she was asking us to wait while she found an English speaker. She returned shortly with a woman who told us how to reach our destination. We had already thanked her and restarted the car when it occurred to us to ask how she came to speak English so fluently. It wasn't common to find inhabitants of such small villages who could speak a foreign language.

"'Of course I speak English!' she replied with a smile. 'My husband is Israeli. And you two should have a *yom tov* – you probably know that means "good day" in Hebrew. You see, my last name is Yomtov.'

"Yosef and I looked at each other, agape. Arik Yomtov was a person on the list of Israeli businessmen whom we had been trying to contact for some time, but whenever we called he was either busy, out, or overseas.

"Sure enough, she assured us the man was her husband and added that he was right there in a nearby cottage, on vacation with his family from the constant buzz of city life. She called him out to meet us.

"'How timely to have met you now,' Arik said, 'I've just purchased a new building and need to have *mezuzos* put up.'

"Arik joined our fledgling Israeli community and has been a loyal supporter ever since."

One of the chassidim of the Rebbe Rashab, the fifth Lubavitcher Rebbe, suffered acute pains. He consulted various doctors, and they all advised him that surgery was his only hope for recovery.

The surgery could have been performed in Petersburg, where the doctors were more renowned, or Vitebsk, which was closer to the chassid's home and more convenient.

Unsure of what to do, the chassid traveled to Lubavitch and asked the Rebbe Rashab. The Rebbe replied: "I don't think you should undergo surgery at all. Go home and all will be well." At the conclusion of their meeting, he advised the chassid: "On your way home, travel first-class."

The chassid was somewhat startled by the Rebbe's answer. He was suffering severely and the doctors had not offered him an alternative. But with faith and trust in the Rebbe's words, despite the extra expense, he purchased a first-class ticket and settled in for the journey home.

During the trip, his pains were too great to endure and he could not help but groan in agony. A well-dressed gentleman from the adjoining compartment approached him and asked if he could help. With some hesitation, the chassid told him of his medical condition.

The man returned to his own compartment, brought back some medication, and explained: "I am a doctor from Berlin. I was called to treat the Russian Czar who is suffering from a similar malady. This medication is not available in Russia. I can promise you that with it, you will be able to treat your condition without surgery."

The chassid was amazed at the unexpected turn of events. He followed the doctor's instructions and was cured.

"*I* was pretty upset when I accidentally backed into a car as I was leaving a parking lot," recalls Maryashie, who is on shlichus with her husband, Rabbi Yossi Deren, in Greenwich, Connecticut.

"To make matters worse, I could see in the mirror that it was a luxury car. I groaned. I was in a rush, and now on top of the time it would take to exchange insurance information, I would have to deal with the angry owner of a damaged expensive vehicle.

"I unlocked my two-year-old daughter's car seat and took a deep breath, prepared for the worst. To my surprise, I met a pleasant woman who, like myself, was holding a toddler as she inspected her car.

"'Don't worry about it,' she reassured me, smiling. 'The best thing about these cars is their ample bumpers! Look, there's no damage at all. Don't feel bad; I could have done the same thing in the cramped space you had available.'

"I was relieved and charmed by this lovely woman who spoke so graciously to me. As we were both standing there with our toddlers in our arms, we introduced ourselves and moved on, soon enough, to 'mother' talk.

"'Does your little girl go to preschool?' my new acquaintance, Carrie Ross, asked. I explained who I was and that Chabad operated a preschool and camp, which my daughter attended.

"'What a coincidence!' Carrie responded. 'We've just moved to the area. My husband has been appointed headmaster of one of the private schools in Greenwich, where many Jewish children attend. But we haven't yet found a Jewish community we can become part of. We would really like our son to be in a Jewish environment and learn about the traditions. We've heard about Chabad, and now you tell me that you have a camp. This may be just what we've been looking for!'

"Little Hal Ross attended our camp and enjoyed the experience, much to his parents' delight and to our own."

"*I* don't know which is the greater challenge – raising Jewish awareness or raising the funds to do so," reflects Rabbi Shlomo Kugel, who operates a Chabad House on the West Side of Manhattan with his wife, Rivka. "In any case, the two are intertwined; the first depends on the second, or so I thought.

"One morning during the week of Sukkos, the pressure of finding a way to fund our activities was really weighing on me, but I didn't have a clue how to proceed. Thinking about the problem only compounded the apparent difficulty. I made a deliberate effort to pull out of that cycle of worry and get a grip on myself.

"My goal in gathering funds is to be able to reach out to Jewish people with mitzvos," I told myself firmly, "so that's just what I'll do!"

"I left my financial concerns at the office, took my *lulav* and *esrog* in hand, and went outside. As I walked through Riverside Park, I saw an elderly couple sitting on a bench. They looked Jewish, so I invited them to fulfill the mitzvah of shaking the four species.

"The two, Zvi and Jane Lavi, were very touched. The husband told me he was a Holocaust survivor in his mid-seventies and had not had a Jewish experience for many years, although he had lived in Israel after the war. He had met his wife, originally from Romania, only recently, after moving to the States. The couple just happened to be taking a stroll near the park that morning. They asked who I was and what organization I represented, and were impressed when they learned of Chabad's outreach efforts.

"This encounter led to a warm relationship. The Lavis frequented our synagogue services and activities and later donated a Torah scroll.

"When they passed away some time later, Rivka and I were deeply moved when we learned that they had left our Chabad House $150,000 in their will."

"There were eight of us en route to New York for the rabbinical conference which is held annually after the holiday of Shavuos," recalls Rabbi Yossi Gordon of Melbourne, Australia. "The two-hour stopover at the Sydney airport left just enough time to hold a *minyan* for the afternoon *minchah* services. Scouting the terminal yielded another Jew, but the group was still one man short. I wasn't about to give up and set out on an additional search."

Twenty minutes later, he caught sight of what appeared to be a Jewish face. Without much time for elaboration, Rabbi Gordon briefly explained the predicament he and his fellow rabbis were in. The man's face lit up.

"Thanks for asking!" he exclaimed, "Of course I'll join! It's my father's *yarhtzeit*[27] and I want to say *Kaddish*."

---

27. The anniversary of a person's passing.

After *minchah*, Rabbi Gordon asked the man if he would like to put on *tefillin*. The man gladly agreed, and said: "I actually attended services this morning to recite *Kaddish* for my deceased father. Everyone around me was wearing *tefillin* and I would have liked to as well. But nobody offered to help me, and I was embarrassed to ask."

"**Y**our car is fine!" the garage attendant declared as he slammed the hood shut. "You can drive her all the way to Timbuktu and back!"

Rabbi Yossi Lew was relieved. He, his wife, Shternie, and their children were planning to meet his brother in Greensboro, North Carolina, that Sunday, and he wanted to be sure his car was in good shape for the long drive from Atlanta, their shlichus city.

So it came as an annoying surprise when the car overheated on the highway. Rabbi Lew pulled over to allow the engine to cool, but to no avail. To make matters worse, it was pouring with rain. Driving slowly to the nearest exit, he pulled off the road and attempted to locate the problem. With his head deep under the hood, he inspected the engine.

"Trouble, eh?" he heard a thick southern accent from behind.

"Water on the brakes?" came another.

Straightening up, Rabbi Lew was surprised to find himself surrounded by a group of locals, each one of them offering advice to help solve his predicament. Their southern hospitality, however, seemed to outweigh their professional knowledge.

Finally, an old fellow, who had kept quiet while the others had offered counsel, spoke up: "It's probably a leak in your radiator."

"But I just took the car to the garage," protested the rabbi.

The man shrugged with the look of an old-timer who has seen it all.

"Let's fill it with water and see if it continues to overheat," the older man suggested.

But the Lews had exhausted their water supply, although they did have some empty plastic cups.

"That'll do," the man stated. "Now come with me to that department store over there. I'll show you how to go to the back where you can get some water."

It took about ten trips with the four cups to conclude that, indeed, the problem must be a leak in the radiator.

"The best thing for you to do is buy some antifreeze at an auto supply store, so you can keep the radiator full 'til you get back home without damaging the engine. Don't use plain water for any length of time. Here, follow me and I'll lead you to a shop that sells antifreeze."

At the entrance to the store the man gave the rabbi directions how to get back to the highway.

Mrs. Lew was effusive in gratitude for the stranger's generosity. "You appeared here like an angel!" she exclaimed.

A strange look passed over the old man, and he was silent for a moment.

"Well, you know," he replied slowly. "A few years ago I had a massive heart attack. I was rushed to hospital and sensed that a team of doctors was all around me. I felt myself being pushed and prodded and pumped in their efforts to revive me. After I had been in a coma for a couple of days, the department head told my family they might as well pull the plug, because I was a goner. And I was gone alright – up to heaven. There they asked me, 'What are you doing here? Your time's not up. You've still got things to do down there.'

"So I came back, and here I am. If I seem like an angel, maybe it's because something rubbed off while I was up there."

With that, the old man wished the Lews a safe journey, got back in his pickup and drove off.

A few weeks later, Rabbi Lew was teaching a class in the Greenfield Hebrew Academy of Atlanta middle school. One of the students, Betty, raised her hand.

"Rabbi, I was wondering what Judaism has to say about pulling the plug?"

Rabbi Lew's mind flashed back to his highway adventure, and he told the class the story.

A few weeks later Betty sent the rabbi an email.

"Remember the question I asked about pulling the plug? It wasn't just theoretical," she wrote. "A while ago, my grandfather was very ill. The doctors gave up and informed my father that he should pull the plug. That day, I came home from school and rushed to call my father. He was about to leave for the hospital to say farewell to my grandfather and end his life. When I told him your story, he decided not to do it.

"Today we all went to visit my grandfather. I thought you'd be gratified to know that he was sitting up, talking and laughing. We spent a great couple of hours together. No one could believe it happened, and I'm still haunted by what would have happened if...."

Betty's grandfather lived a few months longer. The sad news of his passing reached her father, an audiologist, while he was on a lecture trip in Colorado. In his grief, Mr. Nagler called Rabbi Lew, mentioning his additional pain at the thought that he had almost brought about his father's premature demise.

"The Torah teaches us not to be depressed by regret," said the rabbi gently, "but rather to take negative energy and direct it into positive avenues. For a while now, we've been speaking about the importance of Jewish education for your daughter. I wonder if the timing is significant. As one generation passes, it's appropriate to weigh the importance of instilling Jewish awareness in the younger generation. Now, after the passing of your father, it is a good time to enroll her in a Jewish high school. I'm sure her grandfather would have approved."

The rabbi's words made an impression, but Betty's parents were still undecided.

A couple of months later, Betty's father was on another lecture trip to Colorado.

"Sitting in the plane," he recalls, "my thoughts turned to my late father, and I began to weep. I was overwhelmed with a wave of grieving, and my tears intensified. I can't explain what came over me. A flight attendant gently offered assistance, but I couldn't even respond.

"And then I suddenly saw a vision of my father smiling. He seemed to be reassuring me and saying, 'Why are you crying? Just do the right thing, and all will be well.'

"And then, inexplicably, the tears stopped."

When he returned home, he shared what had transpired on the plane with his family, admitting that he was still struggling to understand the meaning of it all.

Betty stood up and said: "I know exactly what it means! It means I need to attend a Jewish high school this fall."

Her parents consented, and next year Betty changed schools.

*M*r. Edward Ives is the owner of a flower drying plant on a large farm in Somis, California, an hour's drive north of Los Angeles. Back in 1995, Mr. Ives had contacted Rabbi Yakov Latowicz, who is on shlichus with his wife, Sarah, in Ventura, California, to establish a Torah class on the farm for the benefit of his Jewish employees and local Jewish businessmen. Subsequently, a successful weekly 'lunch-and-learn' program was launched, taught by Rabbi Latowicz and graciously hosted by Mr. Ives.

Some time later, a former congregant, Mr. Shapiro, who had emigrated to Israel, contacted Rabbi Latowicz to offici-ate at his mother's funeral in nearby Camarillo, California. Mr. Shapiro decided to observe the week of *shivah* mourning in Camarillo, where his mother had lived, and inquired about the possibility of a *minyan* so that he could recite *Kaddish*.

Rabbi Latowicz approached Mr. Ives, and they discussed the possibility of holding the *minyan* at the farm. Mr. Ives was enthused about the idea and kindly offered the use of a house on the property. With a convenient location and the incentive of enabling a fellow Jew to say *Kaddish* during the week of *shivah*, local Jews responded positively about forming a *minyan* in Somis.

The intent had originally been to hold the *minyan* for one week only. But as Mr. Shapiro remained in Camarillo for several weeks, and no one seemed to be complaining, Rabbi Latowicz used the momentum to launch the first daily *minyan* in the area.

When new shluchim, Rabbi Noson and Bassie Gurary, came to the nearby city of Simi Valley, Rabbi Latowicz, always looking for more recruits, asked Rabbi Gurary to help maintain the daily *minyan* in Somis.

"I'll come," Rabbi Gurary replied. "There is a back road, Route 118, that leads from Simi Valley right into Somis. The time involved won't interfere with my local obligations too much." And so the *minyan* carried on.

One morning, on the way back from the *minyan*, Rabbi Gurary's car malfunctioned. He called the insurance company and was told they would soon be on their way. Rabbi Gurary braced himself for a long wait, due to the isolated location of the flower farm. He had been waiting on the side of the road for some time when a car pulled up. A friendly-looking, obviously Jewish man stopped his car.

"Can I help you, Rabbi?" he asked.

Rabbi Gurary expressed his thanks, but assured the man that help was on the way. The man, who introduced himself as Gershon, looked at him quizzically. "Excuse me for asking, but what is a dignified individual like yourself doing on these back roads? This farmland is an unlikely place to see a rabbi, and so early in the morning, too!"

Rabbi Gurary explained about the *minyan* at the flower farm.

"Really?" the man exclaimed. "Please tell me exactly where it is. I can hardly believe my good fortune in spotting you on the road. You see, I lost my father this year, and I've been trying to say *Kaddish* every morning with a *minyan*. I work here on the farms and, with a heavy heart, I often have to forgo the local *minyan* near home to get to work on time. Now you're telling me there's a morning *minyan* right hear, in my work area?! How timely for me to have met you and found out about it!"

The coastal city of Ashkelon in Israel, where Rabbi Mendy and Chanie Gorelick are on shlichus, boasts a beautiful shoreline and antiquities that attract many tourists. But for many local people, the city is just their home, where they struggle to make ends meet. It is for these hardworking, low-income families that the Chabad House operates a popular thrift shop. Rock-bottom prices and service with sensitivity draw many to the shop.

For some, though, even these low prices are beyond their means. Rabbi and Mrs. Gorelick try to be attentive to people's needs and do all they can to help. S. is a local woman who had been struggling financially for some time. Aware of her plight, the Goforelicks made a special arrangement. Every Friday and on holiday eves, she would come to their house and pick up parcels of homemade food. In addition, she would receive coupons entitling her to obtain items in the thrift shop for free.

The woman was very grateful for this arrangement and benefited from it week after week. One Thursday night, just before Pesach, she arrived at the Gorelicks' door anticipating the assistance she had always been given. She rang the bell, but there was no answer. After a few tries, she assumed that the bell was not working.

"It's the night before the holiday," she thought to herself. "They must be home."

She knocked on the door, but still no response. "They're probably busy with holiday preparations and don't hear," she concluded. So she pounded loudly for a short while, to no avail. Finally, realizing that no one was home, she left, intending to come back the following morning.

Indeed, the Gorelick family had gone out to do last-minute shopping. They returned much later than they had planned.

To their shock, it appeared that someone had attempted to burglarize their home! A window was broken, items were turned upside down, and drawers had been pulled open. But strangely, nothing was missing. It seemed as if the burglar had not had the chance to finish his job.

Friday morning, they called the police to report the puzzling break-in. For the police, as well, the attempted burglary was a mystery, and so the Gorelicks put it out of their minds as they prepared for the holiday. That is, until there was a knock at the door. It was S. who had returned to pick up her food parcels and coupons.

She apologized for disturbing the busy holiday preparations.

"I came yesterday, but no one was home. If you had been, you certainly would have heard my loud banging on the door."

Suddenly, everything seemed to fall into place. This unfortunate woman, who had benefited from the Gorelicks' kindness, had unknowingly reciprocated by frightening off the intruder.

∽

"This child has a special soul," Janice commented out of the blue, pointing to her three-month-old son. She was making the observation to Rabbi Sholom Ber Harlig, who was on shlichus with his wife, Chanie, in Rancho Cucamonga, California.

"One day," Janice continued, "he's bound to become a rabbi."

Rabbi Harlig wondered what had prompted Janice to say such a thing. She was not Jewish, although her Jewish husband occasionally visited their Chabad House.

As if reading his thoughts, the woman revealed that the little boy was adopted, and that the agency had mentioned a Jewish biological mother. There was, however, no legal proof of this.

Rabbi Harlig was not sure why Janice had chosen to share such private information with him. She was not seeking help of any sort in probing the matter, and in any case it would be problematic. So he left things as they were, and the issue did not come up again.

About a year later, Rabbi Harlig, accompanied by his young daughter, was driving to the hospital to visit a community member. They were passing through a certain low-class neighborhood when Rabbi Harlig suddenly had an overpowering feeling of thirst.

"I don't remember ever having had such an urgent need for a drink that would compel me to stop and buy one," recalls Rabbi Harlig. "And I really didn't want to do it in that crime-ridden area, especially with my daughter."

But the pressing thirst would not let up, and so Rabbi Harlig pulled up to a convenience store. Holding his daughter's hand firmly, he walked toward the entrance. A woman who had been lingering with a raggedy group in the parking lot approached him.

"Sir, I need to talk to you," she said in a garbled tone. The smell of alcohol and the glassy look in her eyes made Rabbi Harlig quicken his step, but the woman followed him into the store and thrust out her hand.

"Take a look at this. You are a rabbi, aren't you? I want to speak to you."

The woman was clutching a necklace with a Star of David pendant. Rabbi Harlig slowed his pace and nodded in her direction.

"I'm not in a good place, rabbi. I just got out of jail and I have a miserable life. I don't really have a home and wouldn't know how to keep house anyway. I'm a lost cause, but I had a little baby boy that was taken from me. I want him to know that he's Jewish, and I want him to get a good education so he won't grow up to be like me. Would you track him down and take care of that?"

Rabbi Harlig sympathized with the poor woman, privately hoping the appropriate social authorities would notice her plight.

"Do you know anything about your child's whereabouts?" he inquired.

"No, but I once saw a picture of his adoptive parents," the woman answered. She described the couple. When she had finished, she turned and walked away.

Rabbi Harlig purchased his drink. His mind was no longer on his thirst but on this strange turn of events. Later, he verified the details and confirmed his suspicion. It was true: The pitiable woman's Jewish child was indeed the little boy who Janice, his non-Jewish adoptive mother, knew possessed a special soul.

"*B*ut the courts in Los Angeles annulled my marriage," Sharon insisted. "Rabbi, it happened such a long time ago, and it only lasted six hours – a stupid mistake. Done, finished, forgotten forever!"

Rabbi Chaim Mentz of Bel Air, California, listened sympathetically. He really felt for Sharon and Andrew, a nice young couple who wanted him to officiate at their upcoming marriage.

"I understand how you feel, Sharon," he explained patiently. "But you see, Jewish law prohibits marriage if the bride or groom had been married before but not divorced according to Jewish law. A court annulment is not enough. A proper bill of divorce, a *get*, must be obtained."

Sharon and Andrew looked devastated.

"Don't worry," Rabbi Mentz calmed them. "We're dealing with a formality, but behind this formality lies the truism that everything a person does has meaning, and so no action should be taken lightly. I will assist you in the procedure and things will work out for the best."

"Yeah," Sharon thought to herself. "I wonder what good can come from adding extra hassles to my six-page-long list of things to do."

With the rabbi's guidance, Sharon contacted the Jewish court (*Beis Din*) in Los Angeles, and in a matter of weeks she had the *get* in hand. The rabbi at the *Beis Din* wished her well. "Now you can go about planning your upcoming marriage with joy and peace of mind," he concluded warmly.

"We have it all planned already," Sharon assured him with a smile. "We're getting married on the fifth of December."

The rabbi shook his head with concern. "Oh dear, I'm sorry you didn't mention that earlier. You see, Jewish law requires that in a case such as yours, you must wait three months before marrying. As you have already demonstrated a high regard for the law, you will surely continue to do so as you begin your new life. May you be blessed in all your endeavors."

The first thing Sharon did was call Andrew, then she called Rabbi Mentz.

"Rabbi," she blurted. "I can't believe this! All our plans, the wedding, our honeymoon! You mean we have to reschedule everything?!"

Rabbi Mentz gently explained the law and its reasons, and encouraged Sharon and Andrew to abide by it. "Judaism maintains that G-d is the active third party in every marriage. You'll be demonstrating how important it is to have Him as a partner in your life."

After some consideration, Sharon and Andrew informed

Rabbi Mentz that they would comply with the law, and they rescheduled their wedding for January 23, 2005.

On December 26, they realized just how vital to their lives their Third Partner was. This would have been one of the last days of the honeymoon they had originally planned, and they would have been spending it at the now famous Kaafu Atoll Maldives Hotel on Lankanfushi Island. The room they had reserved was one of those swept away by the devastating tsunami of December 2004.

A chassid asked the Rebbe Rashab, the fifth Lubavitcher Rebbe, why he extolled the service of simple Jews so highly.

"They have many superior qualities," the Rebbe answered.

"I don't see them," responded the chassid.

The Rebbe did not pursue the matter and instead turned the conversation to the chassid's business affairs, asking him several questions about the gem market with which he was involved. The Rebbe then inquired if the chassid had brought with him any of the stones in which he had invested. When the chassid answered affirmatively, the Rebbe asked to see them.

"They don't look very special," the Rebbe remarked. "I don't see why they are so unique."

"With all due respect," the chassid replied, "to understand gems, you have to be a maven."

"And to understand neshamos (souls), you also have to be a maven," the Rebbe gently replied.

"*I*n the span of our many years of shlichus in Antwerp, we've had a wide variety of people with a rich assortment of inquiries pass through our Chabad House," relates Rabbi

Shabtai Slavaticki. "But this was the first time someone had come in with a proposal to sell us a *shofar.*"

The owner was a young man of eighteen who presented the item for sale and said it had been recommended that he try his luck here.

"Who told you that we might be interested in buying it from you?" Rabbi Slavaticki asked curiously.

"I found my way to a synagogue in the city, and the people there directed me here," the young man replied.

"What are you asking for your *shofar*?"

"Five thousand euros."

"That's a very high price for a *shofar.* There are some exceptionally crafted types whose value is higher than the norm, but this one is ordinary. Sometimes a *shofar* fetches a high price because it was the possession of a renowned personality. Where did you get it?"

The young man told his tale.

His father was the sole member of his family to survive the Holocaust. In his grief, he denounced his Judaism, married a non-Jewish woman, and never disclosed his origin to his son. The secret was revealed in the form of taunts that classmates in grade school had shouted at the boy. He confronted his father with the name-calling, demanding an explanation.

"Ignore them," his father had responded. "Calling someone a dirty Jew is a figure of speech. People say it as an insult; it's not meant to be a statement of fact."

The boy accepted his father's clarification. But when the taunting continued, he pressed his father for the truth. This time his father admitted his Jewish origin but insisted it was of no significance. Some time later, the boy discovered an object he couldn't identify in the attic of their home. Showing it to his father, he learned that it was a *shofar* and that, as a sacred Jewish item, that it was valuable.

Rabbi Slavaticki listened intently to the young man's account. He was much more interested in the owner of the *shofar* than in the article itself, for a lost Jewish soul is undeniably of highest value. He weighed his words carefully.

"As I told you, this *shofar* doesn't seem to justify your high price, but I also mentioned that the monetary worth of an article of worship can increase due to its illustrious owner. Please mention to your father that, the next time he's in this area, he should come in and we can clarify the matter further."

"Can't it be discussed over the phone?" the young boy asked.

"If this *shofar* is even half as valuable as your price would suggest, it's not for a telephone conversation," the rabbi replied.

Some time later, the father called and made an appointment. The conversation that ensued took place in authentic Yiddish. In the course of their meeting, Rabbi Slavaticki invited the man to fulfill the *mitzvah* of *tefillin*.

"I've come here only to discuss the *shofar* business," he retorted icily.

"You've suffered much pain and loss because of Hitler," Rabbi Slavaticki said sensitively. "You don't have to perpetuate those losses endlessly. You can gain a sense of personal victory by reconnecting to your faith, for which you were persecuted."

"I have already lost that battle," the man said bitterly.

"Hitler wanted to kill Jews. Do you truly think he succeeded in killing the Jew within you? A Jewish soul is inherently powerful. Must you believe that he defeated you?" the rabbi asked encouragingly.

But the man's stooped shoulders shook with a mixture of anger and despair, and he walked out without a word.

For two months, the Slavatickis heard nothing more from him, until one night when their doorbell rang.

Apologizing for the late hour, the man requested entrance to the Chabad House synagogue. "I don't want to inconvenience you," he insisted, obviously uncomfortable with his sudden visit. "Perhaps you could give me the key and I'll drop it into your mailbox as soon as I'm finished," he suggested.

The Slavatickis could see that the man was in the throes of some personal upheaval. Without a word they handed him the key and he hurried out. As soon as he left, though, they had second thoughts. The man was a stranger whom the rabbi had met only once. He had shown interest in selling articles of Jewish value. Maybe they had been too naive and trusting. The Talmud cautions: "One should respect but one may also suspect...."

Rabbi Slavaticki made his way undetected into the women's section of the synagogue. He was moved to the core at the sight of the man clutching a Torah scroll, his eyes streaming with tears as he whispered many, many names. The Rabbi had seen enough. Silently, he made his way out, the man's voice echoing behind, "Dear G-d, I forgive you for what You have done to Your people, please forgive me as well...."

Some time later, the man informed the Slavatickis that he was moving to Israel with his son. He had separated from his non-Jewish wife, and his son had undergone proper conversion.

～

Meira, originally from the United States, and Yaron Grabiner, her Israeli husband, lived for a while in Washburn, Minnesota, teaching in a local school.

Their hope was to establish themselves financially before returning to Israel. They were very pleased to find a rent-free home to live in, owned by a woman named Barbara, a friend of Meira's family. The house was being renovated, while Barbara stayed elsewhere until the work was completed. The noise and disarray didn't bother the younger couple much, and they were happy with the arrangement.

Barbara, a devout Christian, would come into Duluth weekly for Bible classes and a prayer group. She would often stop by at her house in Washburn, checking on the work in progress and visiting with the Grabiners.

On one occasion, the discussion turned to the topic of Jewish identity. The Grabiners explained the principle in Jewish law that a Jew is defined by his or her mother's religion. Barbara was surprised at this notion and later shared it with the participants in her Bible class. The teacher, April Scheer, was astonished. "Why, if that's true, it would make me Jewish!" she blurted out.

Barbara was curious. "My Christian Bible class teacher a Jew?!" she wondered. The next time she visited the Grabiners, Barbara told them what she had discovered. The Grabiners decided that the best people with whom to share this information were their friends, Rabbi Baruch and Rivka Greenwald. As Chabad shluchim who had recently come to Duluth, they were always on the lookout for Jewish people.

In time, Rabbi Greenwald called the Scheer home and introduced himself as the new rabbi in town, interested in contacting Jews.

"I'm not Jewish," April stated flatly.

Rabbi Greenwald responded gently. "In Duluth, I've encountered several Jews who hadn't even realized they were Jewish. According to Jewish law, anyone whose mother is Jewish is a Jew as well."

April was moved to hear this from a rabbi and accepted the Greenwalds' invitation to join their Friday night meal. The Grabiners were also guests that evening, and they marveled as April shared some information about her family. Although the family had intermarried many generations back, nearly all the descendants were female; the few males had either remained single or had never had children. "I have three sisters, two daughters and five granddaughters!" April chuckled.

"That's a lot of Jewish women," Yaron remarked. "I guess G-d really wanted to keep your family Jewish."

One of the Scheer daughters, Celia, took on a Hebrew name, Chaya'le, and went on to attend the Torah study program for girls at Bais Chanah. She now works at the Chabad House in Duluth.

"Shalom. May I speak to the rabbi?"

"This is Rabbi Gluckowsky. Can I help you?"

"I hope so. My name is Sarah Bonchek. I've heard you're an English-speaking rabbi and that you're new to the community. I'm part of a small group of English-speaking seniors who live here in Rechovot. We met through AACI (the Association of Americans and Canadians in Israel), and get together for a weekly Torah class. Our lecturer is an elderly gentleman who unfortunately has a heart condition, so he is no longer able to give the class. We're looking for a new teacher, and I wonder if you'd be willing."

Would he be willing?! Rabbi Mendel Gluckowsky and his wife, Rochel, had just begun setting up their shlichus in Rechovot, and here were people anxious to learn. Nonetheless, he was not able to commit himself on a weekly basis.

"Mrs. Bonchek, I'm delighted to hear of an ongoing study group here in town," he responded. "There is another English-speaking rabbi here, Mordechai Kastel, who may be able to help. I'll ask him if he would share the respomsibility with me. That way, each of us would teach twice a month, and I believe such an arrangement would suit us all."

Rabbi Kastel agreed, and the class was continued to everyone's satisfaction. Sarah Bonchek was the driving force behind the endeavor. Every Monday night she would call to confirm the teachers, remind the participants and arrange for refreshments.

In time, the teachers and students, who numbered between five and fifteen weekly, bonded into a small "community." Rabbis Gluckowsky and Kastel and their families celebrated holidays such as Chanukah and Purim with the group. They shared in each other's family celebrations, as well as bereavements. This interaction served as the glue connecting these elderly people to their heritage.

The class carried on for about seven years. Then Sarah called one day. It was not about confirming the class.

"Rabbi, I want you to know how grateful we all are for your and Rabbi Kastel's involvement. We all thoroughly enjoy the classes and everything that you have shared with us. However, I am getting on in years. My age and health compel me to think seriously about my future, and I have decided to move into an assisted-living complex in Tel Aviv to be near my children. I regret that I can no longer carry on with our group, so I'm calling to thank you and wish you farewell."

So Sarah moved, and another senior couple took over responsibility for arranging the classes.

About two years later, Rabbi Gluckowsky received an urgent call. It was Sarah Bonchek's son from Tel Aviv.

"Rabbi," he said in a shaken voice. "You don't know me, but I've heard about you from my mother. She always spoke fondly of the classes she attended while living in Rechovot. Unfortunately, two days ago she suffered a severe heart attack and was in a coma. Twenty minutes ago, she suddenly regained consciousness and asked me to call for you to come."

Rabbi Gluckowsky was taken aback. He had had no contact with Sarah for two years now and was unsettled to hear that she was asking for him. He immediately canceled all appointments for the day and rushed to Tel Aviv.

He found Sarah weak, but lucid and peaceful. She expressed her gratitude for his prompt arrival.

"Rabbi, you've known me for a long time. You and my friends can vouch for my down-to-earth, rational conduct. All the same, the reason I've summoned you is to share something distinctly other-worldly. I trust you will believe what I have to say.

"As you know, I was unconscious for some time. I felt my soul departing and had visions of a world beyond this physical sphere. An appraisal of my deeds and accomplishments was being presented. I saw an image of a brilliant jewel in a crown intended for me and was informed that this merit was due to my having organized and upheld a Torah class.

"Realizing now how highly valued this activity is in the spiritual realms, I ask you to continue teaching the class for the benefit of my soul."

Rabbi Gluckowsky was very moved by her words and assured her that her request would be honored. A couple of hours later, Sarah Bonchek passed away.

"*A* Chanukah Fair promoting Jewish toys and books for children – that would be a good way to make these educational resources available to families in our area," decided Rabbi Sholom Ber and Chanie Harlig of Rancho Cucamonga, California. The Chabad House of the Inland Empire services a broad Jewish community that, unfortunately, has a high rate of intermarriage. No local entrepreneur was particularly interested in stocking up on such merchandise when the potential market seemed so small and undefined.

That reality led Rabbi Harlig to contact the well known company, Jewish Educational Toys, located in Chicago, and place an order with Mr. Avraham Blumberger. At the end of their conversation, Mr. Blumberger inquired, "Is your wife's maiden name by any chance Cunin, the daughter of Rabbi Pinchus and Bina Cunin, who live in Crown Heights, Brooklyn?"

"Why yes," replied Rabbi Harlig, surprised. "How do you know my wife's family?"

"Well, I come from the West Coast, and my family was not observant. While I was making my journey back to Judaism, I studied at the Morristown *yeshivah* in New Jersey and spent many Shabbos meals in the Cunin home. I remember hearing that one of their daughters had married a Rabbi Harlig. Incidentally, it was about then that I first thought of creating Jewish toys on a large scale."

The two men chatted for a while, no longer talking business.

A few days later, Rabbi Harlig received a phone call from Mr. Blumberger.

"Hello, Rabbi, your order has been shipped, but that's not really the reason for this call. I was filing your invoice and noticed your address and area code. I have a customer who lives about forty-five minutes from you, in the high desert area. We're really a wholesale business and don't usually sell to individuals, but one day this woman called me and requested a special service.

"She told me that she knows we're wholesalers, but asked us to make an exception for her. She explained that she lives in an area where it's difficult to purchase toys with any Jewish educational value. She's determined to provide Jewish content in her children's lives and appealed to us to accommodate her needs.

"We agreed to make an exception for her, and she has become a steady customer.

"Now, we adhere to a policy of customer privacy, so I wouldn't do this under other circumstances, but I thought I should give you this woman's address and number. She's obviously interested in Judaism, and maybe you can help her."

Rabbi Harlig was very grateful.

"I haven't come across any Jews who live in that area, but I will definitely contact her."

That initial contact through the toy supplier in Chicago opened up an entire new realm of Jewish involvement for the woman and her children. Their home became kosher, and they began to observe Shabbos. The children attended Sunday school and brought others along with them.

Incidentally, one day the Harligs met a man named Bob Seigel, who was seeking to connect to his Jewish heritage. In discussion, he mentioned that he had grown up in San Diego and had a best friend who was Jewish. It was a long shot, but Chanie Harlig remembered that the guest in her parent's house, Avraham, often spoke about having grown up in San Diego with a best Jewish friend.

"Would his name be Blumberger, by any chance?" she asked.

It was he!

The Harligs told Bob of Avraham's journey to Judaism, and put the two old friends back in touch with each other. With the Harlig's guidance, Bob Seigel also returned to his roots.

"*R*abbi," said Mr. Bloom, a community member, "a woman I know has inquired about the Jewish burial ceremony and funeral arrangements. Her mother is quite advanced in age, and she'd like to have the information so she won't be caught unprepared when the time comes. Although her mother has lived all her life as a Greek Orthodox Christian, she is in fact Jewish."

Rabbi Shimshon Yurkowicz, who directs Chabad House of Malvern, Australia, with his wife, Rivka, requested the name and address of the elderly woman. The laws regarding burial in a Jewish cemetery are not all that simple, and he preferred to speak with the woman personally to verify some details.

"That would be fine, Rabbi," answered Mr. Bloom. "I must tell you, though, that the woman's mother unfortunately has Alzheimer's disease. Some days are better than others."

Rabbi Yurkowicz assured him he would do his best and made arrangements for a visit to the old-age home where she resided.

As he approached the elderly woman's room, he could see the distant look in her eyes and prepared himself for the effort it might take to communicate. He was caught off guard when the woman turned to face him with indignation, retorting: "I'm not ready to die; you can come back another time!"

Regaining his composure, Rabbi Yurkowicz gently informed her that he had just come to visit. He gradually realized that the woman's daughter had assessed her mother with some approximation; in effect, her fluctuation in and out of reality seemed to be more by the moment than by the day. In the course of conversation, Rabbi Yurkowicz asked numerous questions that might identify her as a Jew. But her responses, he felt, left her status in terms of Jewish law somewhat uncertain. For example, he asked if her mother had lit candles on Friday night. She replied that they lit candles every night, since there was no electricity in those days. Rabbi Yurkowicz resolved to visit her again in the hope of gaining more insight. Just then, an idea came to mind.

"Before I take my leave," he said softly to the woman, "I'll say a Jewish prayer."

Slowly and deliberately he recited: "*Shema Yisroel…*"

The woman cut him off, and concluded the prayer, "…*HaShem elokainu, HaShem echod.*"

No further questions seemed necessary.

When her time came, funeral arrangements were made and all took place in accordance with Jewish law. Rabbi Yurkowicz located the deceased woman's son and instructed him how to recite *Kaddish.* Her children were relieved to fulfill their obligation and honor their mother with a proper Jewish burial.

"We wanted to attract a more sophisticated crowd than usual for one of our evening lectures," relate Rabbi Zalman and Bella Gorelik, on shlichus in Beersheba, Israel. "We were looking for something bigger than our small accommodations at Chabad House – somewhere classy yet intimate. Our first choice was the local municipal library."

The Goreliks knew that special permission was required

before a public hall could be used for a private function, so Rabbi Gorelik approached the city comptroller, whom he knew personally, and presented his request.

"I grant you permission in principle," the official said, "and will write a letter of recommendation to the library supervisor. Be advised, though, that municipal policy puts the final decision in the hands of the supervisor."

Rabbi Gorelik thanked him and made an appointment to see the man.

"As a rule, I don't allow such events," was the supervisor's response. "I get periodic requests of this nature, and my experience has led me to refuse them all. There's no one here to oversee evening activities, you see, and people might tamper with our books and equipment, or they may leave a mess. I will tolerate no damage or loss to the library. True, there is an ongoing weekly class on the Torah portion, but that was begun fourteen years ago, before my time. However, since you are from Chabad, I'll make an exception; I can't say 'no' to Chabad."

Rabbi Gorelik was very grateful. He wondered, though, what Chabad had to do with it.

"It's because of my nephew," the supervisor explained. "My brother and I both live in this city, and our families are close. My brother has a fine traditional family, and has raised lovely children. One of his sons went through the army and, like many other Israelis, embarked on a worldwide trek once he finished. His wanderlust led him through South America and eventually to Canada. In time, he distanced himself from the Jewish lifestyle, made new acquaintances, and was even considering intermarriage. A number of family members tried to direct him back to the faith, but to no avail. Then, while he was in Toronto, people from Chabad somehow found their way to his heart, showering him with patient care and concern.

Thanks to them, today he's a happily married, Torah-observant Jew. Our family has never had an opportunity to thank those Chabad people personally. And so, as a gesture of appreciation, I've decided to make this exception to the rule."

When the man concluded his narration, Rabbi Gorelik, who had been listening intently, took a shot in the dark: "Is your nephew's name Yuval?"

The man was startled.

"How did you know that?"

"Well, as you told his story, the pieces fell into place. When I was a *yeshivah* student, I spent a year studying at the Chabad-Lubavitch headquarters in Brooklyn. That summer, a group of us were asked to assist the shaliach in Toronto, Rabbi Yosef Gansberg, in his outreach activities with Israelis. As you spoke, it came back to me. Beersheba...army service...South America...Toronto.

"I was one of the boys who spent many a night talking with Yuval."

"Shalom," beamed the visitor as he approached Rabbi Mordechai Siev of the Ascent Institute in Tzefat, Israel. "Do you remember me?"

Rabbi Siev, known affectionately as "Big Mo," looked at the young man who appeared like any other *yeshivah* student and had to admit that he did not. This was not surprising; thousands of people pass through the welcoming doors of Ascent every year. Located on a mountain ridge with a magnificent view of the hills and valleys of the Upper Galilee, Ascent draws many spiritual seekers to its attractive and varied programs. Whether one is looking for a Kabbalah-oriented weekend, a class" in chassidic philosophy, a Saturday night sing-along or a rejuvenating hike, Ascent offers it all, and more.

But this visitor reminded Rabbi Siev that he had knocked on his door one Saturday morning in search of something else.

"It was a scorching summer day, and I was roaming the streets looking for a place to cool off," began the young man, "Most places were closed, so I was delighted to find your doors wide open. I walked in and asked if you knew of a pool.

"You directed me to go out, turn left, circle the building and follow the winding street to the end. You told me I would come to a set of stairs. I should go to the bottom and make a left. Straight ahead I would find the pool. You warned me that it was quite small and very cold. I didn't care; all I wanted was to cool off. You even offered me a towel.

"I followed your directions and found the pool. You were right. It was the coldest body of water I had ever entered. And it was much too small to do any swimming. But strangely, as I cooled off, I began to warm up inside. Something in that pool was very powerful, and I stayed in the water a long time, focused on profound thoughts.

"That meaningful introspection was the beginning of a long inward-bound journey, and as you see, I've made significant changes in my life as a result. I've come back to thank you for giving me directions to the pool that watered my faith."

Rabbi Siev smiled and shook the visitor's hand warmly. "It was your own inner conviction, with G-d's help, that guided you," he insisted. "I was only accommodating your request for directions."

Rabbi Siev's directions had led to the most renowned "pool" in Tzefat – the saintly Rabbi Yitzchak Luria's *mikveh*!

Afterword

*I*t was a hit right from the beginning. The weekly Beginners Service at Congregation Kehilath Jeshurun on the Upper East Side of Manhattan has drawn crowds since it was initiated by George Rohr in 1991. Everyone is welcome, regardless of prior knowledge, experience or level of observance.

One Shabbos morning, a first-timer ventured in. She was a bright and articulate young lawyer. Throughout the morning, she confronted Mr. Rohr repeatedly with arguments and objections.

"I tried to reply pleasantly and spice my responses with a touch of humor. I wanted to lighten the edgy atmosphere that her confrontational attitude created," relates Mr. Rohr. "But she did not relent. Time after time she shot back with provoking questions."

"There is something else I want to know," she insisted for the sixth time. "You see, as a rabbi, you – "

"I'm not a rabbi," Mr. Rohr assured her affably. "I am a businessman. I'm here because I identify with many Jewish people who would like to participate in a Shabbos service but find it hard to keep up with a typical *minyan*."

Immediately, the woman softened. "Oh," she exclaimed in surprise. "I didn't realize you were a lay person. I assumed that anyone leading a service and presenting Jewish philosophy would be a "man of the cloth."

From that moment on she grew receptive.

*   *   *

This story communicates one of the Rebbe's fundamental messages: Shlichus is not merely for those who serve professionally in that capacity. Rather, every Jew is a shaliach. Indeed, a Jewish businessperson or professional can often get through to people whom a rabbi could never reach, for people often respond more favorably in settings in which they feel at home. When they meet a peer in the office or in a place of leisure, a Torah thought he offers can leave a profound impression.

This mission relates to us all. Today, there are many – some consciously and some not-yet-consciously – who are seeking more meaning and substance in their lives. When they meet a man or woman whose life reflects purpose, direction, and inner peace, they are motivated to discover their own inner truth.

The ripples of change such conduct will produce can swell into waves. To borrow an analogy from the navigation of a ship: Ships have long been guided by the movement of a rudder. As early ships grew larger, the rudders needed to steer them also increased in size. Moving these larger rudders became difficult. A small rudder known as a trim-tab was therefore attached to the large rudder. This smaller rudder is easier to move; it then moves the large rudder, which in turn changes the course of the entire ship. In today's world, each of us can be such a trim-tab and do our part in pointing mankind toward good – and indeed, toward the ultimate good.

One Sunday, the Rebbe was visited by a CNN news team as he distributed dollars for charity. The reporter asked him if he had a message to share with others. The Rebbe replied that he wished to emphasize that the redemption is imminent and that each of us can bring it closer by increasing our deeds of goodness and kindness.

By living in a way that radiates the joy, meaning, and peace that will characterize the era of *Mashiach*, we can anticipate the eventual diffusion of these qualities throughout the world and in that way precipitate their complete revelation.

Index of Names

Alpern, Rabbi Shabsi
and Esther......................216

Avtzon, Rabbi Mordechai
and Goldie 45

Banin, Rabbi Rami
and Shachar.................... 138

Bentolila, Rabbi Shlomo
and Myriam 106

Bergman, Rabbi Shimon
and Yael............................ 10

Berkowitz, Rabbi Avraham
and Leah 57

Biderman, Rabbi Jacob
and Edla........................... 94

Borenstein, Rabbi Dovid
and Mindy.......................... 2

Brod, Rabbi Menachem
and Miriam 16

Bronstein, Rabbi Asher
and Faigy............................87

Brook, Rabbi Meir
and Sarit............................51

Bryski, Rabbi Moshe
and Matty 13, 121

Cohen, Rabbi Danny
and Bat Sheva 171

Cunin, Rabbi Shlomo
and Miriam 263

Denberg, Rabbi Moshe
and Rivka 44

Deren, Rabbi Yisrael
and Vivi............................142

Deren, Rabbi Yossi
and Maryashie............... 240

Dubov, Rabbi Nissan
and Sarah 164

Eidelman, Rabbi Yosef
and Chana...........................x

Eilfort, Rabbi Yeruchem
and Nechama 145

Engel, Rabbi Moshe
and Nechamah 11

Freundlich, Rabbi Shimon
and Dini.............................6

Friedman, Rabbi Manis
and Chanie......................146

Friedman, Rabbi Yossi
and Miriam 221

Gluckowsky, Rabbi Mendel
and Rochel 28, 260

Goldbloom, Rabbi Arye
and Goldie 18

Goldman, Rabbi Yehoshua
and Chana...................... 109

Goldstein, Rabbi Aharon
and Esther......................130

Goldstein, Rabbi Yitzchak
and Shifra 198

Gordon, Rabbi Sholom Ber
and Miriam 162

Gordon, Rabbi Yehoshuah
Binyamin and Devorah 2

Gordon, Rabbi Yossi
and Mina 183, 243

Gorelick, Rabbi Mendy
and Chanie 249

Gorelik, Rabbi Zalman
and Bella 266

Greenberg, Rabbi Yossi
and Esty 134

Greenwald, Rabbi Baruch
and Rivka 259

Groner, Rabbi Leibel
and Yehudis 93, 220

Groner, Rabbi Yosef
and Mariasha 136

Grossbaum, Rabbi Chaim
and Rivkie 82

Gruzman, Rabbi Yosef
and Tamar 234

Gurary, Rabbi Nosson
and Bassie 248

Gurary, Rabbi Nosson and
Miriam 140

Gurewitz, Rabbi Shmuel
and Sara 11

Hanoka, Rabbi Chaim
and Chanie 48

Harlig, Rabbi Mendy
and Chaya 195

Harlig, Rabbi Shea
and Dina 127

Harlig, Rabbi Sholom Ber
and Chanie 251, 262

Harlig, Rabbi Yossi
and Nechama 222

Hershkowitz, Rabbi Yisrael
and Sarah 232

Holtzberg, Rabbi Gavriel
and Rivki 113

Jacobs, Rabbi Binyomin
and Blouma 89, 102

Jaffe, Zalman 149

Junik, Rabbi Menachem
and Goldie 39 99

Kaminetzki, Rabbi Shmuel
and Chanah 61

Kantor, Rabbi Yosef Chaim
and Nechama 43, 83, 213

Kaplan, Rabbi Baruch
and Rivka 32

Kaplan, Rabbi Shmuel
and Rochel 132

Karniel, Rabbi Benyamin
and Chani 200

Kastel, Rabbi Mordechai
and Batya 260

Katzman, Rabbi Moshe
and Chani 133

Kittner, Rabbi Yirachmiel
and Chanah 190

Konikov, Rabbi Zvi
and Shulamis 165, 203

Krasnjansky, Rabbi Yitzchak
and Pearl 111

Kugel, Rabbi Shlomo
and Rivka 242

Landa, Rabbi Yosef
and Shiffy..........................33
Latowicz, Rabbi Yakov
and Sarah 247
Lazar, Rabbi Berel
and Chanie.................. 53, 66
Lazarus, Rabbi Shlomo
and Yona..........................194
Leider, Rabbi Moishe
and Sura 79
Lesches, Rabbi Baruch
and Shterna.................... 235
Leverton, Rabbi Sholom
and Aliza.........................176
Leviev, Lev 53, 69
Levin, Rabbi Yosef
and Dena.................. 26, 166
Lew, Rabbi Shmuel
and Mindy.......................150
Lew, Rabbi Sholom
and Chana.......................147
Lew, Rabbi Yossi
and Shternie.................... 244
Lifshitz, Rabbi Chezki
and Chanah.........................1
Lihany, Rabbi Y'chiah
and Bat Sheva 50
Lipskar, Rabbi Mendel
and Mashi 8, 48
Lipskar, Rabbi Sholom
Ber and Chani................. 225
Loewenthal, Rabbi Yitzchak
and Rochel 154

Matusof, Rabbi Yehuda
and Tsherna..............180 188

Mentz, Rabbi Chaim
and Charna 206, 253
Myers, Rabbi Baruch
and Chanie....................... 97

Namdar, Rabbi Alexander
and Leah 150, 193

Oberlander, Rabbi Baruch
and Bat Sheva 236

Pewzner, Rabbi Mendel
and Sarah 71
Pinchuk, Mr. Victor.............. 62
Pinson, Rabbi Nissan
and Rochel .... xv, 187
Pinson, Rabbi Yisrael
and Chani 48
Plotkin, Rabbi Avraham
and Goldie 43
Posner, Rabbi Shmuel
and Chanie........................32

Raichman, Rabbi Arye
and Rivka 73
Rapoport, Rabbi Shmuel
David and Tova 174
Raskin, Rabbi Shmuel
and Devorah Leah 236
Rodal, Rabbi Sholom Ber
and Rochel 42
Rohr, George 271
Rosenblum, Rabbi Yehoshua
and Chanie.......................229
Rosenfeld, Rabbi Yisrael
and Sarah 152

Sabag, Rabbi Mendel
and Chanah..............156, 168

Safra, Edmund
and Lilly............................72

Schanowitz, Rabbi Yisroel
and Shternie......................45

Schanowitz, Rabbi Yosef
and Michla...................... 173

Schapiro, Rabbi Moshe
and Shaindel 116

Segal, Rabbi Shlomo
and Chedva xii

Serebryanski, Rabbi Aharon
and Zlata......................... 183

Serebryanski, Rabbi Moshe
and Bluma.......................197

Shemtov, Rabbi Eliezer
and Rochi..................xiv, 189

Shemtov, Rabbi Moshe
and Leah 47, 142

Shemtov, Rabbi Yosef
and Chanie.......................112

Shishler, Rabbi Ari
and Naomi 21

Shmotkin, Rabbi Yisrael
and Devorah..................... 24

Siev, Rabbi Mordechai
and Chana...................... 268

Slavaticki, Rabbi Shabtai
and Richa...................75, 255

Sneiderman, Rabbi Eliezer
and Roni 185

Solomon, Yosef
and Tamar 239

Steinmetz, Rabbi Chaim
and Sora 98, 115

Sudak, Rabbi Levi
and Feige......................... 125

Teichtel, Rabbi Yehuda
and Leah xiii

Trebnik, Rabbi Shneur Zalman
and Chanie..................... 191

Vishedsky, Rabbi Pinchas
and Nechama 104

Vogel, Rabbi Chuni
and Oryah 223

Weg, Rabbi Yehuda
and Devorah..................... xv

Winner, Rabbi Zushe
and Esther................157, 196

Wolf, Rabbi Aron
and Bracha 227

Woolstone, Rabbi Pinchos
and Aviva 225

Yurkowicz, Rabbi Shimshon
and Rivka 265

Zaklas, Rabbi Zalman
and Mimi 54, 66

Zippel, Rabbi Benny
and Sharonne 30

Zirkind, Rabbi Levy
and Chanie..................... 122